CUSTOMS MODERNIZATION INITIATIVES: CASE STUDIES

CUSTOMS MODERNIZATION INITIATIVES: CASE STUDIES

Editors
Luc De Wulf and José B. Sokol

THE WORLD BANK
Washington, D.C.

1818 H Street, NW
Washington, DC 20433
Telephone 202-473-1000
Internet www.worldbank.org
E-mail feedback@worldbank.org

A copublication of the World Bank and Oxford University Press.

1 2 3 4 07 06 05 04

Library of Congress Cataloging-in-Publication Data

Customs modernization initiatives: case studies / edited by Luc De Wulf and José B. Sokol.

p. com.

Includes bibliographic references and index.

ISBN 0-8213-5752-2

1. Customs administration—Developing countries. I. Wulf, Luc De, 1942- II. Sokol, José B.

HJ7390.C87 2004

352.4'48—dc22 2004050364

CONTENTS

FIGURES

FOREWORD

In recent years, policymakers have become increasingly aware of the importance of policies that can facilitate the flow of goods and services across borders. Sound trade facilitation policies are indeed essential if countries are to realize the potential gains available from enhanced market access, lowered tariffs, reduced transportation costs, and improved communications. Such gains can allow countries to achieve higher growth rates and reduce poverty.

Customs administrations are a critical component of this framework and are therefore important catalysts of economic development. Well-designed programs that focus on improving the efficiency of customs administrations can generate significant gains by helping to integrate developing countries into the global trading system. In this context, many countries have undertaken customs reform and modernization initiatives, often with the assistance of the World Bank or other development agencies.

The outcomes of those programs have been mixed because, unfortunately, many programs have failed to meet their objectives. To help our member countries draw lessons from the successes and failures of such reform efforts, the International Trade Department of the World Bank is preparing a series of tools anchored on its *Customs Modernization Handbook.* This publication is a companion to the *Customs Modernization Handbook.* It documents the lessons to be learned from eight case studies that were prepared to inform the *Handbook.* The case studies reflect the realities of extremely diverse countries in terms of development, culture, and geography.

We hope that both the *Customs Modernization Initiatives* volume and the *Customs Modernization Handbook* will contribute to successful reforms that will help developing countries' to integrate into the global economy and achieve their ultimate objective of poverty reduction.

Uri Dadush
Director
International Trade Department

ACKNOWLEDGMENTS

The country case studies are the product of a collaborative effort on the part of customs experts and consultants who either participated in the reform processes in the countries reviewed or have accumulated significant technical knowledge about customs reform and modernization processes in a worldwide context during the course of their professional experience. The studies were prepared using a methodology developed by Luc De Wulf and Michael Lane. The editors have revised and updated the studies submitted by the authors so as to obtain greater uniformity.

The editors reviewed the country case studies on an individual basis, as did a number of peer reviewers, including Amparo Ballivián (World Bank), Michael Engelschalk (World Bank), Carlos Ferreira (World Bank), Guillermo Gutierrez (National Customs of Bolivia), Allan Katiga (Uganda Revenue Authority), David Kloeden (International Monetary Fund), and Michael Lane (formerly with the U.S. Customs Service). The editors also wish to thank the staff members of the Ghana Community Network, who were most helpful to the author in undertaking the Ghana study, especially Emmanuel Darko and Nigel Gregory. Comments were received from the respective World Bank country teams. The contribution of Peter M. Kalil, chief of the Integration Trade and Hemispheric Issues Division, Inter-American Development Bank, is also gratefully acknowledged, particularly in supporting the preparation of the Peru case study. In addition, Paul Duran (consultant) helped the editors ensure the consistency and coherence of all the case studies. The views expressed are entirely those of the contributors and do not necessarily reflect the views of the World Bank Group, the institutions with which the authors are affiliated, or the countries they represent.

This book is a product of the World Bank's Trade Department. It was initiated by the Africa Region under the leadership of Larry Hinkle, who at that time was completing a study on Africa's trade reforms ("How Far Did Africa's First Generation Trade Reforms Go?" Africa Region Working Paper Series No. 58a, June 2003). That study suggested that the benefits from trade liberalization policies would be greatly enhanced by reforms in the trade facilitation area, particularly in customs administration.

The editors are indebted to Melanie Faltas, Zeba Jetha, and Lili Tabada for their excellent administrative support throughout the project. Alice Faintich of The Word Doctor edited the document, which greatly improved its readability. Their dedication has significantly enhanced the quality of this product.

ABOUT THE EDITORS

Luc De Wulf, a Belgian national, joined the Fiscal Affairs Department of the International Monetary Fund in 1972 and later worked on China in the Asia Department before moving to the World Bank in 1988, where he worked in the Africa Region and the Middle East Region. He retired from the Bank in 1999.

Initially, De Wulf's interest in the taxation of foreign trade was driven by the important revenue contribution of taxes in many developing countries. Recently he has worked intensively as a consultant on trade and development issues, particularly in Mauritania and Senegal. During the course of this work, he increasingly recognized that trade liberalization, with its emphasis on improving market access and lowering both tariff and nontariff trade barriers, would not fulfill its promises of growth and poverty alleviation without significant strengthening of trade facilitation. In the area of trade facilitation, customs is a key agency that in a number of countries fails to reduce the cost of trade sufficiently, and its potential contribution to trade facilitation is frequently not fully realized. Hence, this publication emphasizes increasing the effectiveness and efficiency of customs operations.

José B. Sokol, a Panamanian national, joined the World Bank in 1977 following a career as a senior government official responsible for economic, budgetary, and financial matters at Panama's Ministry of Planning and Economic Policy. At the World Bank, Sokol worked in the Latin America and the Caribbean Region and in the Africa Region. He retired in May 2001.

Initially, Sokol's work focused on macroeconomic issues and the contribution that policies in this area can bring to a country's development efforts. His work on Argentina, Colombia, and the Commonwealth Caribbean countries gradually shifted to the area of structural adjustment with an emphasis on trade liberalization, particularly on reducing tariff and nontariff barriers to trade. Later his work in the Africa Region shifted to addressing growth, poverty reduction, governance, and capacity-building issues. His more recent work has focused on evaluating both the impact of country assistance strategies and adjustment operations on growth and poverty reduction and the contribution that trade facilitation and customs modernization can have on strengthening a country's outward-looking growth orientation.

ABBREVIATIONS AND ACRONYMS

ACIT	Administration of Customs and Indirect Taxes (Administration des Douanes et Impôts Indirects) (Morocco)
ACV	Agreement on Customs Valuation
ASYCUDA	Automated System for Customs Data
BOC	Bureau of Customs (Philippines)
CCMS	Computerized Customs Management System (Turkey)
CEPS	Customs, Excise, and Preventive Services (Ghana)
COMESA	Common Market for Eastern and Southern Africa
CSCC	Computerized Support for Customs Clearance
DFID	Department for International Development (United Kingdom)
DIS	destination inspection services
DTI	direct trader input
EDI	electronic data interchange
EU	European Union
GCMS	Ghana Customs Management System
GCNet	Ghana Community Network
GDP	gross domestic product
ICT	information and communication technology
IDB	Inter-American Development Bank
IMF	International Monetary Fund
ITS	Intertek Testing Services
MEF	Ministry of Economy and Finance (Peru)
MOF	Ministry of Finance
MOTI	Ministry of Trade and Industry (Ghana)
NCB	National Customs of Bolivia (Aduana Nacional de Bolivia)
NCS	National Customs Service (Superintendencia Nacional de Aduanas) (Peru)
PSI	preshipment inspection
PTCP	Philippine Tax Computerization Project
SADC	Southern African Development Community
SGS	Société Générale de Surveillance
SPACE	selectivity, postaudit, advance clearance, client self-assessment, and electronic data processing
TCA	Turkish Customs Administration
TIMS	Trade Information Management System
TURC	Technical Unit for Restructuring Customs (Unitade Técnica de Reforma das Alfãndegas) (Mozambique)
UNCTAD	United Nations Conference on Trade and Development
URA	Uganda Revenue Authority
VAT	value added tax
WCO	World Customs Organization
WTO	World Trade Organization

1

OVERVIEW

Luc De Wulf and José B. Sokol

This volume presents case studies of customs modernization initiatives in eight developing countries: Bolivia, Ghana, Morocco, Mozambique, Peru, the Philippines, Turkey, and Uganda. The purpose of these case studies was to obtain a firsthand view of how these countries undertook customs reforms and to assess their success. The overall lessons learned from these studies are presented in chapter 2 of the *Customs Modernization Handbook* (World Bank forthcoming), a companion volume that provides policymakers, practitioners, and project managers from development agencies with an overview of the key issues they need to address in preparing and implementing customs modernization initiatives. The audience for the *Customs Modernization Handbook* is customs officials who are called on to design and implement customs reform and modernization strategies, as well as staff members of the World Bank and of other multilateral and bilateral development agencies who support developing countries in implementing such strategies. All the case studies except for the one on Ghana were prepared using basically the same methodology, which aimed at identifying the origins of the reforms, the main drivers, and the outcomes. The Ghana case study is somewhat different, because it focuses on how the automation of trade and customs processes took the lead in the trade facilitation and customs reform.

The country case studies were prepared by customs experts and consultants who had either participated in the reform processes in the countries reviewed or accumulated significant technical knowledge of customs reform and modernization processes in a worldwide context. The selection of countries aimed to assess initiatives used in different continents in the hope that their unique characteristics would yield interesting insights.

The country case studies were undertaken with a common approach to ensure comprehensiveness and comparability. They targeted five areas of the reform process:

1. The background of the reform and modernization process, including its economic and institutional context, factors leading to reform decisions, supporters, objectives and design, and financial and technical support
2. The issues pertinent to the reform process
3. The reform measures themselves, including legislation; management changes; staff-related questions, such as pay, selection, training, integrity, and corruption; information technology; valuation; experience with preshipment

inspection; special import regimes; and selectivity in pre- and post-release control

4. The outcomes, including the effect of reform on fiscal performance, trade facilitation, corruption, staffing and workloads, and conformity with international standards plus, where available, an assessment of quantitative performance indicators and users' reactions
5. The lessons that each of these reforms contain a judgment about the sustainability of the modernization initiatives

The findings and conclusions of each case study are based primarily on interviews conducted in the field with public sector representatives—mainly customs officials—as well as oversight authorities and private sector representatives, including importers, brokers, carriers, and their professional associations. The findings were at times complemented by further dialogue between the editors and others with valuable insights in relation to reform processes and outcomes.

Interviews were conducted at three levels: (a) with sponsors and originators of the reform process so as to identify the motivating and encouraging actors behind the reform, (b) with customs officials and other officials involved in implementing reform who were in a position to provide details about the reform process and methodology, and (c) with users of customs services who are directly affected by customs operations and who could help assess the reform process and outcomes.

Although the country case studies share the same approach and cover the same topics, they differ in the depth and extent of treatment of the issues examined. This difference reflects the varying expertise of the consultants who undertook the studies, the information available about the details of the reform, the specificity of the country initiatives, and the relative importance of different reform elements in the various programs. Also, because these studies were largely undertaken in mid-2002, some of the findings may be somewhat outdated.

Bolivia

Initiated within the framework of an institutional reform covering the entire government and provided with strong leadership by the vice president, customs reform in Bolivia aimed at total transformation. One of the key elements of the reform was a complete staff renewal, designed to rid the customs service of deeply embedded corruption. Under the reform, new staff members were selected on the basis of competitive recruitment of qualified candidates conducted by outside consultants. With the adoption of the Automatic System for Customs Data (ASYCUDA++) software, the National Customs of Bolivia (NCB; Aduanas Nacionales de Bolivia or ANB in Spanish) was able to achieve random selectivity in the inspection of shipments and limit physical controls to 20 percent of shipments. The upgrading of information and communication technology (ICT) allowed the NCB to monitor customs clearance times closely, thereby enabling it to remedy weaknesses and help design measures to reduce clearance times. The program also provided for a gradual handover of the valuation function to the NCB. In addition to a significant reduction in corruption, smuggling of products of mass consumption declined. However, control of informal trade remains a challenge. In recent years, smuggling activity in the informal sector appears to have increased sharply in response to a deterioration in economic conditions following adverse external and domestic shocks. Also resources earmarked for the NCB to cover its operations appear to be inadequate to sustain the financial autonomy that it was granted as part of the reform.

Morocco

Although not codified in a detailed action plan, Morocco's program of customs reform and modernization reflected a comprehensive vision and covered all aspects of customs operations. Reform actions were undertaken in a deliberate and pragmatic process. The priorities of the Administration of Customs and Indirect Taxes (ACIT; Administration des Douanes et Impôts Indirects or ADII in French) changed significantly, away from revenue generation and law enforcement and toward the facilitation of trade and transparency. The reform process has benefited greatly from the close involvement of the ACIT's private sector partners in designing the reform, which included an overhaul of the Customs Code and the implementation of the Customs Valuation Agreement of the World

Trade Organization. The ACIT actively engaged the entire customs staff in elaborating and implementing the reform while strengthening training and staff incentives. The close involvement of both staff members and users of customs services in the reform effort benefited greatly from the early development of customs communications. Substantially reinforced ICT led to considerable progress in automating customs operations. With selectivity limiting physical inspections to 10 percent of declarations and other process simplifications, customs clearance time was substantially reduced. This result, posted on the ACIT's Web site, put pressure on other public and private sector agents to streamline their operations so as to reduce delays in releasing shipments to importers.

Mozambique

In Mozambique, the most significant characteristic of the reform was the willingness to rely extensively on external consultants to manage and implement the reform and to value imports and exports for customs purposes. Mozambique adopted this unusual approach in the midst of rebuilding a government service that had been totally destroyed after many years of war. The reform design was, from the outset, comprehensive and ambitious; however, its implementation was gradual and phased, with careful monitoring systems built in. Significant foreign financing supported the reform. Under the reform, the Mozambique Customs Administration (or Direcção Geral de Alfãndegas) introduced a modern ICT system and initiated a program of staff renewal, with recruitment based on new standards of qualification and integrity, and a new salary scale. A sizable portion of the existing staff was scheduled to be released. The contract for external consultants was extended twice because more time was needed to prepare national management to direct an efficient and effective customs organization and to gear up for integration into the envisaged new central customs authority. Whether this innovative approach is the best way to ensure the sustainability of reform is yet to be determined. Mozambique has still not completed the process of streamlining its staff. It also needs to develop the ICT system further to deal effectively with persistent corruption and smuggling problems.

Peru

In Peru, customs reform and modernization were high on the agenda of the president, who provided strong political support throughout enactment of the reform. The customs administration was vested with full ownership of the reform and maintained the necessary continuity to see the process through to completion. Peru created the National Customs Service (Superintendencia Nacional de Aduanas) to grant the customs administration the operational flexibility required to improve services and to be held accountable for the results. The reform program was comprehensive, and it was implemented in a systematic way that led to steady progress. An entire series of measures was taken at the beginning, followed by a period of consolidation. Major areas that were addressed included adopting new legislation; streamlining procedures; implementing full automation of operations based on an integrated, domestically developed computer program; introducing risk analysis and postrelease audits; and initiating broadly based personnel renewal. The administrative and financial autonomy granted to the customs administration allowed it to introduce effective management and personnel policies that included the provision of attractive salaries and the removal of unqualified and corrupt staff members. The use of preshipment inspection services illustrates how such services can contribute to effective and efficient customs operations.

Philippines

Decisive factors in the success of the reform in the Philippines included strong, top-level political backing; strong, able, and sustained operational leadership; ownership of the reform by the head of the Bureau of Customs; and support that included some funding by private sector users of customs services. Among the weaknesses of the reform were a failure of customs staff members to commit to it, caused partly by their inadequate compensation, a problem that the Bureau of Customs could not address because it lacked the requisite authority and funding. This lack of commitment, together with the loss of political interest on the part of the subsequent administration, led to later backsliding on reform. In addition, other agencies involved in import and export clearance did not go along with the modernization efforts and continued to impede trade flows. Nevertheless, the adoption of simplified procedures and the significant progress in automation affected nearly all segments of the clearance process. The introduction of ASYCUDA++, with its support of risk assessment and selectivity, contributed to a substantial enhancement of customs controls and a reduction in clearance times.

Turkey

Two goals dominated customs reform and modernization efforts in Turkey: bringing customs legislation and administrative structures in line with European Union standards, and automating customs procedures. The establishment of an independent Modernization Project Unit with strong political support and steady management by the Turkish Customs Administration (TCA; Gümrük in Turkish) was a critical element in the effective coordination of automation activities. Such activities included adoption of a new ICT system and its rapid deployment and application, which permitted automation of the entire clearance process; introduction of risk-based selectivity; and implementation of postrelease controls. The TCA also witnessed a significant improvement in staff quality, as well as improvements in physical infrastructure, which were occasionally funded by private sector contributions. Some regional customs offices lagged in deploying the new ICT system, hiring qualified personnel, and adopting automated procedures. The TCA's lack of autonomy in salary setting and in recruitment hampered its modernization effort. Inefficiencies in the procedures other agencies used to fulfill their own mandates, including the Ministry of Health, Ministry of Agriculture, and Standards Institute, undermined the overall benefits that traders reaped from the customs reform.

Uganda

In Uganda, customs reform has been a long-term process. Started in 1990–91, its main aim was to strengthen revenue mobilization and to combat corruption. At the beginning of the reform, the customs administration became part of an autonomous revenue agency that also managed domestic taxes. Measures were implemented to enhance staff member integrity, in part by significantly upgrading salaries and removing staff members who had been tainted by previous integrity shortcomings. Those efforts were reinforced by a wide-ranging anticorruption campaign. In 2002, the reform also streamlined several steps in the clearance process. The reform process still has a considerable unfinished agenda, because audit controls are at an embryonic stage of development and a realistic database still needs to be developed. Now that ASYCUDA++ has been adopted, the automation of customs processes is making progress. However, no fully fledged risk management system is operational yet, and the physical inspection rate is still close to 100 percent. The fight against corruption has proved to be an arduous task, requiring steadfast efforts with high-level political support. Yet some noteworthy successes have recently been registered. In mid-2002, several high-ranking officials were arrested, and the campaign against corruption is still high on the agenda. As the reform moves ahead, it may benefit from a greater focus on the promotion of integrity and trade facilitation in combination with strong enforcement.

Ghana

The Ghana case study is quite different from the other case studies. It was initially undertaken as a case study of reform that would improve the investment climate and would be used as an input in the *World Development Report* (World Bank 2004). It is reproduced with permission from the *World Development Report* team, because it clearly illustrates how introducing ICT, even in the absence of comprehensive customs reform, can strengthen revenue mobilization and speed up cargo clearance. Ghana has adopted a novel approach to the introduction of ICT by commissioning this task to a joint venture company, the Ghana Community Network. The vision is to connect all members of the trading community in an electronic network so as to facilitate all aspects of the trade transaction for both traders and the government agencies overseeing these transactions, each of which has its own agenda. Progress so far has been good in terms of raising revenue and speeding up customs clearance times. The lessons learned from this experience show that (a) ICT can serve as a powerful force to streamline trade and customs procedures; (b) the sustainability of the improvements registered will depend on modernization of the non-ICT aspects of customs work; and (c) the inclusion of other members of the trading community in the electronic network requires more political will than has been mustered so far.

References

World Bank. 2004. *World Development Report 2004: Making Services Work for Poor People.* New York: Oxford University Press.

———. Forthcoming. L. De Wulf and J. Sokol, eds., *Customs Modernization Handbook.* Washington, D.C.: World Bank.

2

BOLIVIA

Flavio Escobar

Bolivia successfully adopted an open market economy model in 1985; however, economic growth and employment generation have been insufficient for the country to make headway in narrowing its sizable inequalities in incomes and standards of living. In an effort to address these issues, the Bolivian authorities pursued a comprehensive economic reform program that included modernization of the customs administration.

Trade Policy and Taxation

In 1985, Bolivia launched significant reforms in the area of international trade that included reducing tariffs and simplifying controls. Initially the authorities introduced a uniform tariff of 20 percent for capital and other goods, but the tariff schedule is no longer uniform, because in 1987, the authorities further reduced the tariff on capital goods to between zero and 5 percent and lowered the tariff on other goods to 10 percent.

In addition to customs duties, levies on imports include a value added tax of 14.9 percent and a selective consumption tax that ranges from 50 percent on cigarettes and other tobacco products to between 10 and 18 percent on automobiles. Other taxes include a specific tax of Bs 0.15 per liter applied to soft drinks, as well as a specific tax of Bs 0.3 to Bs 1.2 per liter applied to alcoholic beverages. Bolivia also levies a special tax on the import and domestic sale of hydrocarbons and their derivatives; for example, in 2002, the specific tax on diesel oil was Bs 0.66 per liter.

Import taxes account for a significant portion of total tax revenue. As figure 2.1 shows, customs revenue from taxes on international trade represents between 30 and 40 percent of the National Treasury's total tax revenue. Customs revenue as a share of total revenue peaked in 1997 and 1998 because of imports required for the construction of a gas pipeline between Bolivia and Brazil, as well as increases in foreign investment in privatized companies.

Among the contributions of the various taxes on international trade to total National Treasury revenue, the value added tax, which is levied on all final imports of goods and services, is the most important, representing about 21 percent of the total. Customs duties are the second most important source of tax revenue and account for about 8 percent of total tax revenue (figure 2.2).

Figure 2.3 shows the effective rates of import taxes as measured by the ratio of customs duty collection to the total value of imports. In 1999–2001,

FIGURE 2.1 Import Taxes as a Share of Overall Budget Revenue, 1994–2000

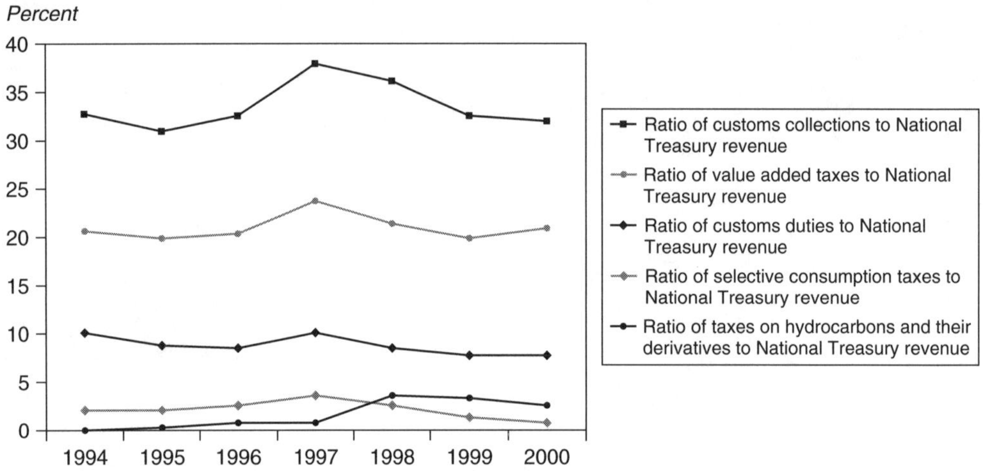

Source: National Customs of Bolivia data.

FIGURE 2.2 Customs Revenue as a Share of Total Tax Revenue, 2000

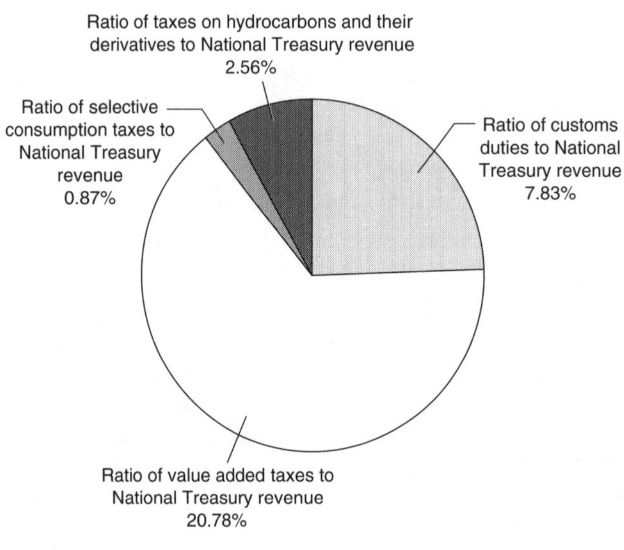

Source: National Customs of Bolivia data.

the effective rate of customs duties was about 5 percent, and the effective rate of all taxes collected by the customs service averaged more than 20 percent. The combined effective rate of all taxes on taxable imports actually amounts to 21.1 percent because not all imports are taxable. The relatively low effective customs rate for all imports is the result of exemptions from import duties included in regional trade agreements and trade agreements with neighboring countries.

Bolivia avoids the use of nontariff barriers and has never taken antidumping or safeguard measures.[1] Moreover, in line with the central tenet of its policy of free trade in goods and services, Bolivia does not require prior permits or licenses for imports except in cases where they might endanger human, animal, or plant health; the security of the state; or the nation's cultural heritage.[2]

1. Except for a safeguard measure against imports of Argentine wheat flour in February 2002, which temporarily suspended tariff preferences granted to the South American Common Market.

2. Supreme Decree Number 24440 of December 1996 establishes free importation for marketable goods without any prior licensing, import quotas, or other nontariff measures.

FIGURE 2.3 Evolution of Effective Customs Rates, 1994–2001

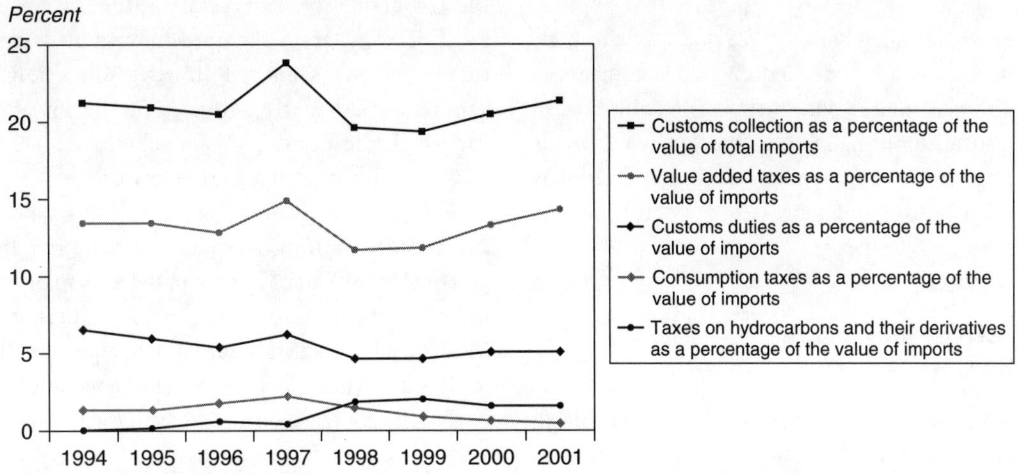

Source: National Customs of Bolivia data.

Even though Bolivia has largely based its trade policy on unilateral liberalization, multilateral and regional initiatives have played an important supporting role. Since 1993, Bolivia has concluded new trade agreements with Chile, Cuba, Mexico, and the South American Common Market. Bolivia has also continued to participate in the Andean Community integration process. Given Bolivia's geographical location, most of these preferential initiatives have the potential of increasing trade and investment.

Customs Administration

The effects of improvements in the trade regime introduced since 1986 were reduced by persistent administrative weaknesses and the resultant unequal application of laws and regulations affecting the administration of the customs service, the heavy reliance on processing imports, the application of intellectual property rights regulations, and the use of sanitary and phytosanitary controls. Difficulties also arose because of the size of the informal sector.

Excise and hydrocarbon tax rates have been changing constantly, the former because of revenue shortfalls and the latter because of the decision to keep domestic prices constant (the domestic price of gasoline has been fixed since 2000). Consequently, revenue improvements for these taxes have been negligible. Also during 1999–2003, total imports decreased by US$300 million, contracting the tax base for customs taxes. However, the progressive devaluations of the national currency have partly compensated for the negative impact on tax collections caused by the decrease in imports.

Before the reform, the general public perceived the National Customs of Bolivia (NCB) as one of the most corrupt institutions in the country because of its links to the political parties: the party in power would take charge and manage the institution however it pleased. Services provided to traders were directly related to the bribes offered, plus almost 40 percent of the total staff consisted of people who did not receive salaries from the NCB but simply kept a share of the taxes they collected for themselves and for whoever had procured the position for them. Overall tax collection was relatively efficient, because collections met the required quota, with the excess allocated to staff as efficiency rewards.

An NCB estimate of smuggling between 1997 and 1998 pointed to a tax evasion level that exceeded US$800 million per year, an amount larger than Bolivia's total foreign financial assistance. Subsequent analyses estimated the revenue losses at an average of US$500 million per year. In recent years, smuggling activity by the informal sector appears to have increased sharply (mainly from the port of Iquique in Chile) in response to the deterioration in economic conditions following adverse external and domestic shocks. Smuggling has a detrimental impact on the formal economy, as reflected by lower tax collection and unfair competition with the formal private sector.

The NCB had traditionally maintained an antiquated legal and normative structure. The applicable legislation dated back to 1929 and was extremely complex, consisting of 285 decrees, 321 ministerial resolutions, and 215 administrative resolutions. In addition, all goods had to be inspected, which made the process of merchandise clearance extremely time-consuming and increased opportunities for rent-seeking activities.

Objectives and Scope of Customs Reform

With a view to addressing these shortcomings, Bolivia implemented a second round of reform in 1997. This round followed the opening up of the economy in 1985 and was aimed at strengthening institutions, with priority given to the customs service and to the gradual integration of informal trade into formal trade channels. The consensus regarding the prevalence of corruption in customs activities led to general agreement on the need for overall reform. The reform aimed at a total reengineering of the customs organization, its staffing, and its processes and procedures. The objective was to make customs activities efficient and transparent so that customs officers could fulfill their proper role of facilitating trade and collecting revenue.

Before the second round of reform, the Customs Police Force was implementing a plan whereby personnel from the Special Unit for Assessing Internal Risk replaced customs staff. The objective was to restore institutional credibility, improve tax collection, and reduce the high levels of institutional corruption.

Reform Team, Support, and Financing

The government set up the National Customs Council during the preparation of the reform to support the reform process. The president chaired the council, which consisted of representatives from the Ministry of the Public Treasury, the Ministry of External Trade, and the private sector. The government dissolved the council following approval of the new Customs Law in 1999, which established the framework for the reform and initiated the reform process.

The vice president, Jorge Quiroga Ramírez, directed the leaders of the Institutional Reform Program during its initial stages (1997–2001), thereby giving it the necessary authority and visibility. The program's main achievement was customs reform. Under Ramírez's direction the cabinet—particularly Minister of the Presidency Alberto Leyton and Minister of Finance Herbert Muller—fully supported the reform.

A new NCB commissioner, Amparo Ballivián, spearheaded the implementation of customs reform, and her forceful management of the reform program was a major reason for its success. The International Monetary Fund (IMF) contributed significantly to the design of the reform by providing technical support to the government and to the reform team.

The private sector participated widely in the reform. The leadership provided by the National Trade Chamber, the National Customs Forwarders Chamber, and the National Industries Chamber is especially noteworthy. The private sector was particularly interested in stemming corruption and fighting smuggling. Private sector representatives voiced the opinion that smuggling by the large informal sector was seriously affecting enterprises' viability and the fabric of domestic industry as a whole. The private sector requested a new set of rules and demanded new legislation that would credibly address corruption and smuggling.

Before the implementation of the contingency plan and the enactment of the new Customs Law, the IMF recommended that the government prepare a medium-term plan for institutional strengthening. As a result, the Reform and Modernization Program of the Bolivian Customs Administration (henceforth referred to as the *Customs Modernization Program*) was designed, prepared, and discussed in detail by the NCB with the government, the main stakeholders, and the international donor community to achieve broad consensus and adequate financial support.

The NCB has received the support of the following international institutions and bilateral donors through credit agreements and grants to finance the Customs Modernization Program: the World Bank; the Inter-American Development Bank (IDB); the IMF; the United Nations Development Programme; the Andean Development Corporation; the Nordic Development Fund; and the governments of Denmark, Germany, Japan, the Netherlands, and Sweden. The World Bank financed the new human resources administration, and the IDB financed the new information technology system.

The innovative aspect of the Customs Modernization Program's design relates to its cofinancing structure, which involves multiple donors. The government set up a special coordination unit that is responsible for (a) coordinating the efforts of the Bolivian authorities, the NCB, and external donors in implementing the program; (b) following up on and monitoring the program; (c) keeping civil society, donors, and the Bolivian authorities informed about the progress of implementation; and (d) designing strategies and preparing terms of reference to ensure adherence to donors' procurement guidelines.

Components of the Reform

The reform focused on the key issues pertaining to the legislative and regulatory framework, as well as on required changes to managerial and operational procedures.

Legislative and Regulatory Framework

A change in customs legislation was one of the main reform measures. The new Customs Law of July 1999 defined a set of rules that changed the law governing customs procedures, regimes, personnel, and administrative structures. It was designed to carry out far-reaching institutional reform and combat corruption, but the issuance of implementing regulations was delayed by almost a year, and as a result the NCB was relatively limited in its ability to provide the legal guidance and transparency that the new legislative framework had aimed for. Nevertheless, the reform was well thought out and its institutional and procedural provisions were eventually implemented. However, Article 4 of the new law posed operational difficulties concerning juridical issues related to the application of the new Code of Penal Procedure and to legal constraints intended to combat smuggling by small traders.

Management Changes

The implementing regulations for the Customs Law came into effect in August 2000. They established a new organizational structure that provided autonomy to the NCB in both financial and normative terms. The NCB's governance structure is based on a board of directors that sets out the operational directives and regulations for managing the NCB. This structure implies that the decisionmaking process is not discretional. The introduction of the implementing regulations was followed in July 2001 by approval of the Institutional Reform Agreement by the NCB, the Ministry of the Public Treasury, and the Technical Unit of the Institutional Reform Program. A local consulting firm was heavily involved in preparing the agreement, particularly those aspects of the agreement that pertained to the NCB's financial sustainability.

The agreement included commitments by the NCB to implement the Customs Modernization Program and by the Ministry of the Public Treasury and the Technical Unit of the Institutional Reform Program to support its implementation. Also important were these entities' commitments of financial resources and technical assistance to ensure the implementation and maintenance of the institutional reform. The Customs Law specified that the NCB would be allowed to retain 10 percent of the revenue from customs duties on imports to defray its expenses. However, this amount turned out to be too low to cover the NCB's costs, thereby undermining the reform's financial sustainability. The authorities are now studying several options to overcome this problem, including consolidating the NCB with the Internal Revenue Service, disbanding the NCB, changing the NCB's revenue sources, and collecting 1 percent of the total value of imports in free-on-board terms. The debate was still ongoing as of the writing of this report. Despite the many changes that have taken place, the NCB's administrative structure is still being reviewed. Joint inspections by the NCB and the Internal Revenue Service as part of an inspection project were delayed because reforms at the Internal Revenue Service have only recently begun.

Personnel and Pay Issues

Personnel reform was part of a comprehensive effort by the Institutional Reform Program and the Customs Modernization Program to reform the overall civil service that was aimed at strengthening the public administration and advancing the fight against corruption. The personnel reform, which was based on the recently adopted Civil Service Statute and Civil Service Program, was fully implemented at the NCB and became an essential element of its transformation into an efficient and transparent organization while significantly reducing corruption (IDB 2001).

The selection and hiring of customs personnel was to be based on transparent and competitive processes. All positions became open to the public, with all senior professional and technical positions given temporary status. All those personnel who had not received salaries but had kept a portion of the duties they collected were dismissed. Specialized consulting firms were hired through public bidding to undertake the selection process so as to enhance the overall transparency of the operation. At the same time, the NCB's Human Resources Department developed a new market-based pay system and offered competitive salaries and promotion opportunities.

Openings for top and mid-level positions and for professional and technical positions were advertised in October 1999 and April 2000, respectively. The outcome of the effort to recruit senior and mid-level staff was disappointing because of a lack of publicity, which meant that fewer applications were received than had been expected; the hasty rejection of a number of applications for border positions; and an unreliable software system. Because many positions remained unfilled, a second round of recruitment for senior and technical personnel was initiated in January 2001.

Implementation of the selection process required a series of prior actions, including defining the ideal profile of a customs officer (in terms of education, experience, and personal integrity) and quantifying staffing requirements, which were set at slightly more than 700, of which 575 positions were open. The personnel consulting firms evaluated candidates on the basis of their professional backgrounds and their technical abilities as determined by tests. A minimum score was established for each position. The consulting firms also screened candidates to eliminate those who had previously been found guilty of violating customs regulations or committing a felony in the service of the NCB. Once the tests had been graded, a shortlist of applicants to be interviewed was provided to the NCB. A final evaluation was conducted by means of a structured interview to evaluate the information provided by the consulting firms, verify that all requirements had been met, and determine the candidate's suitability for a specific position. The final selections were carried out by a committee of the NCB's board of directors, which submitted a report with recommendations to the board or general management. Appointees were required to undergo a three-month probationary period before being given permanent positions.

A total of 12,563 candidates applied during the two recruitment periods and, because they were allowed to apply for up to three positions, filed 37,698 applications. Of the 8,763 candidates who fulfilled all requirements, 2,718 passed the tests. Following screening and interviews, 1,653 candidates were shortlisted. The personnel consulting firms submitted reports to the NCB that included short-lists of candidates for each position and a list of positions for which no suitable candidates had applied. By July 2001, approximately 87 percent of positions had been filled.

Under the new salary structure, salaries were raised by 73 percent for management staff, by 22 to 28 percent for mid-level officials, and by 41 percent for support personnel. The maximum monthly salary rose from Bs 14,000 to Bs 29,000, while the minimum increased from about Bs 1,200 to Bs 1,300. Regulations do not permit performance bonuses, but good performance is taken into account during the promotion process. Although a promotion reward system exists for teams that exceed predetermined goals, those rewards are constrained by the NCB's budget.

The customs reform opened up employment to the general public and put it on a merit-based footing. The staff training program was to be strengthened with World Bank support in the context of the Civil Service Statute.

Integrity and Anticorruption Policies

Upon entering the customs service, all staff members must sign a sworn declaration that they will abide by NCB rules and familiarize themselves with the Code of Ethics. The staff training curriculum includes modules on corruption, smuggling, fraud, and the Code of Ethics. The General Law of Customs provides for civil or penal procedures for violating customs regulations and for customs felonies. The Office of Ethics handles internal administrative procedures, and the Superintendency of the Civil Service considers appeals against dismissal.

Training

Since the customs reform was carried out, education requirements have become stricter; they are now defined according to the responsibilities of particular categories of positions. Staff training has not yet been sufficiently strengthened. This insufficiency has occurred partly because, between 1999 and 2002, the NCB concentrated on hiring personnel and was not in a position to provide the requisite training. To date, and in the absence of a customs training academy, training is outsourced.

Customs officials must undertake a minimum number of hours of training each year. The Strategic Training Plan anticipates that individual training programs will be set up and provides a time frame for their implementation. Progress in implementing these training programs will be reflected in the individual performance evaluations of staff members. Importers are also given the opportunity to benefit from specialized training intended to acquaint them with the new customs procedures and facilitate their trade processing activities. Preshipment inspection (PSI) companies provide 320 hours per year of courses and internships for NCB officials.

Information and Communication Technology

Before the 1999 reform, the NCB used a software program called SARA, which is basically a register of operations. The software it currently uses is the Automated System for Customs Data (ASYCUDA++), which has proved to be an important factor in NCB's transformation. This new system was chosen because of the low cost of the software, the technical assistance provided by the United Nations Conference for Trade and Development, and the possibility that Bolivia could benefit from the experience of other countries that use this system. With the automation of operations, a considerable number of staff members were freed for redeployment elsewhere in the civil service, a process that has not yet been completed.

Based on the assumption of users' good faith, the new information system made it possible to limit physical inspections. In accordance with Article 79 of the new Customs Law, physical inspections of merchandise are to be limited to a maximum of 20 percent of declarations. Shipments are selected randomly by means of an automated procedure, which runs counter to best practices, whereby goods are selected for inspection based on their risk profile. Goods are designated for one of three channels: red, yellow, or green. Red channel goods undergo physical and document inspection, yellow channel goods are subject to document inspection, and green channel goods are not inspected. For all the products that enter through the yellow and red channels, reference prices can indicate whether there are reasonable doubts concerning the validity of the declared value and can form the basis for a revised valuation.

The reform seeks to automate the entire process of entrance, exit, and clearance. For instance, control systems have been installed for the entrance of goods from the Port of Arica, Chile, and for clearance in any of the customs offices in the Tambo Quemado–La Paz circuit. Before the reform, one of the main complaints of importers and customs brokers was that the customs administration treated them differently depending on which office they chose for the clearance process. The NCB used to argue that this inconsistency occurred because of the lack of an integrated system and the excessive turnover of customs personnel. The implementation of the new legislation and the installation of the ASYCUDA system have eased import and export procedures, but some customs offices and some inspectors are still using old procedures for both imports and exports. Thus, further mainstreaming of the new, simplified procedures is required.

Valuation Issues

At the time of the customs reform, Bolivia was using a valuation system based on the Brussels definition of *value.* The system was administered by two PSI companies: the Société Générale de Surveillance and the Inspectorate. Bolivia has signed the World Trade Organization's Valuation Agreement but, like many other developing countries, it was granted an implementation delay of several years. Now that this period of delay has ended, the main challenge for Bolivia is to correctly implement the agreement, which specifies that customs valuation should be based primarily on the invoice price. This effort is expected to require a building up of the NCB's valuation services and a move away from reliance on reference prices. In this context, the NCB decided not to renew its contracts with the two PSI firms and to progressively assume the customs valuation function.

The NCB originally turned to PSI companies because it distrusted the values declared by importers. The PSI companies charge 1.75 percent of the free-on-board value of imports for their valuation services. Whereas some people, including IMF staff members, doubt whether the PSI companies have contributed to raising customs revenue, the companies assert that they have prevented a significant decline in customs revenue. They assert that discontinuing the use of their services would be risky as long as the NCB does not have the expertise to undertake the valuation responsibilities on its own.

NCB staff members may still inspect imports that have a proper PSI certificate, a step that obviously delays customs clearance. The NCB is planning to phase out its reliance on PSI. Under this plan, PSI companies would gradually restrict their intervention to those tariff categories where such intervention is still warranted because of the revenue importance of the imports. In June 2002, the NCB exempted 48 chapters from PSI. In January 2003, all PSI ceased, in preparation for which the NCB had strengthened it capacities to undertake pre- and post-release valuation control.

Experience with Free Trade Zones

The Customs Code specifies two types of free trade zones: commercial and industrial. Bolivia has a total of 15 free trade zones, including 12 commercial free trade zones, 2 industrial free trade zones, and 1 that is a combination of the two.

Sectors with activities in the commercial free zones include vehicles, food, alcoholic and nonalcoholic beverages, clothing, electrical appliances, home and office furniture, industrial inputs, and machinery and industrial equipment. The two industrial free trade zones have only one active firm each, one of which manufactures wooden furniture and the other of which manufactures circuit boards. According to current law, goods brought into commercial free trade zones can remain unprocessed for an unlimited amount of time until they are either imported for domestic consumption, admitted with exemption from customs duties, temporarily admitted for re-export in the same state, temporarily admitted for active improvement, transferred to another free zone, or re-expedited.

In the industrial free trade zones, goods from abroad and from elsewhere in Bolivia are approved and then either imported for domestic consumption or exported abroad. The activities in those zones include storage, splitting of goods shipments, ordinary handling, retail sales, and goods finishing.

In these free trade zones, the NCB certifies the entry and exit of goods, vehicles, and people. This control is achieved by means of customs documents, such as shipping manifests, commercial bills, and shipping documents. The concessionaires, which the Ministry of External Trade and Investment and the Ministry of Finance entrust to develop and manage the free trade zones, manage controls inside the zones.

Achievements and Deficiencies of the Reform

After only two years, and notwithstanding some shortcomings, the reform of the NCB has yielded positive results, particularly in substantially reducing the pervasive and long-standing corruption. It has also served as a model for the reform of other institutions in the country. New procedures have been enforced gradually, in accordance with the new Customs Law, although further progress could be made. The reform is still ongoing and continues to require support. Important challenges remain, ranging from achieving financial sustainability to rendering new procedures irreversible and improving revenue collection.

Regarding financial sustainability, the deputy minister of taxation has proposed increasing the amount of customs revenue that the NCB retains to cover its expenses to a 3 percent share of total customs revenue, including, in addition to customs duties, value added, consumption, and energy taxes on imports. The NCB considers this proposition to be insufficient, as it would not provide it with the resources needed to operate efficiently. Alternatively, a charge equivalent to 1 percent of the value of imports could be earmarked to finance the NCB's operations. Such a charge would not represent a new burden on trade, as it could replace the fee for valuation services that the PSI companies charged.

The planned merger of the Internal Revenue Service with the NCB may be premature, because the two agencies have not yet consolidated their own reforms. Over the medium term, the government could consider putting a sole revenue authority in place, but any integration of the two agencies would benefit substantially from continued efforts to modernize the NCB and to make further progress with the reforms at the Internal Revenue

Service. In addition, efforts under way to better coordinate activities at both agencies should yield tangible results before further integration could have good payoffs in terms of the effectiveness and efficiency of revenue administration in general.

Bolivia's sizable informal sector raises important issues for the reform process for which no easy solution is available. Because smuggling is an important source of income and employment in many regions, combating smuggling would have a significant short-term social cost. Therefore Article 4 of the Customs Law inhibits control over the domestic retail trade, thereby preventing full attainment of the original objective of imposing sanctions on smuggling and hindering the NCB's attempts to contain smuggling as much as it might otherwise have done. As a result, traders who pay all required import duties complain of unfair competition.

Factors Contributing to the Reform's Success

Several factors have contributed to the success achieved by the reform process thus far. The most important are the following:

- *Leadership role.* The role played by the NCB's recent director general was crucial to the implementation of the key reform measures. The director general was supported by a customs board and management team that provided consistent direction and follow-through for a complex reform.
- *Replacement of NCB personnel.* The drastic overhaul of NCB staff radically reduced the prevalence of corruption. However, this staff renewal has had a cost in terms of services being provided by personnel who are inadequately trained. Only sustained efforts to train staff can overcome this aspect of an otherwise successful reform component.
- *Financial support.* The financial assistance that international institutions have provided to support customs reform has been crucial to its success.
- *Private sector involvement.* The private sector has participated actively in the reform process. Its participation in drafting the new Customs Code is noteworthy, even though the final draft did not retain all the private sector's recommendations. The NCB keeps the private sector informed of the achievements and progress of the reform program through the Customs Modernization Program's follow-up committee, its quality committee, and its contracts with the National Association of Freight Forwarders. In addition, the private sector has been given the opportunity to comment on drafts of forthcoming regulations and appreciates the fact that on many occasions its views and suggestions have been taken into account.
- *Information technology.* The substantial upgrading of information technology has allowed the NCB to introduce selectivity into the process of physical inspections and to start monitoring customs clearance time.

Outcomes

The outcome of the reform can be judged in terms of its effect on corruption, customs clearance time, customs controls and selectivity, enforcement, and revenue performance.

Corruption Private sector traders recognize the drastic curtailment of corrupt practices as one of the main achievements of the reform. Even though corruption has not been completely eradicated, the present situation stands in stark contrast to the situation before the reform, when corruption was rampant.

Customs Clearance Time The reform has resulted in a drastic reduction in the long clearance times that characterized the period before the reform and that traders greatly resented. For them, corruption meant a major increase in their costs, in some cases proving to be as much a trade impediment as tariffs. As table 2.1 shows, during January–July 2003, customs clearance time averaged 39 hours for goods designated to the green channel (no inspection),[3] 49 hours for the yellow channel (document inspection), and 71 hours for the red channel (physical and document inspection). Mendoza

3. Although clearing merchandise that has been slated for the green channel appears to take 39 hours, the actual clearance time for this channel is zero. Once the system assigns green to an import declaration, it clears it immediately with no further ado. Thirty-nine hours is merely the average time that the importer or its customs agent takes between the moment it registers the declaration in the system and the time it picks up the merchandise; it has nothing to do with the time that customs officers take to authorize the goods.

TABLE 2.1 Customs Clearance Time, January–July 2003 (average hours and minutes per shipment)

Clearance Process Steps	Green Lane	Yellow Lane	Red Lane	Average
1. Completion of documentation and payment of duties	10:15	9:41	9:11	9:43
2. Request for and decision about lane designation	10:46	9:04	11:02	10:17
Subtotal 1 + 2	21:01	18:45	20:13	20:00
3. Customs control and inspection	0	17:28	33:50	17:06
Subtotal 1 + 2 + 3	21:01	36:15	54:04	37:07
4. Preparation for exit of goods from customs warehouse	18:23	12:49	16:44	15:59
Total 1 + 2 + 3 + 4	39:25	49:05	70:48	53:06

Source: Mendoza and Gutierrez 2003.

and Gutierrez (2003) compiled these data using ASYCUDA++, and they detailed the delays that take place between the various steps of the clearance process.

Clearance time is measured from the registration of the import declaration until the exit of the goods from the customs warehouse. Excluding the time required to exit the customs' warehouse after customs inspection, the average clearance time reached some 54 hours for the red channel, 36 hours for the yellow channel, and 21 hours for the green channel. Table 2.1 shows the average length of time taken for the various components of the customs clearance process.

These data have only recently been compiled and have led the NCB's management to consider measures to further streamline the customs clearance processes and to introduce targeted actions to reduce the relatively large difference in clearance performance between customs offices, which appears to result from failures to adequately follow the prescribed procedures. The failure to follow procedures is in all likelihood traceable to poor training and officers' lack of familiarity with the simplified and streamlined procedures.

Customs Controls and Selectivity Compliance with customs laws and regulations is significant, and the application of the principle of good faith largely prevails. In conformity with the Customs Law, only 20 percent of the merchandise is physically inspected, with the selection randomly determined. Some traders interviewed noted that the change in customs procedures has still not yielded satisfactory results; inspections are still excessively detailed and cumbersome, and the truthfulness of the declaration is all too often cast in doubt even for traders who have a consistently good reputation.

Enforcement To date, no precise indicators have been established to measure the improvements in efficiency and the reduction in illegitimate trade. According to secondary indicators, customs reform has reduced smuggling compared with the previous situation. These indicators include the number of judicial cases against smugglers; the volume of confiscated merchandise subject to auction; and the prices of some products, such as cigarettes and alcoholic beverages. A reduced level of smuggling is evident for products of mass consumption for which controls are better, such as flour and cigarettes, but lower-volume trade has found ways to enter the country illegally. As noted earlier, controls on the informal import trade deliberately have been lighter than would otherwise have been the case.

Collection of Customs Taxes Customs performance can be measured through the evolution of effective customs tax rates before and after the reform. Subsequent to the customs reform in 1999, imports have declined, reflecting the economic slowdown, the reduction in investments by privatized companies, and the completion of the Bolivia–Brazil gas pipeline. However, the drop in imports exceeded the decline in customs revenue, resulting in an increase in effective tax rates after the reform (figure 2.3). This result points to the favorable effect of the reform on customs efficiency, notwithstanding the possible adverse effects of the staff changeover on expertise and of weaknesses in the implementation of new regulations. The assignment of more staff members to inspections and more expedient enforcement of the new regulations might have enhanced the effects of the reform on revenue.

Users' Reactions

Traders in general are satisfied with the results of the reform, particularly with the success that has been achieved in stemming corruption and the reduction in clearance times, as well as with the streamlined import processes. Traders have also expressed their appreciation of the increased transparency of the clearance procedures. Nevertheless, at times traders criticize how the reform was managed or the way in which some operational steps run contrary to traders' immediate interests.

Exporters note that they have not benefited as much from the reform as they had hoped, because they still encounter major problems with obtaining timely drawback refunds. Some exporters claim to have curtailed their operations. They largely blame this failure on the introduction of the computer software, which has not been helpful in speeding up traders' receipt of adequate drawback refunds. The NCB recognizes this problem and attributes it to the fiscal difficulties under which the Ministry of Finance operates.

The reforms could likely benefit from some modifications to the Customs Code, from further improvements in customs automation, and from improved customs infrastructure at borders, as well as from personnel training.

Much could be gained from shifting the selection of shipments to be inspected from a random basis to one based on risk analysis. If well executed, such a program could further reduce the number of physical inspections and feed into the postrelease verification program, without jeopardizing the NCB's revenue raising responsibilities.

Private users have various recommendations for improving the customs service. They suggest the following:

- improving coordination with companies that manage customs warehouses
- ensuring that changes in release procedures are implemented in such a way as not to cause problems for exporters
- extending the NCB's workday beyond the present eight hours when required by trade flows
- generalizing the practice of accepting the principle of good faith in establishing penalties levied in the case of inaccurate completion of documents
- devising a solution to the problem of smuggling by small traders in the context of regulations that allow and encourage informal sector activities.

Traders are also worried that the NCB will attempt to ensure adequate financing for its operations by increasing the fees and charges for its services. They note that increases would undermine their competitiveness and further benefit the informal traders who are already sheltered from strict application of the Customs Code.

Risks for Sustainability

The sustainability of the reform will depend greatly on continued political support, as well as on the financial support provided for the NCB's operations. Political interference in staffing matters and in favor of exceptional treatment for particular import shipments constitutes a major problem for the sustainability of the momentum of the reform. The reform will also require that coordination between the Treasury and the NCB be maintained or even improved. The anticipated withdrawal of the PSI inspectors also means that the NCB will have to strengthen its own capacities in the area of customs valuation.

Maintaining the trading community's support for the reform is important. If the private sector is convinced that it realizes benefits from the customs reform, it will provide support against backsliding and may even ensure that adequate budget allocations for the NCB are forthcoming. Therefore, a good strategy for communicating with the private sector should be put in place.

Disseminating performance indicators, such as the recently produced data on customs clearance time, on a regular basis may help. In other countries, making sure that all relevant data and regulations are transparently available on the Internet has also helped customs authorities maintain private sector support. Also critical to the continued progress of the customs reform is whether the judicial system can be sufficiently strengthened to support the enforcement of the rule of law and of the sanctions that are meted out against infractions of customs regulations by the trading community and by NCB staff members.

Lessons Learned

Carrying out such extensive reform as is called for in the case of customs procedures and processes requires a clear political decision from the highest authority. In Bolivia, support came from the executive branch of government and from the National Congress, which approved the Reform Law by a majority of more than two-thirds. This endorsement provided the legal and administrative framework to implement the reform. The general public appreciated the benefits to be reaped from the reform and was generally supportive. The further success of the reform will depend on maintaining this support by the body politic as well as by the stakeholders.

The reform cannot succeed without dedicated and well-focused leadership, both from the director general and from the Customs Board and the top management team. The reform also cannot succeed without a vision of and strategy for its implementation. In this case, the vision of administrative improvements benefited from the application of lessons learned from studying the best practices of customs reforms elsewhere and of strategies to combat corruption.

Good management is needed to implement the vision and strategy. In this case, some elements of the reform could have been managed better. For example, the personnel renewal would have been more successful if priority had been given to recruiting staff members who were well versed or trained in customs inspections. Also, the cost of the transition to the ASYCUDA++ system was high for some exporters, who claim that because of it they did not receive adequate refunds under the drawback system. Either the system needed to be better explained and implemented or a financing mechanism should have been put in place to prevent the problems resulting from the Ministry of Finance interference with the payment of tax refunds due to exporters.

Budgets tend to call for the NCB to generate excessive revenues and set the organization up for apparent failure to live up to the revenue expectations included in the budget. Also, the NCB claims that funding for its operations is inadequate, thus jeopardizing its sustainability. This claim may have to be reviewed in light of NCB's operational efficiency and the costs of running a customs organization in other countries.

Large-scale reforms, such as the one implemented in Bolivia, may have significant social costs and benefits. Some are explicitly recognized, and other are not addressed. Bolivia was in the throes of an economic crisis at the time the reform was implemented. Job loss among customs staff and potential loss of income for traders operating in the informal sector were issues. By contrast, exporters, whose jobs would be protected, benefited, as did consumers, who gained from the lower transaction costs that eventually translated into lower prices. The cost-benefit analysis could have been made more explicit and explained to the public at large. Although transitional measures have somewhat protected informal traders, such measures should have been phased out and not enshrined in the Customs Code.

References

IDB (Inter-American Development Bank). 2001. "Bolivia: Institutionalizing Human Resources Management in Bolivia's Customs Administration." In *Customs Best Practices in East Asia and Latin America.* Washington, D.C.

Mendoza, Jaime, and José Eduardo Gutierrez. 2003. "A Methodology to Measure the Time Required for the Release of Goods." Working Paper WP/01/03. National Customs of Bolivia, La Paz.

3

GHANA

Luc De Wulf

Ever since the World Trade Organization meeting in Singapore in 1996, international trade discussions and negotiations have focused on trade facilitation. Trade facilitation was a key agenda point at the World Trade Organization Summit in Cancún in the fall of 2003. That is just one recent illustration of how trade negotiators see trade facilitation, together with policies that reduce trade barriers, as a powerful way to help countries integrate better into the world economy and thereby enhance their growth prospects.

Singapore's achievements in speeding up trade transactions and linking most members of the trading community by means of a single data network, known as TradeNet, have attracted the attention of a number of observers. Mauritius has replicated Singapore's system, and Ghana has recently moved toward introducing key features of this approach to its own trading community. This chapter briefly describes the origins and achievements of Singapore's TradeNet and what other countries that want to facilitate trade transactions might learn from Singapore's experience. The chapter then turns to Ghana's experience to date, including the results achieved and what Ghana still needs to do to fully capture the benefits that TradeNet has to offer.

The Singapore TradeNet

The Singapore TradeNet links multiple parties involved in external trade, including 34 government units, to a single point of transaction for most trade-related activities, such as clearing customs and paying duties and taxes, processing export and import permits and certificates of origin, and collecting trade statistics. The introduction of this system in 1989 drastically simplified trade transactions (King and Konsunski 1995; United Nations Economic and Social Commission for Asia and the Pacific 2003). TradeNet's main achievements since 1989 include the following:

- The processing time for cargo clearance was reduced from two to four days to only minutes.
- The number of documents required for cargo clearance fell from a range of 3 to 35, depending on the transaction, to 1.
- The number of trade transactions processed per day rose from 10,000 to 30,000.
- The freight forwarders estimate that their costs of handling trade documentation have fallen by 20 to 35 percent.
- The customs service receives customs duties payments much faster than before.

- The compilation of trade statistics has improved substantially, benefiting both the trading community and the national authorities responsible for trade policy and economic surveillance.

TradeNet was not created overnight. The idea originated as early as 1979, when a high-level government committee recommended that Singapore should make maximum use of information and communication technology (ICT) to overcome the handicap presented by its small size. A first step in that direction was to expand the skill base through accelerated training in ICT and to computerize government agencies. The government chose to focus on the foreign trade sector as a priority area where results could be achieved quickly, particularly in speeding up the clearance time for exports and imports. The objective was to enhance the competitiveness of Singapore's economy, an issue that became more urgent in 1985, when Singapore experienced its first recession.

The authorities made the Singapore Trade Development Board (officially renamed International Enterprise Singapore in April 2002) responsible for coordinating the aims, concerns, and activities of the trading community. The board reviewed trade documentation and proposed reducing the multiple trade document requirements to a single online form that would serve nearly all the country's trade documentation needs. The board viewed this task as crucial, because automating the multiplicity of forms and data requirements that prevailed at the time was virtually impossible. The challenge of coordinating the different agencies involved and their data requirements into a set of coherent and simplified procedures that could be automated was in many cases more political than technical.

In December 1986, the initiative received high-level backing when Trade Minister B. G. Lee, currently deputy prime minister, publicly endorsed the initiative and gave the TradeNet project full political backing. Lee announced that TradeNet would be launched in January 1989. In 1990, the government created Singapore Network Services (whose name was changed to CrimsonLogic in 2002) to own and operate the TradeNet system, with the Singapore Trade Development Board, the port and civil aviation authorities, and the international airport as stakeholders. Singapore Network Services carried out an intensive review of the proposed TradeNet system and prepared initial designs. This step permitted the launching of a competitive bidding process for a systems integrator. IBM won the contract to develop an electronic data interchange system that would allow computer-to-computer exchange of business documents among connected members of the Singapore trading community.

The focus was on accuracy and speed. The system was to be designed so that a trader would submit one document to TradeNet, which would then forward it to all pertinent agencies and partners. Agencies that needed to make decisions would then be able to do so promptly to permit the trade transaction to proceed smoothly.

The system became operational as of January 1, 1989, and traders were invited to adopt its protocols on a voluntary basis. By the end of the year TradeNet was being used for 45 percent of all air and sea shipments, a share that rose to 95 percent by mid-1991, when the use of TradeNet had become mandatory, two years earlier than originally planned. Extensive training and continued high-level political support sustained the adoption process for traders, particularly small traders.

Progress in linking all members of the trading community benefited greatly from the fact that many of them had already acquired substantial computer knowledge and were relying on sophisticated computer equipment for doing their work. This factor was in part an outcome of Singapore's well-implemented government strategy to foster the use of ICT. Publicizing TradeNet's benefits early on contributed to overcoming initial reluctance to participate among the various government agencies and the trading community.

Background in Ghana

In the 1990s, Ghana undertook fundamental trade policy reforms, a move that bilateral and multilateral donors strongly supported. The United States provided support through two trade and investment projects, and the World Bank and International Monetary Fund provided substantial adjustment lending as well as support for the development of private enterprises and exports. This reform drive benefited from the strong personal support of the minister of trade and industry, in line with the government's vision of a Ghana that was open to the rest of the world and that could attract foreign direct investment and promote business competitiveness. The vision implied an open economy, low tariffs, and well-performing institutions. The reforms therefore included reducing and then eliminating import quotas and export taxes, lowering the level of import tariffs, and reducing the number of applicable tariff rates. Nontraditional exports were to be promoted so as to diversify the economy and create much-needed jobs.

By 1998, Ghana had implemented many of the policy reforms, but foreign direct investment was still lagging. A number of reviews by the World Bank, the International Monetary Fund, the Foreign Investment Advisory Service, and the Multilateral Investment Guarantee Agency, among others, suggested that for the policy reforms to have the desired impact on trade, foreign direct investment, and growth they had to be complemented by the lifting of a number of structural investment constraints. In particular, the government needed to improve the operational efficiency of frontline agencies at facilitating investment flows. Such frontline agencies included the customs service, the immigration authorities, the port authorities, and the Investment Promotion Council. The government took those suggestions to heart and decided to launch the Ghana Gateway Project, for which it solicited support from the World Bank. Ghanaian civil society, as well as the foreign donor community, broadly shared this vision of Ghana as the world's gateway to West Africa. The government envisaged that the project not only would enhance the competitiveness of domestic business entities but would also make Ghana the most competitive investment destination in West Africa, compared with other destinations such as Côte d'Ivoire, Nigeria, or Senegal.

Although Ghana was more competitive in terms of costs than Nigeria as a transit corridor for the Sahelian countries, its cost parity was about the same as that of Côte d'Ivoire, but Ghana lacked the Ivorian infrastructure backbone. Thus Ghana saw the introduction of an automated system for customs clearance, along with other reforms initiated for the frontline agencies, as steps that would bring Ghana up to Côte d'Ivoire's level, if not actually giving it a competitive edge over Côte d'Ivoire.

In search of new ideas and to investigate trade facilitation and promotion programs introduced elsewhere, official delegations visited Malaysia, Mauritius, New Zealand, and Singapore, countries with which Ghana enjoyed excellent relations. These missions included representatives of the private sector and of industry, the minister of trade, the chief executives of the Ghana Investment Promotion Center, and members of the Ghana Export Promotion Council. Those involved eventually became a broader stakeholder group of public and private sector representatives. The delegations found the visits to Mauritius and Singapore particularly fascinating. They saw in the TradeNet approach a system that provided the dual benefits of speeding up trade transactions without jeopardizing government revenues while streamlining trade transaction processes by bringing the various members of the trading community into an integrated network.

Under the leadership of the Ministry of Trade and Industry (MOTI) the delegates identified the key elements of the approach that Ghana intended to pursue to rapidly achieve a major breakthrough in trade facilitation. The scheme's design was heavily influenced by Singapore's TradeNet and by the desire to rely on strong outside financial and technical support. Having seen the Singaporean model and its Mauritian adaptation firsthand, the delegates were convinced that a combination of strong political support and excellent technical implementing capabilities would be required to attain the objective of facilitating trade and investment while protecting, if not increasing, budget revenue. The implementation of such a system, along with other policy measures, in Mauritius propelled the country into becoming a leading textile and garment exporter. With this example in mind, MOTI took the lead in these initiatives with a view to making trade the engine of future growth.

The Ministry of Finance, which has ministerial oversight responsibility for the Customs, Excise, and Preventive Services (CEPS), supported the initiative. It was attracted to the project mainly because of the possibilities the project offered for strengthening customs services and increasing budget revenues. Even though CEPS had to undertake much of the initial implementation, it was not asked to manage the project because, at that time, CEPS did not have the same vision with respect to trade facilitation or the required implementation capacity. In addition, the government saw trade facilitation as involving more than just customs operations.

The major elements of the proposed strategy were as follows. A committee, the Inter-Ministerial Gateway Oversight Committee, with its own secretariat, was to oversee the various components of this ambitious initiative. A capable public servant was chosen to head the secretariat. After the committee reviewed proposals from various software and systems integrators, the government invited the Singaporean firm that managed TradeNet, CrimsonLogic, to provide the electronic data interchange system that would become the core of Ghana's version of TradeNet. Although CrimsonLogic had successfully transferred the technology to Mauritius and had convinced the Gateway team of its ability to do the same in Ghana, it was not prepared to commit investment funds directly for the development of the electronic data interchange, as the government required. This undertaking was assumed by the Société Générale de Surveillance (SGS), which had a strategic partnership with CrimsonLogic as an investor and lead technical partner. SGS also had extensive experience in providing trade assurance services for Ghana.

Thus Ghana adopted a customs management system that had been designed for Mauritius and interfaced smoothly with its version of TradeNet. As part of the arrangements, a company was to be created that would be charged with implementing both Ghana's version of TradeNet and the Ghana Customs Management System (GCMS) for CEPS by means of what virtually amounted to a build-own-operate-transfer contract.

With a view to ensuring broad stakeholder commitment to the project, various private and public entities were invited to participate in the equity of the company that would manage TradeNet and help computerize customs operations. In particular, the government approached communications infrastructure companies, several banks, chambers of commerce and industry, and associations of ship owners and freight forwarders. However, most declined because of a lack of either vision or capital. Since the rollout of the system and as its effectiveness and financial viability have become apparent, most banks and some stakeholders, such as the Ghana Institute of Freight Forwarders, have sought to subscribe to the company's equity.

The company, known as the Ghana Community Network (GCNet), was created as a joint venture company with SGS (60 percent), CEPS (20 percent), the Ghana Shippers Council (10 percent), and two local banks (5 percent each) as its shareholders. SGS had operated the Ghana preshipment service until 1988, had expert knowledge of the country, and wanted to expand its portfolio of services to the government. By participating with a majority stake, SGS strove to meet its accountability obligations by having the necessary operational authority. In November 2000, GCNet was incorporated with equity of US$5.3 million (total investments to date are now estimated at US$7 million). CEPS's contribution consisted of in-kind equity (namely, computer equipment that it had procured with World Bank funding under the Gateway Project). The other equity partners contributed cash.

GCNet operates under a service contract with MOTI. The contract specifies that GCNet must install the electronic data interchange and customs management systems. The contract does not include any clear performance indicators or targets, only the requirement to report periodically on the progress of the project and its results.

Rollout of the Vision

Implementing the vision of efficiently connecting all members of the trading community involved both simplifying the existing customs procedures and building the institutional and infrastructural capacity to manage the new procedures.

The Situation before Reform

The GCNet vision was to transform a spaghetti-like network that had connected the various agencies and entities involved in the trade transaction process into a single network of trading community members. Figure 3.1 shows the various communication links that had existed in the years before reform. Each agency required a unique set of documents that had to be submitted only to it and that it did not share with other members of the trading community, even though those other members may have required similar documents. Thus, a great deal of paperwork was required, and the transcription of multiple copies was error prone.

All this effort was time-consuming and costly. Various studies reported that clearing a consignment involved 23 steps (see the appendix for more details). These steps included submitting

FIGURE 3.1 The Pre-Reform Trade Transaction System

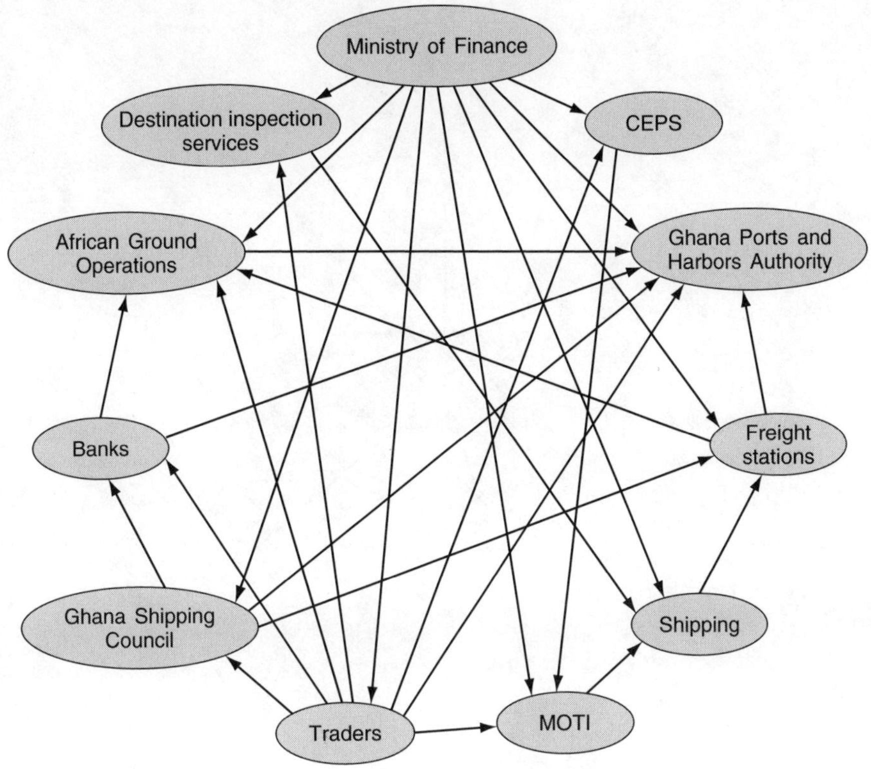

Source: GCNet.

an import declaration form, inspection reports, and a certificate or permit from the relevant regulatory bodies—for example, the Food and Drug Board, the Ministry of Interior, the Free Zone Board, and the Ghana Chamber of Commerce and Industry. In meeting these diverse agency requirements, trade operators were obliged to criss-cross from one agency to another to chase documents being processed, because the agencies were neither networked to communicate with each other nor able to access to a common database.

For instance, the carrier had to submit 13 copies of the shipping manifest to CEPS. CEPS then transcribed this information into a different format and used it as a basis for checking the manifest to ensure that all cargo that the carrier brought in had been declared. This process was time-consuming and error prone and did not provide a transparent method for auditing whether all cargo had indeed been declared. The Statistical Service compiled statistics by collecting all the documents on paper or on diskettes and compiling them into different sets of statistical tables (kind of trade, countries of origin and destination, and so on). The transmittal and manipulation of the information needed to produce the desired statistical data again took a great deal of time, was not particularly accurate, and was produced only after long delays.

This situation created many opportunities for soliciting and providing "facilitation money" to speed up transactions, to be permitted to jump the line, or simply to adjust a customs declaration to suit the particular objectives of those involved. The overall lack of transparency left a weak audit trail, and in most instances left no trail at all. All those problems impeded the competitiveness of the Ghanaian economy.

Figure 3.2 portrays a vision of a totally interconnected trading community, one that is similar to Singapore's TradeNet and constitutes the objective of GCNet. The idea is that the trader submits one document online to GCNet that contains the

FIGURE 3.2 TradeNet Concepts

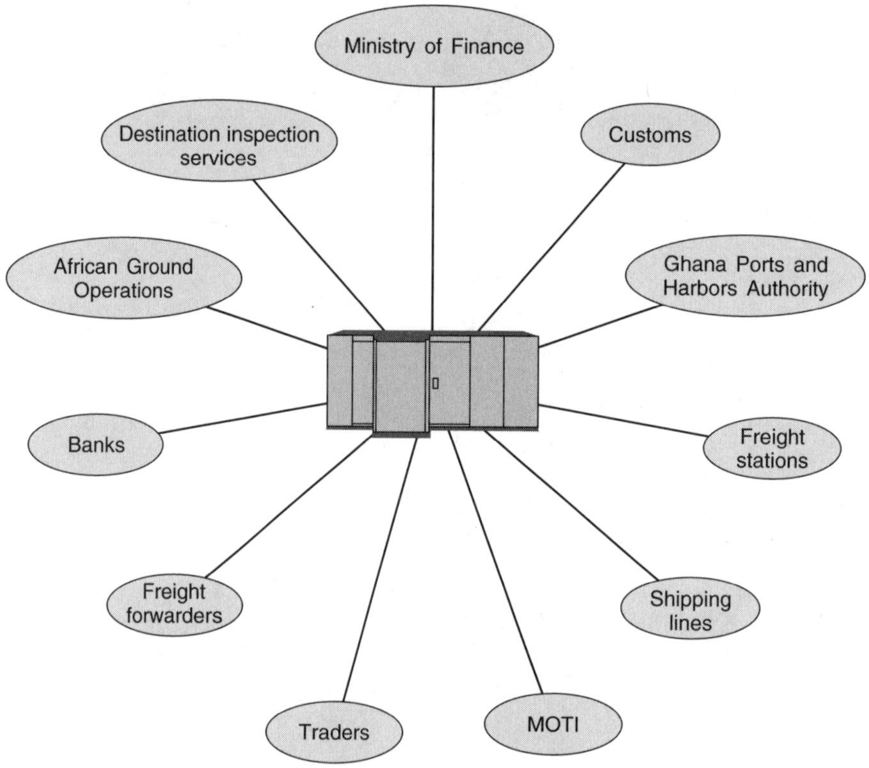

Source: GCNet.

information all pertinent agencies require either to fulfill their regulatory functions or to provide the necessary permits. GCNet then sends the information to the relevant agencies, which respond immediately either with requests for further information or with the necessary permits. The objective of integrating all traders into a community of this kind is to reduce traders' transaction costs and to make the government's regulatory operations more effective and efficient.

The Efficiency of Customs Transactions

During the 1990s, customs operations were subjected to a number of reviews sponsored by the World Bank, in the context of preparing the Gateway Project. The reviews noted the commitment of customs service officers and their general acceptance of an obligation to meet revenue targets. The reviews also judged the legal framework for CEPS operations to be satisfactory, albeit requiring some modifications. However, the reviews also noted several weaknesses. First, the structure and organization of CEPS, its ICT, and its human resources management structure and tools were inappropriate for meeting the demands of modern, effective, and efficient customs operations. Second, the system for data capture was extremely labor intensive and slow. Numerous manual records were kept, and the software in place, the Automated System for Customs Data (ASYCUDA), was grossly underused and poorly maintained, thereby offering little value added. As a result, customs operations were inconsistent among the different clearance stations; inspection companies were called in to assist in valuation work; transit trade was hindered by the requirement that vehicles involved in transit trade be accompanied by customs staff during the transit voyage to ascertain that they had left the country; and revenue leakages resulted from weaknesses at every point of the clearance process, from manifest declaration, to warehouse control, to payment of duties.

Various observers frequently made proposals to strengthen ASYCUDA, but no improvements that had lasting results were undertaken, largely because of the absence of a real champion for change, the lack of budgetary resources, and the inadequate support provided by the developers of the software. CEPS staff members were also somewhat complacent, because the situation let them benefit in terms of significant payments of facilitation money. Clearance times were extremely slow, with much of the blame falling on slow operations at CEPS, even though other factors also accounted for significant clearance delays. No accurate estimates are available of the time importers had to wait between declaration and clearance, but importers note that the fastest clearance time at the seaports was four days, while the average clearance time was several weeks. Clearance at the airports was faster than at the seaports.

As installed and used in Ghana, ASYCUDA was unable to turn a declaration around in fewer than 24 hours. Hence, a drastic upgrade of customs operations was required if the government was to attain its trade facilitation aims. To this end, Ghana adopted a phased program that would start with CEPS simplifying its trade procedures and acquiring a modern customs management system. This system would consist of the various modules required to manage imports, exports, warehousing, and the transit trade—that is, all relevant customs operations from the declaration of cargo to the payment of duties and clearance. The system would need to be as modern as possible and be modeled on systems that were fully operational elsewhere. Once the new software system was entrenched, a fully fledged customs modernization program could be initiated. This strategy was risky, as the new customs management system could run into the same problems that had caused ASYCUDA to fail. Special safeguards were therefore required to reduce this risk. Entrusting GCNet to support CEPS with the introduction of the system was intended to address this risk.

The Rollout of GCNet

The rollout of GCNet was plagued with problems. The timing of GCNet's incorporation, November 2000, was only one month before the December 2000 national elections. The opposition won the elections and did not install a new cabinet until March 2001. This power vacuum, and the transition period before the new cabinet members reviewed policy decisions made by the previous government for due diligence purposes, seriously affected the implementation of the Gateway Project. It prevented the secretariat from making operational decisions, including the procurement of the computer hardware that was to be CEPS's contribution to GCNet. In addition, the appointment of many new ministers meant that GCNet did not get the political backing that had been expected at its creation, when a powerful MOTI stood behind the project and envisaged integrating the various trading partners into a single trading community.

At CEPS, the leadership was initially not fully informed about the reforms that the introduction of the new customs management system required, particularly the documentation and process simplification it required. As a result of this information gap and the uncertain political support, CEPS took 14 months to provide GCNet with its capital contribution. It also took until July 2002 for the legislation to be modified to permit the automation of customs operations. However, once the new administration had completed its due diligence on the relevance of the project and the operational modalities to be followed, it supported the project as a key feature of its revenue mobilization aims and its role as a facilitator for trade operators.

GCNet's service contract with MOTI contained a commitment to help implement the electronic data interchange system and the GCMS at CEPS. In return, it was to be paid a fee set at 0.4 percent of the transacted value for each declaration processed by TradeNet. In other words, GCNet was to be the systems integrator and needed to select the various systems that would make up the overall package. With respect to the data interchange system, the choice was relatively simple, as the initial inspiration had come from seeing the CrimsonLogic platform operating in Singapore and its subsequent modification for Mauritius Network Services. As a result, GCNet secured the services and support of both CrimsonLogic and Mauritius Network Services—itself a joint venture company between the Mauritian telecommunications provider, the Mauritian government, and CrimsonLogic—to roll out its service.

GCNet had a hands-on approach during this whole process, even when political commitment was lackluster because of the political transition. In addition, GCNet provided assistance to CEPS not only for training its staff, which was included in the service agreement with MOTI, and installing the electronic data interchange technology, but also for some infrastructure and maintenance expenses for which CEPS claimed not to have the budgetary resources. Indeed, GCNet stepped in wherever necessary to ensure that TradeNet and the GCMS would operate smoothly, which included providing air conditioning for some offices, ensuring that backup generators for the GCMS were provided with diesel fuel, and making sure that maintenance contracts were paid up. GCNet also provided assistance in setting up a national customs selectivity team to coordinate and implement risk assessment and in training CEPS staff to undertake postclearance audits.

GCNet's Operations

GCNet operates a customized electronic system for processing trade and customs documents and for recording the results of this processing and validation and the related duty and tax payments. It does so using two systems: the Ghana TradeNet and the GCMS. Through the Ghana TradeNet's electronic data interchange platform, users can interface with the GCMS and can transmit messages to the various parties connected to the system and receive replies electronically. These parties include key public sector agencies (such as MOTI, the Ministry of Finance, the Bank of Ghana, and CEPS), as well as entities in the private sector (for instance, the shipping lines, African Ground Operations, freight forwarders, and banks). TradeNet thus provides a medium for exchanging trade information between businesses and government agencies, thereby making GCNet a business-to-government company.

To enable users to access its services, GCNet has established its own private communications network. This network consists of a fiber optic broadband link between the GCNet office and CEPS. The link is complemented by radio links that cover CEPS's collection stations, plus dedicated leased lines and points of presence in locations outside Accra. This network links CEPS offices throughout Ghana and, in so doing, facilitates easy access to the system by its users. The development of this private network also ensures that the system will always be up and running and will not suffer any communications hiccups, unlike the normal, unreliable communications networks. In the absence of a well-articulated national communications strategy, this new communications network stands in isolation without the necessary interface with other agencies.

GCNet has worked closely with CEPS to reengineer CEPS's operational processes, including the preparation of new customs procedures codes that meet standards set by the World Customs Organization. The Ghana customs tariff book, which provides for only four rates—0, 5, 10, and 20 percent—has also been reviewed extensively and updated to ensure that it meets standards set by the harmonized system of the World Customs Organization.

Throughout the development of its systems, GCNet has sensitized all key stakeholders—for example, ship owners, clearing agents, importers, exporters, and banks—and has engaged them in interactive consultations to ensure that the systems address their concerns and meet their expectations. In addition, GCNet has embarked on an extensive training program for CEPS staff and declarants to ensure that all system users are adequately trained in those aspects required for their trade and customs transactions. GCNet has also prepared user guidelines and posters, and explanations of procedures are available on CD-ROM and on a Web site. Copies of the various documents are available at GCNet's offices for registered declarants.

GCNet rolled out the TradeNet and GCMS systems gradually. It began by conducting tests at Kotoka International Airport. On completion of the tests, full rollout started. The systems were introduced to small groups of traders at a time so that the learning process was spread over a number of months, thereby permitting CEPS's employees to acquaint themselves with the new procedures and traders and their representatives to be trained in using the system. The first electronic data interchange declarations were lodged at Kotoka International Airport in October 2002 for import transactions. The transition was completed by December 2002. From March to June 2003, the system was implemented at Tema Harbor, also for import declarations. In November 2003, the system was introduced at the port of Takoradi and also started recording exports. Other clearance stations will be connected in the coming months.

A Typical Import Transaction

The following description of the steps involved in the import process illustrates the advantages of the new procedures (see the appendix for an outline of the procedures that prevailed before the launch of GCNet). It also presents some of the problems that still need to be tackled before Ghana can fully master the challenges of trade facilitation. Of course, there are a number of special import regimes and transit and export transactions, for which GCMS foresees specialized modules. Figure 3.3 provides a schematic view of the full customs clearance process, which can be divided into eight steps.

- *Step 1.* The importer obtains an import declaration form from MOTI at a cost of ₵50,000 (recently increased from ₵5,000). This aspect of the process is not connected to GCNet. Banks use import declaration forms for payment purposes and the destination inspection services (DIS) companies use them merely as a notice of intent to import the goods listed on the form.
- *Step 2.* The importer requests a destination inspection form from one of the four DIS companies engaged by MOTI. Only two of these DIS companies are members of the International Federation of Inspection Agencies, which certifies and regulates the operations of inspection companies. At times, those DIS companies that are members of the federation draw on resources from the federation's members abroad. One DIS agency relies heavily on scanning to examine containerized cargo. Scanning equipment is on order for the other DIS companies. The DIS

FIGURE 3.3 Simplified Import Procedures

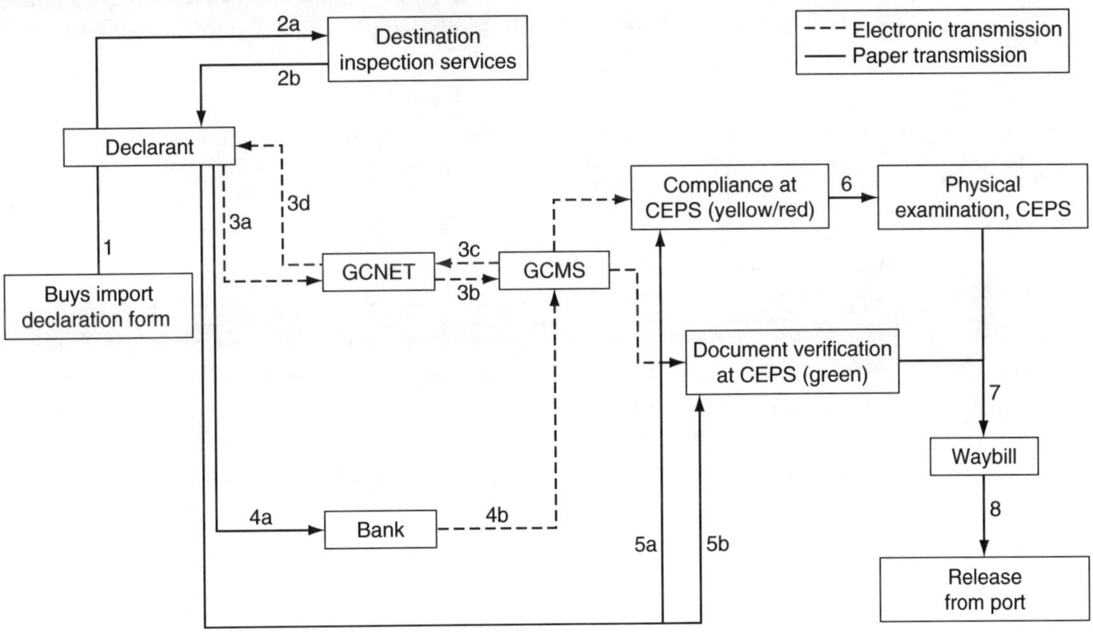

Steps

1. Declarant buys import declaration form at MOTI
2a. Declarant submits import declaration form, invoice, and bill of lading to destination inspection services company
2b. Destination inspection services issues report
3. Declarant electronically validates customs declaration through Ghana Customs Management System (GCMS) and obtains response, consignment manifest is sent electronically from shipping agent to CEPS for electronic checking
4a. Declarant proceeds to bank and settles all duties and taxes
4b. Bank confirms payment electronically to GCMS
5. Declarant proceeds either to customs document verification (green channel) or to customs compliance (yellow or red channels)
6. Compliance routes declaration electronically to examination officer who conducts examination (no examination on green channel)
7. Officer releases consignment electronically
8. Waybill is issued and consignment is physically cleared

companies charge importers 1 percent of the cost, insurance, and freight value of the shipment for the DIS certificate. The companies provide the trader and CEPS with a final classification and valuation report on paper.[1]

- *Step 3.* The declarant (importer or shipping agent) prepares an electronic customs declaration on a computer that has GCNet-installed front-end software and submits it to TradeNet, which is located at GCNet's headquarters. The declaration provides data required for that particular category of import. It also provides customs data, such as valuation, weight, Harmonized Commodity Description and Coding System classification, origin of the cargo, and taxes and other fees due, as well as data required by the Ghana Standards Board and any other agency. The declaration is electronically forwarded to CEPS's headquarters. The GCMS validates the declaration, a process that takes only a few minutes, and electronically notifies the declarant of validation or sends it back through GCNet to the declarant to provide further information or to resolve inconsistencies. In the meantime, upon arrival of the imported goods, the carrier's manifest is transmitted electronically to TradeNet, with copies to CEPS and to the Ghana Port and Harbor Authority. Thus CEPS is able to verify whether all cargo included in the manifest has been declared within a reasonable period of time and to remind the owners of cargo that they must make a declaration or forfeit the goods.
- *Step 4.* The declarant prints the validated declaration and pays the required taxes and duties at one of the two banks connected to TradeNet, branches of which are located at CEPS's clearance offices. The bank electronically notifies the GCMS that the taxes and duties for that particular declaration have been paid.
- *Step 5.* The declarant provides the supporting documentation (printed declaration, invoice, certificate of origin, DIS certificate, and so on) to either the document verification section or the CEPS compliance office at the clearance point, depending on the risk profile. The risk analysis module of GCMS determines whether the cargo is to be cleared without further ado (green channel), will be subjected to document verification (yellow channel), or requires physical inspection (red channel).
- *Step 6.* The GCMS randomly assigns the inspector who will do the physical inspection. The GCMS informs the freight station of the inspection requirements.
- *Step 7.* The GCMS issues the clearance statement and notes whether the declarant must make additional payments and then releases the consignment electronically to the port authorities and to the declarant. The port authorities issue the waybill (manually for the moment, but plans are being finalized for electronic issuance by mid-2004).
- *Step 8.* The goods leave the port.

In addition to these steps for customs clearance, the declarant must also complete cargo handling and warehouse procedures and comply with controls pertaining to such regulatory agencies as the Ghana Standards Board and the Food and Drugs Board. Step 3 through the first part of step 7 are managed electronically.

Outcomes

Although it is too soon to make a full assessment of the results, some preliminary observations can certainly be made.

Revenues Are Up

At Kotoka International Airport, revenues for July to September 2003 were nearly 40 percent higher than during the same period in 2002. Five percentage points of this was due to the depreciation of the cedi against the U.S. dollar during that period. The increase does not appear to have been caused by

1. The author did not consult directly with the DIS companies. However, from discussions with a MOTI representative, he learned that the largest DIS company claimed that in September 2003 it had increased the declared value of imports by about 75 percent. For 62 percent of invoices, the company changed the Harmonized Commodity Description and Coding System classification, and for 65 percent of invoices, it increased the values without changing the declared classification. The company claimed that in September it realized additional payments of US$5.4 million. None of the importers had to pay fines. As is the case in many other countries where DIS or similar companies operate, their intervention is heavily criticized by importers and by customs officials, who claim that the companies lack integrity and that their processes are time-consuming. The author did not examine the operations of the DIS companies in detail.

an increase in the volume of imports, because estimates indicate that import volumes have stagnated year to year. With no real change in the activities of the DIS companies during this period, GCNet operations are conservatively estimated to have added 30 percent to the customs revenues from airport traffic.

Clearance Times Are Down

No firm statistics are available about clearance times before the introduction of GCNet, but traders unanimously assert that improvements with respect to the time taken to clear goods both at Kotoka International Airport and at Tema Harbor are major.

With respect to Kotoka International Airport, GCNet notes that average clearance times have dropped from three days to four hours (18 percent of goods clear in fewer than two hours and 75 percent clear the same day). Customs document review, which in the past averaged 24 hours, now averages 10 minutes. Bank payment, which used to average a few hours, now averages 10 minutes.

With respect to Tema Port, GCNet claims that clearance times have been reduced from a week, on average, to a few days. Customs document review averages 15 minutes instead of 24 hours (14 percent of goods clear the same day and 30 percent clear in 24 to 48 hours). Bank payments average 10 minutes, compared with a few hours in the past.

Community Networks Are Being Initiated

A start has been made at connecting various members of the trading community, with the result that trade transactions are easier for traders and that government and regulatory agencies are beginning to have access to a centralized data source. Much work still needs to be done, but the following members of the trading community have already been connected:

- The shipping lines provide electronic manifests to GCNet, which transfers them to the Ghana Ports and Harbors Authority.
- The Ghana Shippers Council obtains all information about the movement of ships and airplanes and, since early 2004, has stopped demanding paper documentation from shippers.
- The customs declarations are provided to CEPS electronically.
- The banks inform CEPS electronically of payments made.
- The Statistical Service is connected to receive all relevant trade statistics from CEPS. Unfortunately, the Statistical Service has not yet taken advantage of this opportunity.
- The Ministry of Finance can download all trade information, as well as all transactions by taxpayers identified by a tax identification number. The Ministry of Finance has not yet taken advantage of this connection, in part because its own management system is still based on manual procedures.
- The Value Added Tax Service accesses information on imports made by firms that must pay value added taxes.

Some Have Won and Some Have Lost

The clear winners of the GCNet initiative have been the traders, who benefit from faster clearance times through customs and a reduced need to provide facilitation money. Representatives of shipping owners and agents, as well as freight forwarders, were vocal in their support of GCNet, because they now have to produce less documentation and because vessel turnaround time has been reduced. The Treasury also benefits from higher revenues and from faster access to tax payments.

The losers are those CEPS personnel who had previously benefited from substantial facilitation payments that traders had offered to accelerate cargo clearance, to close their eyes when cargo left port premises without a declaration, or to accept declarations that included underinvoicing and erroneous product classifications so as to lower the amount of duties due. Some CEPS personnel are clearly unhappy with the current situation, afraid that any further modernization of CEPS will further undermine their entrenched positions and involve drastic changes with respect to recruitment and training requirements. Such personnel invariably tend to frustrate traders with a view to extracting payments or delaying the process. Others have tested the system to try to find any loopholes that they might be able to exploit. Decisive action against such officers, albeit not as severe as might have been expected, serves as a deterrent against such actions.

Lessons Learned and the Road Ahead

A number of valuable lessons have been learned during the course of implementing the new system. First, partnerships between the private and public sectors can work. GCNet anchored the reforms and ensured the continuity of and a focus on the reform objectives during a period of political transition, when no other local organization had the wherewithal to effect such a drastic transformation of trade and customs procedures. If CEPS or the Gateway secretariat had been in charge of implementing the trade facilitation project, it probably would have made little progress to date. The build-own-operate-transfer concept can be extremely effective when local institutions are relatively weak, especially in relation to trade facilitation. It has been tried in only a few countries, including Mauritius, Singapore, and Tunisia, where its community-owned concept was favorably received. Further replication is worth looking into when the circumstances warrant.

Second, making use of ICT can yield rapid results. It took only from early 2001 to mid-2003 to roll out TradeNet and GCMS in ports that account for more than 90 percent of all Ghana's trade. Clearance times and revenue performance exceeded expectations during this short period of time.

Third, hands-on technical support to customs operations can speed them up. Whereas the customs service had struggled for years to upgrade its information system and make the best use of it, the reform required an outside push and hands-on implementation support to force the process simplification that was required and the adoption of advanced ICT processes.

Finally, top-level support for a project is extremely helpful in launching and sustaining it. Initially the project benefited from top-level MOTI support that was perceived as bringing with it the support of the whole government. When that support wavered after the December 2000 elections, the project floundered for a year and the Gateway secretariat could provide no real support. It was during that time that GCNet had to wait for more than 14 months to obtain approval from the National Communications Authority to use a secure radio frequency as part of its communications network. Also, the absence of dedicated support for the project made it difficult to ensure that the various trade-related agencies were fully integrated into the network.

In terms of necessary actions to complete the trade facilitation project, customs reform must now be tackled seriously. So far the reforms at CEPS have been limited to introducing the GCMS and its associated process simplification; however, CEPS is still an outmoded and inefficient organization. Its organizational structure suffers from serious shortcomings that will prevent it from fully internalizing the ongoing reforms and from taking advantage of the possibilities they offer. Consider the following issues:

- CEPS has limited specialized capacity in customs valuation to provide support to the officers in charge of document compliance checks. Most customs organizations have a valuation department or unit staffed by specialists in various commodity categories. CEPS should gradually take over such work from the DIS companies or could rely much more selectively—and more economically—on valuation support from the DIS companies.
- The Ministry of Finance should take over the supervision of the DIS companies' activities from MOTI.
- CEPS does not have a team that can draw operational conclusions from the plentiful data that have become available to support modern management techniques.
- Modern risk analysis is absent. In October 2003, nearly 99 percent of all cargo arriving at Tema Port and 88 percent of that arriving at Kotoka International Airport were physically inspected. This high proportion is only partly explained by the rigid requirement of MOTI and the Ghana Standards Board to inspect a large share of total imports, by the difficulties presented by the imports channeled by informal traders, and by the shipments made by occasional importers that have no track record with the customs authorities. Proper risk analysis could drastically reduce those numbers, if only by permitting large traders with recognized track records to automatically pass through the green channel with a possibility for later audits. Some 10 percent of traders probably account for 50 to 70 percent of all imports; therefore, the introduction of a "gold card scheme"—that is, automatic green channel

routing and exemption from DIS—would drastically reduce trade impediments.

- Staff training and recruitment will need to be revised substantially.[2] In the future, customs techniques will depend increasingly on fast clearance with minimal physical and document inspection, requiring that teams perform efficient postclearance inspections. Such a shift implies that staff will be reassigned from physical inspection in the ports or airport to postclearance monitoring and audits, assignments that require substantially different skills. Staff without the requisite skills will no longer be needed.[3]

More members of the trading community should be part of the GCNet community. Obviously, overcoming the lack of computer literacy at some organizations will take time and require persuasion, as will eliminating the latent rivalry between them. High-level visible support will help.

In the immediate future, the government should support ongoing plans that will allow the Ghana Ports and Harbors Authority to issue waybills electronically. In addition, the Statistics Service should activate its connection and start downloading trade statistics. The Value Added Tax Service and the Internal Revenue Service, which are already connected, should prepare themselves to use the data provided by the GCMS, for which a streamlining of tax identification numbers will be needed. Such data could be extremely useful for their own audit work, particularly when full-year data become available. The Bank of Ghana and MOTI could do likewise for the online, real-time collation of trade data that they require for preparing various statistical trade reports.

In the near future, it should also be possible to connect MOTI, with respect to the issuance of import declarations if they are still required in the future, as well as the documentation of the DIS companies that operate under MOTI contracts. Early connection of the Food and Drug Board and the Ghana Standards Board would also benefit trade greatly by permitting greater streamlining of inspections. Similarly, connections could be made by a whole range of agencies, such as the Ghana Free Zone Board, the Investment Promotion Center, the Driver and Vehicle Licensing Authority, and the Minerals Commission, which have key roles to play in processing trade documents and clearing cargo.

Clearance time is not only a function of CEPS's operations. Other agencies also need to carry their weight. Now that CEPS's operations are faster and less costly than in the past, efforts should be made to reduce the overall clearance time by improving the operations of the DIS companies (which average one week or more), as well as those of the ports.[4] Some observers suggest that the drastic reduction in the time CEPS takes to clear goods has overwhelmed and exacerbated inefficiencies elsewhere in the transport logistics chain. In any event, assessing the improvements in clearance times resulting from improvements in customs procedures has had a major result, such that blame for the delays can now be laid where it belongs. That may be a major side benefit of carefully measuring clearance times and making them public, in that such publicity may energize or shame other responsible parties into improving their own performance.

2. The training commitment that the DIS companies have recently signed with MOTI does not appear to be integrated with CEPS's business plan. Similar training commitments in other countries have never been able to replace a dedicated training effort managed by the customs authorities themselves.

3. Some CEPS staff are functionally illiterate and incapable of contributing to running a modern and efficient customs service.

4. The Ghana Ports and Harbors Authority is currently commissioning a new management tool that could provide substantial support for improved port operations. This system should be integrated with GCNet.

Appendix 3.A.: Import Procedures Before GCNet

Before TradeNet and the Ghana Customs Management System were rolled out, all formalities required for an import transaction to take place were reviewed in detail. After this review, the procedures were substantially simplified to take advantage of the possibilities offered by TradeNet and the Ghana Customs Management System.

A description of a typical import process before the reforms follows. For special import regimes the procedures could be substantially more complicated. Multiple face-to-face contacts between importers or their representatives and customs officials could easily lead to integrity problems.

1. The shipping agent submits 12 copies of the shipping manifest.
2. The importer or the importer's agent obtains shipment notifications.
3. The declarant purchases an import declaration form.
4. The declarant submits documents for DIS.
5. The declarant buys 13 copies of the customs declaration form.
6. The declarant submits the final classification and valuation report from a DIS company.
7. The declarant pays self-assessed duties at the bank. Only one bank accepts payments. This bank is located at the point of entry, which is usually overcrowded and wracked with delays.
8. The bank issues a payment receipt and passes it on to CEPS, which is located at the same point of entry.
9. The declarant submits the declaration with supporting documents to CEPS.
10. CEPS reviews the declaration.
11. CEPS enters the declaration into ASYCUDA, which takes a minimum of 24 hours.
12. CEPS prints the ASYCUDA form and confirms or alters the tax liability.
13. CEPS numbers the declaration and affixes a date and hologram seal.
14. CEPS detaches the 13 copies and dispatches them to the various recipients.
15. CEPS's verification unit receives its copy of the declaration.
16. An examination officer is assigned to the particular shipment.
17. The results of the inspection are entered in the landing accounts book.
18. The entry in the landing accounts book is signed and given to the declarant.
19. The declarant pays handling charges to the port authority and the shipping agent as required.
20. The port authority issues a waybill.
21. The goods are moved to the gate, where frequently they are again inspected before the release can take place.
22. CEPS checks the manifest.
23. Shipping agents report to CEPS on their activities every month.

References

King, John, and Ben Konsunski. 1995. *Singapore TradeNet: A Tale of One City.* Case Study 9-191-009. Cambridge, Mass.: Harvard Business School.

United Nations Economic and Social Commission for Asia and the Pacific. 2003. "Trade Facilitation Framework." Expert Group on Trade Facilitation and Electronic Commerce, Bangkok. Draft report.

4

MOROCCO

Marcel Steenlandt and Luc De Wulf

In the early 1980s, Morocco's political leaders decided to open their economy to world markets despite the danger of economic vulnerability. They adopted a series of priority measures to attract foreign investors into the country and ensure the safety of their investments. Because Morocco has abundant skilled labor, the government encouraged foreign industrial and financial institutions to invest in major sectors such as textiles, electronics, and automobile accessories. These export promotion efforts not only increased exports substantially but also encouraged export diversification. The Moroccan economy is now open and trade barriers are almost nonexistent.

Modernizing customs administration is an integral part of trade promotion, and Morocco began reform of its customs administration and customs services early on, before reform became an urgent necessity. The country's pragmatic, open-door policy called for three major areas of focus, namely:

- enhancement of customs management quality
- development of an improved tariff schedule
- simplification of customs procedures

After summarizing the factors that led the Administration of Customs and Indirect Taxes (ACIT) to opt for modernization, this chapter describes the process that led to the definition of a strategy, presents the framework for reform implementation, describes the new working environment, and analyzes the results achieved to date.

Background to Customs Reform

Several factors facilitated the customs administration reform: clear goals, abundant human and institutional resources, and expert management guidance.

Problems and Goals

In the early 1990s, to foster economic development and to sustain an infant processing industry, King Hassan II envisaged a series of measures to boost foreign trade. During the implementation of these measures, serious malfunctions were detected in the customs service, for which some high-ranking officials were held accountable. In response to those problems, the minister of finance issued clear-cut directives to his staff to analyze the criticisms leveled at the customs service, assess the existing system, and propose reforms adapted to developments in the international trading environment. Morocco has been a member of the World Customs Organization since the inception of that organization in

1995 and has adjusted its approach to international trade in accordance with the World Customs Organization's successive conventions and agreements. In this context, it reformed its customs administration to facilitate customs clearance transactions while securing customs revenue.

Institutional Resources

The customs administration was already disciplined and properly structured, which facilitated the attainment of the reform objectives. Staffers in all positions were able to emerge from a culture of exhaustive controls to lend their full support to trade facilitation measures that were introduced progressively. In addition, representatives of the trading community attended meetings designed to enlist the active participation of customs administration staff members.

Foreign consultants reinforced the contribution of national actors. France provided high-level experts to propose changes in the Ministry of Finance. Experts from the International Monetary Fund contributed to an impartial initial diagnosis and the formulation of recommendations for an efficient strategy attuned to the most innovative international practices. The World Bank consistently supported and backed those initiatives. Specialized private firms applied their experience and skills to specific, highly technical aspects of the reform, including human resource management and the formulation of a master plan for customs computerization.

Robust, Comprehensive, and Pragmatic Approach

The customs administration did not limit its analysis and action to tackling immediate problems and constraints. Rather, it developed an ambitious, overarching strategy. Morocco's commitment to a pragmatic approach has translated into implementing technical measures already included in a 1995–96 master plan. More important, the government has focused its energies on delivering better service. The sustained participation and commitment of civil service staff have helped internalize the reform objectives, thereby turning them into a set of commonly shared values.

The first task was to identify what reforms were needed for the customs administration to implement its mandate correctly. On the external front, Morocco needed to honor its commitment to join the community of trading nations and to implement the trade facilitation measures appropriate for an emerging economy—for instance, support for the development of the export processing sectors (textiles, electronics, and so on). On the internal front, it needed to assess its legal framework, reorganize the operations of customs services, reduce customs clearance time and costs, and review personnel and equipment management procedures. This approach allowed the customs authorities to set guidelines for devising a realistic strategy. They constantly analyzed proposed solutions in light of their own and other entities' experiences and adopted relevant suggestions.

With the coherence of the project design assured, the customs authorities provided continuous training to enhance overall efficiency and recruited highly qualified university graduates to provide sophisticated technological expertise and to counter any internal resistance to change. The approach was pragmatic, well thought out, and built in coherent phases. The authorities conducted the entire reform of customs services expertly in terms of both human resources and funding.

Diagnosis and Strategy

An initial assessment of the functioning of the customs administration found four major areas on which the reform process should focus, namely:

1. resource management
2. information exchange and relations between the private sector and customs staff
3. tariff policy
4. organization of services.

Instrumental in the success of the reforms was the revision of the legal and statutory framework within which the customs administration operated; the simplification of procedures; and the introduction of a mode of management that incorporated staff participation, programming of assignments, and improved communication.

Initial Observations

In 1996, customs clearance operations were slow, cumbersome, contentious, unpredictable, and completely ill-adapted to modern logistical requirements for handling goods. In the port of Casablanca, releasing a container took 18 to 20 days, and half of that time was directly attributable to customs formalities. Customs officers were regarded as having sweeping powers and few traders dared to clash with them.

The main objective of customs administration personnel was to collect revenue. International trade facilitation was not their concern. They imposed exhaustive controls and justified them by the need to enforce the Customs Code, collect correct amounts of customs duties and taxes, and fight customs evasion.

The customs computerization scheme introduced in the early 1990s did not produce sufficient changes in customs procedures and working methods. The management of temporary imports was complex, and many related documents were not processed by the time of the last reexportation.

The reform process solicited the support of operators in searching for practical solutions to the obstacles they confronted.

Resource Management

Improving the ACIT's performance required heavy staff involvement and better use of resources.

Human Resources Modernizing a country's customs service requires active participation by the entire staff as essential agents of change. To that end, the customs administration set out to accomplish the following:

- Promote cooperation between headquarters staff and staff of the regional directorates and the districts in defining realistic objectives and implementation methods. (Note that customs staff members are encouraged to express their views so as to better integrate regional concerns into policy, and the director general's annual policy paper reflects such comments and suggestions.)
- Improve staff training and keep staff members better informed.
- Strengthen employees' motivation to make valuable contributions to the ACIT's mandate, including through bonuses and benefits.

The rigidity of civil service regulations sometimes hampered efforts to strengthen incentives. Thus, the customs administration took steps to improve the regulations as they applied to customs staff. For example, paying bonuses for good work requires a system for grading performance, but the existing evaluation system, which periodically graded staff members on their professional skills, efficiency, output, and conduct on a scale of 0 to 3, was too unsophisticated to permit remuneration based on merit. The system was replaced with semiannual appraisals whereby staff were evaluated on the basis of five criteria, using a graduated scale of scores ranging from 1 to 10, along with more individualized assessment systems, such as face-to-face meetings with staff members and their supervisors to discuss their performance, career paths, and training needs.

As a result of being openly based on efficiency and merit, human resources management has become more transparent and coherent. Nevertheless, some operational staff members do not fully appreciate the changes, because they penalize inefficiencies and provide for greater differentiation in staff remuneration.

Decentralization allowed the transfer of most personnel management tasks from central to local levels. Customs staff members perceive this change as a positive step, noting that they now can make their opinions known more readily and that they now are better informed. At the same time, decentralization improved the organization of work. The involvement of decentralized units in decisionmaking has allowed staff members in those units to enhance their management skills and to become more efficient.

The customs authorities set up a regional body to ensure the coordinated transfer of skills and authority from headquarters to local entities. In 1996, seven regional directorates were established, each covering two or more districts and having jurisdiction over a number of geographic areas and functions. This new setup was coupled with a redefinition of district managers' responsibilities. The operational services became more autonomous, and the role of the central administration was reduced to arbitration, consultation, and provision of expertise. Thus, decentralization resulted in the strengthening of regional units in relation to the center and the elimination of unnecessary levels in the management hierarchy.

The modernization that the customs administration hoped to achieve by enhancing its human resources was based on an analysis of job and skill requirements. Based on this analysis and on workload indicators, the following steps were taken:

- To optimize productivity and raise the quality of services provided, the customs administration reorganized customs services.
- To better specify the qualifications required by staff members holding positions of responsibility and to clarify career paths, the administration ranked customs offices and subdivisions by importance.
- To improve mobility so as to enhance job satisfaction, the administration redeployed staff members over time to positions that better matched their qualifications.
- To ensure uniform approaches by the different customs bureaus, the administration put together a manual of customs procedures.
- To build staff versatility and to allow staff members to rotate among different functions, the administration designed a training program.
- To reduce corruption, the administration encouraged integrity and compliance with professional ethics not only by means of legal sanctions but also by clear signals that any abuse of power would not be tolerated.

Financial Resources In fiscal year 1999–2000, the ACIT began to decentralize financial resource management and to engage contract staff members from the Ministry of Finance. The extent of the decentralization of budget funds has grown. Some 4 percent of funds were decentralized in 1999–2000. This figure rose to 13 percent in 2002 and now stands at 26 percent of the operating budget and 20 percent of the investment budget (excluding funds allocated for computerization). Responsibility for credit management was transferred to new specialized units in the regional directorates. Pertinent staff members attended training courses and seminars on public expenditure management.

Financial decentralization has not yet fully achieved its goal. The regional directorates still emphasize expenditures that are driven by existing operational needs rather than by envisaged service objectives, which have not been clearly specified. Regional use of the decentralized funds still covers expenditures through purchase vouchers for maintenance and rentals and still covers payments through utility stamps for water, electricity, and telephone service. Those expenditures and payments reduce the real effect of the sought-after fiscal decentralization. In addition, assessing the true cost of services is difficult because of a lack of data on the costs of staff salaries and benefits.

The planned computerization of customs management will improve expenditure estimates and execution. The customs administration's Integrated Resources Management System will permit expenditure forecasting, control, monitoring, and analysis much more effectively than traditional management methods. In fiscal year 2003, for the first time, the Ministry of Finance provided funds for computerizing customs operations. Streamlining and continuous monitoring of expenditures led to savings of DH 7.5 million, generated largely from such items as uniforms (only field personnel now wear uniforms), administrative forms (many forms have been consolidated), telephone bills (telephone use is more closely controlled), and maintenance (which is managed more efficiently).

Dialogue with the Private Sector

One key to the success of Morocco's customs reform is the inclusion of the private sector. Bolstered by broadly based public relations and information campaigns, the open door policy adopted by the General Directorate of Customs reflects radical changes at all levels of the customs service. Those changes, which were geared toward transparency, efficiency, and partnership, resulted in economic operators acknowledging the customs administration's responsiveness and understanding. These characteristics were particularly appreciated in a state agency and indicated a measure of corporate social responsibility.

The customs administration seeks to enter into partnerships not only with firms in good fiscal standing but also with professional associations. Implementation in 1998 of the World Customs Organization's customs valuation principles, which are based on invoice prices, gave the customs administration an opportunity to reinforce its relationships with importers and licensed customs brokers. The ACIT organized an effective information, training, and support campaign that simultaneously consolidated revenues and improved public relations. However, valuation remains difficult, and customs officers have remained attentive and vigilant, because some traders still tend to undervalue their imports.

The customs administration has gone beyond minimal statutory requirements. It has set out to foster the spirit of the International Convention on the Simplification and Harmonization of Customs Procedures (known as the revised Kyoto Convention) and to meet firms' concrete needs. Today, any change in procedures is subject to prior consultations with the private sector. For example, dialogue with the textile industry resulted in substantial modifications to the management of the temporary admission regime.

The customs administration aims for a trusting relationship with firms. For several years, the regional directorates have offered consulting service to firms. In addition, extensive information is available through a Web site (http://www.douane.gov.ma).[1] The ACIT also offers direct technical services by telephone, by electronic messaging, and through the Internet. To reach the general public, the customs administration publishes and disseminates brochures and pamphlets.

Tariff Policy

Despite tariff reforms in the early 1980s, no coherent, structured tariff policy existed before the customs reform of the late 1990s. The number of customs duties and taxes had been cut from 26 in 1987 to 13 in 1994, and the 1996 Finance Law further reduced the number to 6. In 1986, the maximum rate was reduced from 100 percent of the value of imports to 45 percent, but an analysis of nominal rates revealed that some rates were not being used.[2] In addition to customs duties, a special import tax, created in 1916, was imposed. This tax had gradually been reduced from 15 percent to 5 percent. In 1988, the special import tax was consolidated with other levies, such as customs stamps, into an import tax with a single rate of 15 percent (drugs and capital goods were exempt). This irrational tariff and duty policy undermined the continuity and predictability of the import regime and was exacerbated by the use of reference prices for more than 400 products (reduced to 210 in 1996), which increased the effective protection of those products. All these successive changes were designed to protect local manufacturers. The use of reference prices has since been abandoned.

Morocco has now merged its external tariffs with the import tax (eight rates, including a zero rate), and has introduced a basic most-favored-nation tariff (four nonzero tariffs and a maximum rate of 40 percent). Under its association agreements with the European Union (EU), which took effect in 2000, Morocco will gradually remove its duties on imports from the EU. Trade with the EU represents more than 60 percent of the value of Morocco's foreign trade. Other bilateral and multilateral agreements, primarily with Arab and African countries, also affect the development of Morocco's tariff policy. Agricultural products are not included in these arrangements, and their rate of taxation may vary from 2.5 to 329 percent. Rates in excess of 50 percent are to be reduced at a rate of 2.4 percent per year, according to Morocco's World Trade Organization commitments. Since 1992, customs tariffs have been based on the harmonized system nomenclature recommended by the World Trade Organization and the World Customs Organization.

Organization of Customs Services

In parallel with the reform of human resources management, a review of the organization and the functioning of customs services was undertaken with a view to creating regional centers that would be responsible for the daily management of customs activities in the field. This decentralization had two objectives: it focused headquarters on the design and revitalization of the regional network and it brought the management of routine procedures and problems closer to customs service staff and users. Such customs decentralization also fostered pragmatism and efficiency.

Since 1996, the ACIT has been organized on the basis of regional jurisdiction and decentralized powers. The seven regional directorates are responsible for management decisions, auditing

1. The site has a wealth of information on such items as regulations, the Customs Code, tariffs, and international trade statistics. It is constantly being updated and upgraded, and will soon include an online decision support system. The site also permits access to software that assists clearance through customs of imports of goods and provides all information about import taxes and regulations under normal import regimes as well as under preferential import regimes.

2. In 1994, the 10.0 percent, 22.5 percent, and 40.0 percent rates were inactive. At the extremes, 32.8 percent of the value of imports was taxed at 0 percent and 0.2 percent was taxed at the 45 percent rate.

and control functions, and staff training. Customs clearance offices are distributed across the country. Mobile inspection forces ensure overall surveillance of the country and of the customs zones.

The headquarters of the ACIT was transferred from Casablanca to the administrative capital, Rabat, to strengthen ACIT's ability to monitor and implement the reforms. The relocated headquarters is better integrated into the system of those who make national economic, financial, and fiscal decisions.

The creation of regional centers was necessary to meet decentralization objectives, but it has had some limitations. Some bureaucratization is emerging, and some regional management staff members still refer too often to headquarters for decisions that they could make at the regional level, thereby inhibiting the optimal use of management close to where transactions take place. However, decentralization has led to clear improvements in the organization of customs clearance, the general surveillance of the territory and borders, and the development of the audit function.

Customs Clearance To make the customs system more efficient, the customs administration emphasized the facilitation of processing customs declarations. Systematic computerization, coupled with the improvement in customs procedures, reinforced control over customs clearance and ensured the effectiveness of the fight against commercial fraud.

The General Directorate of Customs sought to balance the organization of its services with the goals of facilitating trade and ensuring revenue. To make the overall system of goods processing more coherent, it initially focused its efforts on the quality of customs declarations (with the support of computerization) and then turned to postclearance controls. The shift from a system of instant verification to one of deferred controls after the release of goods required the following:[3]

- a mechanism for selective control and inspection in customs clearance operations, including provision for selective, automated customs release without inspection (which is now applied to a significant share of total declarations)
- the progressive redeployment of staff members on the basis of their qualifications
- the dissemination of documentation and information about deferred controls.

Surveillance The approach adopted in the fight against smuggling and other forms of fraud was practical and adaptable. Surveillance of the territory was initially organized through units located along the borders and the major highways. Because of the geographical distribution of smuggling, units along the northern border were assigned more staff than units in central and southern Morocco. In addition to this frontline defense, deterrent action was sustained throughout the country and antismuggling units were reinforced and their intervention methods enhanced.

The geographical distribution of antismuggling units and their staff members has changed. An attempt to curb smuggling only in the border zones became unrealistic in the 1990s, and highway controls were reduced while control of places where smuggled goods were stored was strengthened. More emphasis was also given to gathering and exploiting smuggling-related intelligence.

Audit Function The ACIT added an audit function to its inspection services to ensure the integrity of overall customs operations. The audit and inspection function has recorded significant advances. In addition to verifying that management practices conform to legal and statutory standards, the function is designed for the following:

- to ensure better use and enhancement of manpower and material resources
- to assess adherence to procedures
- to help simplify and standardize procedures
- to evaluate organizational performance and assess the efficiency of services
- to contribute to the development of preventive, anticipatory controls to avoid errors.

The new function reflects a shift from an inquisitorial, repressive system to one that provides consultative services to assist in decisionmaking. At the same time, the new audit function helps ensure that the behavior of ACIT personnel is ethical.

3. Deferred and ex post controls are intended to supplement immediate controls. Deferred controls are based purely on customs declarations and associated documents. Ex post controls apply at a later stage and involve reviewing the accounting books and registers of importers and other foreign trade operators.

The New Working Environment

To enhance the competitiveness of Morocco's private sector without reducing the quality of public services or the collection of revenues, the ACIT exerted considerable efforts to improve customs procedures and adapt them for computerization.

Improving Procedures

Before the reform, all the principal functions of the customs administration seemed to be aimed at collecting duties and taxes. Users complained that the customs clearance process was long, cumbersome, and often unpredictable. Those complaints and the need to adapt to international trade requirements were among the primary reasons for the reform. Morocco was one of the first nations to ratify the provisions of the Kyoto Convention as amended in June 2000. The ACIT, in cooperation with representatives of other public sector agencies and the private sector, carefully reviewed existing procedures and then began adapting them to international rules, giving priority to efficiency and simplicity.

Enhancing the Quality and Efficiency of Customs Clearance Operations The customs administration has made adaptation of its procedures a constant priority, along with the maximum use possible of an enhanced, open computerization process that encourages communication. In this connection, its main actions were the following:

- improving cargo control for both exports and imports
- setting up customs clearance sites outside port or airport domains
- introducing selectivity in controls
- computerizing document processing.

The customs administration made a careful study of existing cargo control procedures with the aim of making them more efficient and user friendly. It imposes two obligations on common carriers: (a) going directly to border crossings (ports, airports, access roads) where customs facilities exist and (b) providing a summary declaration of their freight upon their arrival at such locations. Those procedures were reviewed in comparison with best practices and in terms of what was achievable using electronic data interchange. With computerization, the entire cargo control process is now much better managed, resulting in more efficient clearance of manifests and enhanced revenue assessment and collection.

Customs clearance sites outside port and airport premises permit the temporary storage of goods in approved areas before clearance (see box 4.1). The

BOX 4.1 Customs Clearance Sites Outside Customs Zones

Increased foreign trade created storage and handling problems in ports and airports. In addition, the intensive use of road transit necessitated the prompt acceptance of cargo consignments to reduce unnecessary stops and offloading.

Customs clearance sites outside customs and port premises help reduce the time goods remain in bonded warehouses and help prevent the underutilization of vehicles and containers. Those efficiencies reduce firms' transaction costs and enhance their competitiveness.

The creation of customs clearance sites requires prior authorization from the customs administration, which approves site locations and layouts. Customs clearance sites are private, restricted premises for the temporary storage of goods pending import or export declarations that may be company specific or may be accessed by multiple users. They are fenced and have only one entrance. The customs administration is responsible for the oversight of customs clearance sites and must be given unrestricted access rights. The management of warehouses must post a bond or statutory guarantee.

Operators understand that customs clearance sites can improve traffic control and have progressively opened such sites throughout the country, although those facilities are currently concentrated around Casablanca, the country's principal port. Extension of the use of customs clearance sites will encourage the building of inland logistics platforms.

In 2002, a total of 92,476 customs declarations was registered in the customs clearance sites of the Casablanca external bureau, of which 57,554 were for imports. Those operations represented 14.6 percent of all declarations registered nationally.

BOX 4.2 Improvement of Risk Analysis

The warehouse data system collects data and integrates it into a single database that helps staff members with monitoring and carrying out customs clearance operations. The foreign trade module deals with all information about commercial imports and exports. The revenue module provides for close monitoring of trends in different categories of customs revenue. The data select module is a decisionmaking application operating in the management information system that allows users to work with selectivity data and to observe the general activity of customs officers and traders. Users also have indicators needed to follow up and improve automated selectivity modules for imports and exports.

sites help reduce congestion at wharfs, warehouses, and airports and have demonstrated the advantages of conducting customs clearance operations outside border-post premises.

The customs reform has been based on restricting examinations to only selected declarations and on improving the method by which goods are selected for examination. The customs administration has set a goal of releasing 95 percent of filed declarations without immediate physical verification. The objectives are to increase transparency and fairness and, indirectly, to reduce customs processing times. Doing so would allow inspectors to concentrate on verifying 5 percent of declarations thoroughly, without undue time pressures. At present, the inspection rate is 10 percent, down from 100 percent in 1996 and 35 percent in 2000. The use of selective examinations reduced the time required for issuing release notes to an estimated average of one hour in mid-2003.

The electronic customs management system makes it easier to select shipments for inspection, and customs officials' ability to detect prosecutable offenses has improved significantly as a result. The customs administration now hopes to improve the selection mechanism even more through econometric processing of data coming into the management information system database (see box 4.2).

Customs operations are carried out as expeditiously as possible and in close cooperation with customs brokers or traders. As noted earlier, the physical examination of imported goods has also become more focused. Nevertheless, the effects of those changes on the total time it takes traders to obtain possession of their goods has so far been limited: operators now average a waiting time of 10 days before their containers can leave the port, compared with an average of 18 days before 1997. Limiting the reform to customs operations without involving other pertinent private and public agencies may be ineffective.

Improved and computerized procedures should speed up the processing of all declarations and, in the future, allow electronic payment of most duties and taxes. Further reforms will eliminate the need to file paper declarations or keep archives of paper documents. For their part, traders will have clear obligations, including tendering to the inspection services, on demand, any documents mentioned in their electronic declarations, such as invoices and certificates of origin.

Simplifying Procedures for Imports under Special Import Regimes The principal characteristic of Moroccan foreign trade is the importance of certain imports for which duties and taxes are temporarily suspended.[4] In 2002, imports for domestic processing of eventual exports represented 35 percent of the value of total imports and 85 percent of the value of total exports. These figures explain why special import regimes apply to such imports.

Customs reforms started with regularization of the accounts of exporters whose past duty-free imports had not been fully accounted for. Indeed, in late 1996, more than 70,000 records for imports under temporary admission accounts were still awaiting regularization. Some files had been submitted before 1990. About 30,000 other files were for accounts with values below DH 1,000 (US$55). A number of factors contributed to the backlog:

4. Special imports procedures with temporary relief of taxes and duties cover four key areas: storage, processing, use as inputs, and transport. In customs terms, they cover warehousing, free industrial warehousing, temporary admission for inward processing, temporary admission for outward processing, temporary exportation, transit, processing under customs control, and drawback.

BOX 4.3 Personalized Management of Special Import Customs Procedures

The simplification of procedures enables firms to act swiftly, efficiently, and predictably. All three characteristics are crucial for the consolidation and expansion of foreign trade. The customs administration has sought an effective way to enhance the competitiveness of export firms. The management of suspended regimes has been streamlined to make control and declaration processes as simple and efficient as possible without detracting from the efficiency of verification. The customs service has detailed the exporter-specific import coefficient needed to effect account reconciliation. This change tailors the standard convention to the needs and work methods of each trader.

The traditional methods associated with customs clearance operations, declarations, and reconciliation of suspended regimes have been overhauled in the course of a few years. Compulsory practices, such as systematic sampling and exhaustive controls of manufactured products for reexport, have been eliminated. The innovative methods of control, divorced from import and export operations, are now part of normal customs management.

inappropriate management systems, indifference to the economic stakes and financial risks involved, excessively meticulous handling of accounts, and insufficient determination to improve the prevailing legal and practical requirements that governed customs agents.

To deal with those problems, the customs administration adopted a pragmatic approach along with periodic campaigns to restore integrity to the management of these accounts. It decided to do the following:

- facilitate access to preferential arrangments for processing firms (mostly work-to-order enterprises serving foreign customers), notably through the free industrial warehouse system (industrial firms with at least 85 percent of total turnover devoted to exports can benefit from this system)
- relax and simplify customs clearance procedures for trade in samples, damaged goods, and exports below a certain value
- simplify account management, especially in relation to the treatment of the value of waste
- expedite the final reconciliation of accounts for imports that entered under suspensive regimes by arranging for the relevant remittance certificates to be issued to traders at the premises
- promote the drawback system as an incentive for exports and extend it to cover energy products consumed during the manufacture of certain goods
- rely on more open and better adapted software to give traders direct access to their accounts and release their guarantees
- revise the guarantee system to make it more accessible and less expensive.

The customs administration has introduced new types of guarantees for special import customs procedures with suspended regimes. Customs officials can now perform the following:

- allow exporting firms to post bonds as guarantees
- exempt subcontractors' imports from surety obligations when the inputs remain the property of the foreign principals
- authorize a combination of bank and personal guarantees
- allow a global guarantee that consists of a down payment backed by a bank guarantee in an amount agreed on by the customs administration and the trader.

The customs administration further pursued its partnerships with firms. It has developed a framework to assure firms of personalized management of their accounts following the firms' own specific procedures (see box 4.3). More than 30 firms now use a personalized management facility. Those firms account for 22 percent of the country's total exports, amounting to DH 18.5 billion.[5]

Traders are no longer always treated as potential smugglers but are increasingly seen as full-fledged partners. At present, only large firms are eligible for the streamlined system of management: their

5. Key products exported by these companies include phosphoric acid, electronic components, natural and chemical fertilizers, and food products.

imports represented 27 percent of total imports in 2001–02. The facility is expected to be broadened in the near future.

To simplify further, the customs administration is studying a more innovative accounting system that will shift from a product-based management system to one that manages the suspended taxes and the credit provided at the time of export. This new approach illustrates the commitment of the General Directorate of Customs to reconcile traders' needs for trade facilitation and process simplification with the government's need to ensure that revenues due are actually paid.

Adapting Information Technology to Customs Clearance Management

The ACIT first used information technology in 1992 when it adopted the Computerized Support for Customs Clearance (CSCC) System (known locally as the Systeme de l'Administration des Douanes et Impôt Indirect et de l'Office des changes, or SADOC). The CSCC System is essentially a way to computerize the processing of customs clearance formalities and the monitoring of special import customs procedures. It has made an invaluable contribution to the success of the reform; however, newer technology would allow better organization of data processing and better integrated trade management.

The Contribution of the CSCC System The master plan for customs computerization rests on a transitional strategy, including a five-year system migration to an open standard system (UNIX) that offers robustness, transparency, and amenability to upgrades. The customs administration has also taken steps to strengthen its capacity. It recruited computer scientists and consulted with private traders in an attempt to reorganize its work, so that it could be more responsive to the needs of its customers and could improve the quality of system support by means of revised procedures, standardized operations, and documentation of changes. New features were added to the system and have significantly improved its reliability. For example, the so-called assistance to users feature focuses on the availability of a telephone line that promptly became a standard communications channel between such users as customs officers and traders and CSCC System staff members.

Improving communications and listening to users gave the computerization project credibility and solved numerous vexing problems. Customs brokers, in particular, expressed satisfaction with the direct information, assistance, and support now made available. Computerization improvements were the primary reason for the positive public reputation of the customs service. The improved CSCC System lets brokers and importers benefit from an instrument that handles almost the entire customs clearance process without waiting for a new computer system. Clients have completely reversed their opinion of the customs administration and now consider it an example for other agencies.

Improving the existing computer system was extremely expensive, but the benefits were not limited to enhanced services and reputation. Computerization improvement also reinforced improvements in customs procedures and services. The customs clearance system has improved considerably, and many new functions have been introduced, including the following:

- computerized processing of cargo manifests and of customs transit operations and termination, including computer-based management of the customs clearance sites
- control over the coherence, plausibility, and compatibility of data
- selectivity of examination of declarations
- automation of price references for inspectors
- computerization of the integrated tariff and of electronic payment of duties and taxes
- consultations with traders on the status of declarations during all stages of processing
- date stamping during each phase of the customs clearance operation
- consultations on the cancellation of bonds upon the completion of bonded transactions
- management of accounts and consultations with traders on the status of their accounts for special import procedures with relief from taxes and duties
- management of guarantees
- use of price estimates.

The customs administration has had success with the electronic storage of manifests. Ninety-five percent of manifests in the port of Casablanca (55 percent overall) are now sent by electronic data interchange. Air transport manifests are transmitted to the customs administration the same way. In addition, a successful pilot experiment of electronic payments conducted with a local bank is being extended to other banks and operators. Finally, all controls over the movements of goods through the warehouses and customs clearance sites at the airport in Casablanca are now computerized.

The Development of New Computer Systems The customs administration is developing several new computer applications, largely with internal resources, but occasionally these resources are supplemented by contractors. A service firm is preparing a new customs clearance application, but customs computer experts have worked alongside the service provider and expect to assume day-to-day management after the system has been launched.

The Customs Computer Network System Despite recent improvements, the CSCC System has outlived its usefulness and a more versatile information technology system, the Customs Computer Network System (Base Automatisée des Douanes en Réseau), is being rolled out. This system will be based on state-of-the-art technology and will complement the CSCC System's features with new modules for litigation, vehicles released for consumption, parcels, and postal packets. The Customs Computer Network System will incorporate new, highly innovative concepts, such as anticipation and online management of requests for modification, and will also offer the user total transparency through multicriteria lists and research services. In addition, the Customs Computer Network System will include the management of the special import customs procedures, which will be based on the reconciliation of accounts rather than on the reconciliation of the relevant detailed import and export documents. The system's cargo control module went into service in September 2003. The full system should be operational by early 2005.

The Management Information System The customs administration has created a management information system (Système Automatisée d'Aide a la Décision). The system uses information and data from other systems (a form of data warehousing)—primarily from the CSCC System—to provide the customs service with an integrated system for information and decisionmaking. It works for both statistical and monitoring purposes. The customs administration is already using the system for help with customs revenue, foreign trade, litigation, selectivity, and special import customs procedures.

The Integrated Resources Management System The Integrated Resources Management System (Ressources Intégrées de l'Administration) reflects the customs administration's goal of creating an integrated computer system for managing all its resources—staff, financial, and equipment—at both central and decentralized levels. The system will be developed internally, and its functions will include human resource management and planning, inventory management, procurement, and budget management. It will be user friendly and will include decision support functions. The Integrated Resources Management System is based on the same technologies as the Customs Computer Network System (UNIX, Java), and access will be through an intranet. Some parts of the Integrated Resources Management System will be ready to come into service in late 2003.

The Application for Managing Imports under Investment Conventions The Application for Managing Imports under Investment Conventions (Application pour la Gestion Informatisée des Listes Annexées aux Conventions d'Investissement) manages the lists of duty-free imports that are annexed to investment conventions. It is accessible through an intranet arrangement and allows continuous, real-time monitoring of the flow of duty-free imported goods.

Involving Public Sector Partners

In addition to being attuned to its economic environment, the customs administration has strengthened its cooperation with other government agencies and has set up ways to share information, both with public sector partners such as ports and with private sector partners such as forwarding agents. However, those initiatives have proved slower and more difficult to implement than other aspects of the reform.

Not all government agencies have attained the same level of modernization, and some initially could not keep pace with changes in the customs administration. Some agencies are now actively reforming and have started their own equipment programs. For example, the taxation service is now using unique taxpayer identification numbers, which in the future should facilitate the exchange of information between the taxation and customs authorities. This freer exchange should enhance the efficiency of overall revenue administration and should, to some extent, compensate for the fact that trade liberalization may reduce revenue from customs duties.

The Ministry of Trade, the Ministry of Industry, the Foreign Exchange Board, and the commercial banks should all help enhance the efficiency of public administration by eliminating compartmentalization and by better adapting their procedures and statutory instruments to economic needs. The planned introduction of an electronic payment system involving private sector banks is a step in that direction.

Ports and airports often use the same information as the customs service, such as freight and cargo manifests. Coordinating efforts in data collection, validation, and use will be crucial to simplifying overall trade procedures. However, teamwork has been difficult to implement for various reasons, including internal resistance in other agencies, fear of losing independence, incompatibility of computer and security systems, lack of funds, and national regulations and legislation. Mechanisms to ensure the sharing of information among ship owners, forwarding agents, and customs agents are progressively being applied. Progress is slow, but information sharing has started to bear fruit in the area of cargo manifest management.

The benefits of expeditious processing of customs clearance transactions have now been widely recognized and have spurred other agencies to improve service delivery. Implementation of the Customs Computer Network System could help consolidate the links among all actors in the transport system.

Employing Additional Instruments for Monitoring Reform

The success of the ACIT has relied on the proper sequencing of a number of other reform initiatives—namely, the following:

- overhauling the legal framework
- consolidating communications with partners and staff
- adopting simple, controllable performance indicators
- supporting work plans with a project management tool for monitoring the progress of reforms.

Statutory Law The customs administration secured reform of the Customs Code by focusing on the basic changes required for improved operation and for the prosecution of major offenses. The administration examined the code in 1997 in close consultation with customs clearance professionals and professional associations. The revised Kyoto Convention served as an inspiration in the drafting of the new Customs Code.

The new Customs Code was submitted to national consultative bodies and was then passed by parliament with ease. The most restrictive provisions of the previous code were either abolished or revised to comply with the spirit and letter of trade facilitation enshrined in the Kyoto Convention. At the same time, the ACIT issued a number of regulations that emphasized decentralization and the improvement of customs procedures. The trading community supports the new regulatory framework.

Communications Strategy Institutional communication was integral to the reform process. It brought widespread understanding of reform measures. The customs administration has created a modernized, consolidated communications service, building on lessons learned in pilot projects. The following have been the major recent achievements of the communications service:

- Creating a Web site: http://www.douane.gov.ma. Launched in 1997, the site has since been substantially improved. Users can submit questions and suggestions directly to the director general. Every message gets a personal reply.
- Launching an intranet site for all staff members that contains professional information; provides a space for the exchange of personal messages; and offers a number of services, such as discussion forums, library access, analytical extracts of interesting articles, and newspaper excerpts.
- Organizing periodic meetings with the media. This public relations effort has been sustained with press briefings, books, thank you notes, and other communications and has resulted in the

press conveying a broadly positive image of customs operations.

- Being receptive to and providing information and guidance to users as part of a partnership with the general public.
- Launching a program of public information through the distribution of technical pamphlets and brochures. These publications have clarified the opaque and often complex customs laws and regulations.
- Organizing staff meetings and conferences to contribute to better mutual understanding of work-related issues.
- Publishing regulations in the official bulletin from time to time. This bulletin is available on the Internet and can be delivered by e-mail.

The effect of the communication strategy was much appreciated by customs staff members, staff members from other agencies, members of the economic community, and members of the general public. In addition, it was well received in other countries.

Management Indicators To support modernization, the customs administration prepared a set of management indicators, including performance indicators that measure the efficiency of its work and assess the costs of its services. Periodic reviews and revision of this set of indicators, supplemented by a review of control functions, proved instrumental for decisionmaking in a complicated reform environment. It also encouraged active participation by staff members in the modernization process.[6]

Programmatic Approach The customs administration has adopted a systematic approach to its business plan to ensure transparent management, to better define and plan its actions, and to ensure their consistency with the working environment. This approach contrasts with the lack of a forward-looking and coherent management approach in earlier years.

Programming and project implementation is monitored through a computer application that is accessible to all staff members through the intranet. The customs administration opted for project management software that would serve as a forecasting and monitoring tool during the reform. Once all the reforms have been implemented, the same software will become a day-to-day management and evaluation tool.

From the plan of action, projects are divided into subprojects, then into basic tasks, then into detailed activities. Each basic task is evaluated in terms of workload (person-days) and scheduled to match available means. The person responsible for each task is identified by name and is given the task of regularly updating the software. This assignment enables the evaluation, monitoring, and readjustment of the entire planning mechanism during implementation. The rigorous monitoring of the implementation of all tasks has not only enabled detection of negligence and malfeasance but also allowed for timely responses to unexpected problems.

Reform Outcomes

This section assesses the striking achievements of the customs administration's reform and modernization initiatives.

Customs Revenue

Morocco's experience clearly illustrates that trade facilitation does not necessarily reduce revenue. During the period of reform, commercial activities developed steadily and revenue increased. Although fraud was not completely eliminated, it did not cause excessive revenue losses—despite some customs officers' resistance to the idea of selective inspections, based on their claims that fraud would increase as a result. Examination of foreign trade statistics (table 4.1) shows the steady growth of the value of imports that enter Morocco under the new special import regimes.

Table 4.1 shows that revenue from import taxes and duties has remained stable since 1998 despite progressive tariff reductions (particularly on imports from the EU). Revenue losses from agreements with the EU, estimated at DH 1.3 billion in 2001 and DH 1.5 billion in 2002, reduced the tariff burden on capital goods and inputs not

6. The indicators include data on the number of travelers; the volume of imports and exports; the activity of the customs service (for instance, the number of declarations); the results achieved (for example, revenue collected and the number of lawsuits); and the available resources used (such as vehicles, computers, active staff, and staff on annual leave or sick leave).

TABLE 4.1 Imports, 1996–2002 (DH millions)

Import Regime	1996[a]	1997[a]	1998	1999	2000	2001	2002
Imports other than for home consumption	62,109.1	63,515.1	69,708.8	74,064.4	88,208.5	87,147.3	91,840.4
ATPA imports	22,809.3	27,315.4	29,086.1	32,016.5	34,780.2	37,493.8	37,953.5
AT imports	1,294.2	1,193.3	2,209.5	2,370.7	2,423.4	2,675.4	1,543.6
Imports in warehouses	133.3	17.6	44.3	30.6	3,193.4	1,830.5	2,338.2
ATPA re-exports	27,297.2	29,733.8	46,043.4	50,129.0	53,850.1	56,9283	62,967.6

AT—Temporary admission.
ATPA—Temporary admission for inward processing.
a. Value of raw materials in ATPA not included for export.
Source: ACIT data.

TABLE 4.2 Customs Revenue Indicators, 1998–2002 (DH millions)

Indicator	1998	1999	2000	2001	2002
Customs revenue	34,386.2	34,997.6	36,089.4	36,735.8	37,029.5
Import taxes	12,782.6	12,552.8	12,775.5	12,317.0	12,192.8
Tax revenue	74,005.0	75,632.0	74,034.0	77,123.0	80,496.0
Gross domestic product	34,6952.0	34,3131.0	35,4316.0	38,2897.0	40,9430.0
Value of imports	98,676.0	105,931.0	122,527.0	124,641.2	127,978.3
Value of imports net of special customs regimes	69,708.8	74,064.4	88,208.5	87,147.3	91,840.4
Customs revenue as a share of tax revenue (1/3)	46.5	46.3	48.7	47.6	46.0
Customs revenue as share of gross domestic product (1/4)	9.9	10.2	10.2	9.7	9.0
Ratio of import duties to gross domestic product (2/4)	3.7	3.7	3.6	3.2	3.0
Rate of tax burden (2/5)	13.0	11.8	10.4	9.9	9.5
Average effective rate of import taxes (2/6)	18.3	16.9	14.5	14.13	13.28

Source: ACIT data.

manufactured locally. This revenue loss led to a reduction of the effective rate of taxation (import duties as a percentage of the value of imports) from 13 percent in 1998 to 9.5 percent in 2002. The revenue reduction was offset by a rise in value added tax revenue from imports, so that customs revenue remained a constant proportion of overall budget resources, around 46 percent or slightly more, from 1998 through 2002.

Customs revenue increased by about 7.7 percent between 1998 and 2002 (table 4.3), primarily because of increased commercial activity, but also

TABLE 4.3 Customs Revenue by Category, 1998–2002 (DH millions)

Category	1998	1999	2000	2001	2002
Import duty	12,872.6	1,2552.8	12,775.5	12,317.0	12,192.8
Inland consumer taxes	9,448.7	10,329.6	9,561.9	10,047.4	10,095.3
Inland consumer taxes on energy products	(8,661.1)	(9,618.4)	8,797.3	9,239.2	9,308.1
Value added tax	10,977.1	11,007.8	12,263.5	12,816.4	13,200.4
Value added tax on energy products	(1,494.6)	1,705.0	2,119.5	2,285.0	2,130.2
Royalties on the exploitation of phosphates	598.6	589.9	568.4	596.6	616.3
Royalties on the gas pipeline	226.1	262.7	634.3	707.3	670.4
Other revenue	263.1	254.8	285.8	251.1	254.3
Total	34,386.2	34,997.6	36,089.4	36,735.8	37,029.5

Source: ACIT data.

because of the improved quality of declarations, the increased customs productivity, and the quality of controls. Thus, customs facilitation and the opening of borders are not in themselves obstacles to sustaining the value of customs receipts.

Efficiency of Service

The customs service does not yet deliver uniform services to firms throughout the nation. Remote regions have not yet benefited fully from the simplification of transit procedures and from the extension of customs clearance to the traders' premises. Because traders in Casablanca and Tangiers benefited disproportionately from recent reforms, the customs service supported the creation of logistic platforms and facilities such as warehouses and customs clearance sites in other locations. At the same time, the customs administration simplified transit formalities and permitted customs clearance at firms' premises for those with regular shipments.

At the national level, the reduction in average processing time for customs clearance has been one of the most impressive achievements of the reform. The time between the validation of a customs declaration and the release of the goods is now less than one hour (table 4.4), a figure that places the ACIT among the most efficient in the world. The processing time for clearing goods imported under suspended regimes is less than for other import arrangements: 40 minutes in July 2003 compared with 55 minutes for imports under the ordinary arrangement.

TABLE 4.4 Average Time for Customs Clearance, January 2001–June 2003

Month	Minutes
January 2001	84
June 2001	92
December 2001	111
June 2002	64
December 2002	60
June 2003	57

Source: ACIT data.

Anticorruption Strategy

The customs administration believed that the overall process of modernization would reduce corruption and that existing legal remedies were sufficient. Indeed, the customs administration does not have a specific code of ethics. It explains observed improvements as a consequence of the following:

- increasing efficiency
- enhancing staff motivation by improving the image of the customs service

- revising job descriptions for customs staff and increasing staff accountability
- increasing mobility for staff members in sensitive positions, which has helped forestall irregularities
- introducing work programming and regular controls that have helped improve integrity
- enhancing the organization of procedures and reducing paperwork, which have reduced the scope of staff interventions
- introducing clearer procedures (including a listing of offenses and penalties), which have considerably simplified litigation and made it unnecessary for traders to enter into protracted negotiations with customs officials
- initiating the outreach program with the private sector, which has led to improved dialogue with traders, as well as to behavioral changes on the part of customs staff members
- introducing frequent communication campaigns aimed at the media, traders, and the general public.

In addition, the customs administration has attempted to enforce discipline more effectively by

- reacting more severely to dishonest behavior
- expediting the processing of disciplinary cases and shortening deadlines for their resolution
- adjusting the penalties in line with detected irregularities
- introducing an awareness campaign to publicize the effect of ethics on the success of the reform
- organizing an annual "customs week" to reinforce employees' loyalty and their sense of belonging to the customs corps.

Conclusion

The changes made by the customs administration in recent years have transformed it into a modern, efficient entity that has adapted to its economic environment. Foreign trade operators now unanimously acknowledge that the customs administration is credible, industrious, and open. Such unanimous support and approval by foreign trade professionals is relatively rare. In most countries they are more inclined to criticize or to be exasperated with the customs service.

The principal objectives of the reform have largely been attained: processing times for customs clearance have been reduced drastically; major procedures indispensable for trade facilitation are all in place; guarantees are no longer a financial handicap for processing industries; and conditions for passing through customs are clear, transparent, and predictable. In addition, the customs administration has shown that trade facilitation does not necessarily reduce tax revenue.

5

MOZAMBIQUE

Anthony Mwangi

Mozambique's reform of its customs operations was initiated in a difficult postconflict environment, which was characterized by a substantial disruption of government services. The approach chosen was unique in that it relied heavily on outside contractors to manage customs services for some time while preparing national authorities to assume full responsibility for them. This experience contains useful lessons for other customs organizations that face similar circumstances.

Background

Mozambique is located in southern Africa and has borders with Malawi, South Africa, Swaziland, Tanzania, Zambia, and Zimbabwe. It has a population of 18.1 million and a total surface area of 489,192 square miles, with 2,841 miles of land borders and 1,535 miles of coastline.

Regional and Preferential Trading Arrangements

Mozambique is a member of the Southern African Development Community (SADC) and of the Cross-Border Initiative. Under the SADC trade protocol, many goods exported from Mozambique, largely raw materials, are exempt from duties in other SADC member countries. Mozambique has signed a preferential trade agreement with South Africa and is currently negotiating bilateral trade agreements with Algeria, Cuba, Egypt, India, Kenya, Malawi, Mauritius, Russia, Zambia, and Zimbabwe. Mozambique's exports enjoy preferential access to the European Union market (under the Cotonou Agreement) and to the markets of industrial countries in general through the Generalized System of Preferences. In addition, Mozambique's exports are eligible for duty-free import into the United States for commodities that qualify for the Africa Growth Opportunity Act. Mozambique is also a member of the World Trade Organization (WTO) and the World Customs Organization (WCO), and it has signed many of the agreements and declarations of those organizations.[1]

Economic Reform Program

After Mozambique achieved independence in 1975, its economy contracted severely during the next

1. Mozambique has made use of the WCO's services in various areas, including (a) hosting the International Conference on Integrity in Customs: The African Response, which was held in Maputo in March 2002; (b) training in the Agreement on Customs Valuation; and (c) training in shipping, handling cargo, and examining containers.

10 years because of civil war and because of inadequate economic policies. In 1987, the government launched its Economic Rehabilitation Program with the support of the International Monetary Fund (IMF), the World Bank, and bilateral donors. The major reforms undertaken under the Economic Rehabilitation Program include (a) unifying and stabilizing the exchange rate, (b) eliminating most price controls, (c) privatizing public enterprises, (d) introducing extensive financial sector reforms, and (e) undertaking significant tariff reform and trade liberalization. Mozambique has made impressive economic gains under the program. During 1987–97, real gross domestic product and exports grew, on average, by 6.8 percent and 15.6 percent, respectively. However, Mozambique remains a relatively poor country—its gross per capita income was US$210 in 2001—with social indicators that are below average for countries in Sub-Saharan Africa.

A key component in the overall process of economic reform was the 1995 decision by the minister of planning and finance to reform and modernize the customs service, primarily to improve the government's revenue-raising capacities and to control trade and transit flows better. The key features of the reform were the creation of a special unit to initiate and oversee the reforms and the engagement of foreign companies to manage key parts of the reform process and implement preshipment inspection (PSI) procedures.

Customs Reform Objectives and Innovative Approach

The government initiated customs reforms to accomplish the following:

- Increase budget revenue. Customs revenues had been on a downward trend since 1992. In 1994, this trend accelerated when a large volume of imports was exempted from import duties under a variety of special programs. In addition, extremely high customs duties encouraged tariff evasion.
- Facilitate legitimate trade by combating corruption and smuggling:
  - — Domestic industries, the sugar and tobacco industries in particular, complained repeatedly that they could not compete with smugglers in the domestic market.
  - — Civil society criticized the government for a lack of transparency in customs operations, for poor management, and above all for a lack of perceived dedication to tackling corruption.
  - — Smuggling rings were firmly entrenched in Mozambican society, and many believed that without a drastic change in customs management, breaking them up would be difficult.
- Create a modern, effective, and reliable customs administration capable of sustaining and building on improvements made during the reform program.

During the end of 1994 and the early part of 1995, the government, together with multilateral donor agencies (in particular, the IMF and the World Bank), agreed on a drastic reform of the customs administration to enhance revenue mobilization and ease trade impediments. The approach selected to solve those problems was a combination of drastic trade liberalization and radical reform and modernization of the customs administration. The latter would cover all key aspects of the customs administration: legislation, structures, management competencies, operational methods, staff training, asset acquisition and management, auditing, enforcement, and a comprehensive anticorruption program. Novel aspects of the approach were to bring in external expertise to manage customs operations and to rely on PSI services to help determine the dutiable value of imports.

Funding

The U.K. Department for International Development (DFID) helped prepare the contract with Crown Agents (the details of which are explained later) and contributed about US$16 million of the total US$37 million cost of the first three years of the contract. The government financed the balance of US$21 million. The IMF supported the reform by providing a legal specialist from 1996 to July 1999. The World Bank provided financing for the Technical Unit for Restructuring Customs (TURC; Unitade Técnica de Reforma das Alfândegas, or UTRA, in Portuguese) from its inception in 1995 until December 1999. The United Nations Development Programme paid for a customs specialist and a part-time macroeconomist.

In view of the need to sustain and build on the successes of the first phase of the reforms, and following a comprehensive contract compliance investigation carried out by the DFID, the government approved a six-month extension to the initial three-year contract with Crown Agents, which was followed by a further contract of three years to consolidate the reforms. The cost of the extension and consolidation phases amounted to US$26 million, of which the government financed US$15 million and the DFID paid US$11 million. With the eventual scaling down of Crown Agents' activities, Crown Agents' fees fell substantially, and for the last year of the consolidation phase they amounted to only about one-third of what had been budgeted for the first year of that phase. The DFID also helped fund a further extension of the contract with Crown Agents for two years (starting in mid-2003), with the objective of strengthening the capacities of the customs agency and helping set up the Central Revenue Authority.

Key Institutional Reform Elements

The minister for planning and finance created TURC in 1995 to manage the reform process. A Mozambican senior manager headed the unit, supported by consultants provided by the IMF and the United Nations Development Programme. Although the private sector was not directly represented, its participation was ensured through strong coordination with the Customs Higher Technical Council, which has a large number of private sector representatives. Strong participation by the private sector in the reform was guaranteed when the proposed new customs legislation was discussed in the council. The plan was for TURC to manage key policy aspects of the ongoing work of the customs administration and to accomplish the following:

- coordinate customs restructuring and represent the minister of finance in all matters relating to customs reform, including serving as a liaison to both private and public sector institutions inside and outside the country
- coordinate the drafting of all customs legislation, including the Tariff Code and customs procedures
- establish the links required with other ministries in light of the needs of the customs restructuring process
- prepare and manage the bidding process for selecting companies that would manage customs services and carry out PSI of imported goods
- supervise the execution of the contract by the successful bidders to ensure that the government gained the maximum benefit from their services
- manage the computerization of customs services.

External Support

In 1996, TURC invited international bids for a company to implement the customs reform process. The major elements of the terms of reference were as follows:

- take over the complete management of customs, including training
- appoint key customs officials to perform the contracted functions in accordance with local employment laws
- supervise imports and other external trade operations subject to the customs legislation, as well as to prevent fraud and the evasion of tax and exchange control regulations
- maintain customs assets in good order and prepare an effective assets inventory system
- procure and maintain equipment assigned to the reform project, including vehicles and data processing software and hardware.

A team that included representatives of the minister of planning and finance, TURC, and the IMF analyzed the bids. Crown Agents was awarded a three-year contract commencing in January 1997 and ending in December 1999. By April 1997, Crown Agents had proposed work plans for each of the activities to be implemented during the contract. Operational management began in mid-1997 in the south of the country and was progressively extended elsewhere.

A senior Crown Agents consultant was appointed as delegated manager of customs and was responsible for implementing the reform program in accordance with the terms of the Crown Agents contract. A Mozambican was retained as deputy national

TABLE 5.1 Number and Types of Crown Agents Consultants, July 2000–January 2003

Work Area	July 2000	January 2001	July 2001	January 2002	July 2002	January 2003
Customs operations	35	22	17	11	1	1
Sensitive operations	9	9	9	9	9	9
Development	3	3	2	2	1	1
Total	47	34	28	22	11	11

Source: Mozambique Customs Bureau data.

director of customs to provide a legal basis for action in cases in which the legislation did not confer the necessary powers to a nonnational or to someone who did not belong to the Mozambique civil service.

At the end of the three-year contract in December 1999, some of the anticipated results—particularly in the institutional development areas, had not been achieved—and the newly created customs service remained fragile. The newly appointed senior customs managers were not yet ready to fully assume their managerial responsibilities, such as financial planning, formulation of management policies, and monitoring, which thus far had been assumed by Crown Agents consultants. Many staff members were relatively inexperienced and were not considered sufficiently advanced in acquiring the necessary skills to take over from the consultants. Moreover, some of the institutional development objectives had not been addressed because of the need to assign local staff members to support the external consultants in operational areas. In addition, some of the operational procedures and information systems were not sufficiently established to yield their expected results.

This situation led to the extension of the contract with Crown Agents until mid-2003. Under the extended contract, which was referred to as the consolidation phase contract, the role of Crown Agents changed from an executive one to a supervisory and mentoring one, except in the areas of investigation and intelligence, staff irregularities, audits, and anticorruption, where Crown Agents maintained its executive role. During the consolidation phase, Crown Agents was to maintain and advance the improvements made in customs services and to introduce the necessary new systems and procedures. A major objective was a controlled handing over of responsibilities to ensure the establishment of a sustainable customs service that would operate without external consultants. The contract specified that the number of Crown Agents consultants was to be reduced from 47 in 2000 to 11 by mid-2003 (table 5.1).

In August 2002, a review of progress under the consolidation phase undertaken by the DFID and TURC concluded that sustainability would not be achieved by mid-2003 because senior management was still considered fragile. Thus, the contract with Crown Agents was extended by another two years. This extension period was to cover a bridging phase until the creation of the new Central Revenue Authority, into which customs activities would be integrated. The main objectives of the bridging phase are to strengthen management at the level of the Customs Board; upgrade skills and processes at all management levels; strengthen capacity in investigations, intelligence, anticorruption, information and communication technology (ICT), and auditing; make further progress with the development of new legislation and control systems; and reinforce the capacity of managers at borders, at terminals, and with mobile teams. Crown Agents was scheduled to focus its support on training, developing, and mentoring managers, while no longer assuming direct management responsibility. The contract called for 11 full-time consultants to be engaged for 2 years and for 3 consultants to be engaged for 18 months.

Intertek Testing Services

To assist with valuation work, TURC launched a competitive bidding process to recruit the services of a PSI company, which resulted in TURC awarding a three-year contract to Intertek Testing

Services (ITS). The reason for employing a PSI company was the lack of control capacity by the customs service and the donor agencies' lack of confidence in the transparency of trade procedures. The PSI company was to check for value, tariff coding, quantity of covered imports, and prohibited imports. The contract also called for ITS to verify the expiration dates of medicines and food products and the value of smaller shipments, which were exempt from PSI requirements, to prevent importers from disaggregating consignments to avoid inspection requirements.

The customs administration paid the fee for the preshipment. Importers were initially liable for a penalty payment of 30 percent of the value of the goods that were selected for PSI but lacked PSI certificates on arrival. This penalty was reduced to 10 percent in February 2003 in parallel with a decision to sharply reduce the number of imports subject to prior inspection.

ITS was appointed to start work in January 1996, a full year ahead of the customs modernization process. PSI was initially applicable to virtually all imports; however, starting in 1999, coverage was progressively reduced using risk management techniques that were developed and operational at that stage within the Crown Agents Trade Information Management System (TIMS). A new tender for PSI services took place in 2000, although evaluation of this tender did not formally take place until early 2002, and the services to be provided were not fully determined until July 2002. In the intervening period, ITS continued to provide PSI services under extensions to the contract signed in 1996. In August 2002, ITS was asked to train local staff through coursework and in-the-field assignments in the areas of local inspection, postshipment, and General Agreement on Tariffs and Trade valuation procedures. ITS also provided support equipment for training.

Accompanying Trade and Fiscal Reform

Mozambique has drastically liberated its trade regime since 1987, including dramatically reducing the number of tariff rates and their levels. It eliminated many special import exemptions that had existed under earlier trade regimes. Most export restrictions and foreign exchange controls were also eliminated. The applicable tariff rates were zero for essential goods, 2.5 percent for raw materials, 5.0 percent for fuels and capital goods, 7.5 percent for intermediary goods, and 30.0 percent for consumption goods. As of January 2003, the maximum tax rate was reduced to 25.0 percent. Mozambique uses the 2002 version of the Harmonized Commodity Description and Coding System. The appendix presents a detailed classification of goods under each tariff structure and a comparison with neighboring Common Market for Eastern and Southern Africa (COMESA) and SADC countries.

The tariff structure is progressive, and tariff rates depend on the extent to which imports are processed. The simple average applied tariff was 13.8 percent in 2001 (down from 15.7 percent in 1998), which is among the lowest in southern Africa and compares with 20.1 percent in Zimbabwe, 24.0 percent in Tanzania, and 24.4 percent in Mauritius. Of neighboring COMESA and SADC countries, only Malawi has a lower rate (5.2 percent), whereas Zambia's rate is roughly the same as Mozambique's. The trade-weighted tariff with COMESA and SADC countries also fell from 10.7 percent in 1998 to 8.7 percent in 2001, which is well below that of Tanzania (19.8 percent), Zimbabwe (19.3 percent), Malawi (14.1 percent), and Zambia (12.9 percent). With four nonzero rates, Mozambique's tariff structure is also among the most streamlined in the region. In comparison, Malawi has 6 rates, Mauritius has 8, and Zimbabwe has 14. To facilitate the lowering of tariffs without excessive overall revenue losses for the budget, Mozambique introduced a 17 percent value added tax (VAT) in 1999. The country also levies excise taxes on automobiles, luxury goods, alcoholic beverages, and tobacco products.

A number of nontariff barriers still impede the smooth flow of trade transactions—namely, the complex standards testing, the labeling and certification requirements, the government's procurement rules, and a lack of adequate intellectual property rights. However, the government has embarked on an aggressive program to eliminate most of these barriers in line with WTO rules. Barriers are being sharply reduced, while government procurement is being simplified. In addition, corruption and smuggling act as deterrents to the growth of legitimate trade. The government has therefore formulated policies and strategies to combat corruption, including sponsoring the African Conference on Integrity, which representatives from the customs services of 50 African countries attended, and the appointment of a third adjunct director general of customs responsible for internal controls and for the development of strategic policies and action plans.

Components of Reform

Mozambique's policymakers conceived of the customs reforms as a comprehensive program, and they therefore entailed a set of complementary and interlocking policy measures.

New Customs Code

Customs laws dated mostly from the colonial period, particularly from the 1940s and 1960s. Not only was the legislation obsolete in terms of the control philosophy, approach, and methodology required in a modern customs service, but also the enforcement powers assigned to the customs service were unclear and inadequate for effective action against customs crimes. Control systems were based on 100 percent physical checks rather than on risk assessment and the targeting of customs resources to consignments that presented the greatest likelihood of irregularities or fraud. Consequently, the systems were slow and inefficient. The outcome was a combination of inefficient public service and poor results in terms of revenue collected and fraud prevented. The new Customs Code was issued in 1998 and was made available on CD-ROM and on the customs administration's website, which also provides other relevant information, such as recent legislation, tariff classification codes, and answers to questions frequently asked by importers and exporters. The computer software in operation is user friendly and easily accessible to companies, importers, and exporters. The Customs Code was updated and reissued at the end of 2002 and encompasses all pertinent legislation and procedures.

Change Management

A steering committee made up of representatives from TURC, the IMF, the World Bank, and the DFID oversees the process of change management implemented by Crown Agents. This committee has been meeting quarterly. In addition, the committee carries out yearly reviews that benchmark and document progress against the original objectives. No such oversight exists with regard to the PSI contract.

Staff, Pay, and Training

Before the reforms, customs personnel were underqualified. In 1996, about a quarter of the staff had not completed high school, and one-third of those had only the most basic educational qualifications (table 5.2). About 10 percent of all staff members had a university degree.

Pay levels were low and no adequate health care plan was in place. In addition, salary payments were irregular. Working and living conditions were poor, especially at border posts, where even such basic necessities as water and electricity were lacking.

TABLE 5.2 Academic Qualification of Customs Staff after the Reform, 1996

Academic Qualification	Number of Staff	Percentage of Total
Postgraduate degree	52	4
University graduate	82	6
Technical or commercial qualifications	284	22
High school graduate	529	43
Completion of ninth or tenth grade	217	17
Basic education or less	108	8
Total	1,272	100

Source: Mozambique Customs Bureau data.

TABLE 5.3 Planned Staff Profile

Staff Category	Before Reform	Changes During Reform	After Reform Total
Customs commissioners	33	(18)	15
Customs supervisors	15	29	44
Customs officials	8	58	66
Agents, trainees, assistants	146	731	877
Guards	125	63	188
First- and second-class auxiliaries	38	44	82
Total	365	907	1,272

Note: The parentheses indicate a reduction in staff numbers.
Source: Mozambique Customs Bureau data.

This situation called for a major reform in human resources. Table 5.3 shows how the staff renewal was envisaged at the outset of the reforms.

The overall staff size was to increase gradually from 365 before the reform to 1,272 at the end of the reform. However, of the 945 staff members on board in 1996, 750 were to be removed; 776 staff members were to be recruited according to newly established standards. However, civil service procedures did not permit the implementation of the staff renewal process as rapidly as had been scheduled. Even after the transfer of some staff members to the new VAT department and to some Planning and Finance Ministry departments, by the end of 2002 about 260 staff members still needed to be released to complete the staff renewal project. New recruitment focused on attracting better-educated personnel. Between 1997 and 2000, 82 postgraduates, 52 university graduates, and 813 mid-level staff members (with high school, technical, or commercial certificates) were added to the staff.

Recently, the target number of customs staff members was further increased to 1,851. This increase was justified by the need to enhance managerial capacity; to improve anticorruption operations, legal investigations, special operations, and postimportation audits; and to reopen closed border stations. (Mozambique has approximately 63 border posts.)

The reforms included the introduction of a new salary scale for customs officers. It is higher than that prevailing for other civil servants and compares well with private sector pay. The remuneration comprises a basic salary and a customs allowance, which varies and is merit based. The new compensation package also included health insurance and a staff pension plan. These changes were agreed to by the Ministry of State Administration, which is responsible for state employees, and were effected through a series of ministerial decrees. This compensation package has not been extended to the rest of the civil service, where the proposed civil service reform is expected to make drastic changes.

Recruitment procedures were substantially modernized and came to rely heavily on academic tests and, in the case of senior staff members, on psychometric tests conducted by independent national institutions and on individual interviews. Background and integrity checks are carried out only for senior managers and for those appointed to sensitive posts. Induction training for new employees now includes paramilitary as well as basic customs training.

A process of continuing education is in place. Consideration is being given to setting up a center for public finance studies that would cover all units in the Ministry of Planning and Finance. The idea would be to start with a customs module. The authorities undertook a feasibility study and a survey of training needs in 2003. In the meantime, the Customs Training Unit, which was established by Crown Agents, uses an institution owned by the Ministry of Health. ITS experts carried out a comprehensive analysis of training needs and assist local trainers by providing technical specialists to present training activities and develop training materials, particularly in the area of valuation. For specialized customs training, customs agents might be able to use the training academies of South Africa and Zambia. The customs service does not provide training to importers, brokers, or forwarders.

Integrity and Corruption Issues

Before the reform, corruption was rampant, and there was no reliable system for detection and punishment. Importers and customs officials frequently colluded in undervaluing and misclassifying imports. Management failures compounded the problem: superiors acquiesced in corrupt practices by staff members under their control and probably shared in the bribes paid. Management and control systems for customs assets were completely absent.

Mozambique is a signatory to the 1993 WCO Arusha Declaration, and the customs reform program is based on the key points of that declaration. Mozambique also signed the WCO 2002 Maputo Declaration on integrity. Against this background, action on integrity and corruption issues centered on a tough program of disciplinary action against staff members who violated the rules. Between 2000 and 2003, 171 customs officials were fired by means of a rigorous disciplinary process. During this period the government created the Directorate of Internal Control, which comprises the Department of Personnel Irregularities and the Anticorruption Unit. Parliament approved anticorruption legislation toward the end of 2003.

Information and Communication Technology

Customs operations did not have any substantial ICT support before the reform project was initiated and the staff was unfamiliar with it. The introduction of modern ICT was carefully phased in so as to be in line with the introduction of modern customs release and management processes. The software selection process entailed a detailed comparison of the advantages and disadvantages of introducing either TIMS or the United Nations Conference on Trade and Development's Automated System for Customs Data. TURC performed this review, with the assistance of an IMF representative. The detailed findings were not made available for this review.

The decision to adopt TIMS was influenced by TURC's limited technical capacity, which hampered its ability to coordinate contracts under the customs modernization and reform program. However, TIMS depends on technical and logistical support from London (like the Automated System for Customs Data, which depends on support from Geneva). The initial cost to the government of the latter was estimated at US$3 million.

TIMS was especially tailored to Mozambique's needs as it implemented its newly adopted customs procedures. The system was first introduced in the south in 1998 and now extends to the whole country. Data transfer to the PSI company by e-mail began in June 2000. Generalized and specialized training preceded the system's introduction. The main functions covered by TIMS include entry of manual declarations, duty payment (not electronic), manifest management, intelligence, risk management, trade zone management, export processing, warehousing, and exemptions. Crown Agents maintains and updates the computer system. The government invested in computer hardware to equip various divisions at customs headquarters.

TIMS is not connected to banks, brokers, ports, or railway authorities, but a proposal is under consideration for establishing a central declaration processing unit in Maputo that will accept declarations made by e-mail and process them automatically. Such a unit would significantly reduce the number of declarations keyed in at clearance points and would speed up the overall clearance process.

Valuation

Since the end of 2002, Mozambique has officially adhered to the WTO Agreement on Customs Valuation, which is based on transaction values as reflected in invoices. ITS maintains a valuation database to which the customs service does not currently have access. However, as of August 2000, its valuation data have been made available to the government through ITS's Advanced Trade Assessment System, as part of the contract with ITS. This system includes information about all inspections performed on imports into Mozambique, such as declarations by importer and exporter, price per exporters' invoices, importer and exporter details, country of supply and origin, harmonized system codes, declared mode of transport, and form of payment. In addition, the database contains data on the results of ITS pricing and coding inspections; comparisons with identical or similar shipments in similar or different quantities; and price trend analyses indicating the lowest, highest, and average prices during any given period. The database also contains other statistics derived from the Internet and trade journals, commodity prices, and so on. Data on ITS inspections in other countries are not revealed for reasons of confidentiality, but they do enhance the work of ITS inspectors. In mid-2002, informal reference prices still existed for most products, but this situation changed in 2003 with the implementation of the WTO Agreement on Customs Valuation.

No reconciliation is carried out between data provided by the PSI company and the final calculation of duties and taxes. ITS had initiated such reconciliation in 1997 with support from the customs service and the National Statistics Institute, in connection with World Bank conditionality attached to the release of US$50 million in debt relief. The reconciliation was designed to (a) compare import values certified by ITS and accepted in the calculation of duties and taxes, (b) identify clearances where the variation between duties assessed by ITS and duties actually paid varied by more than 10 percent, (c) verify the existence of exemptions from PSI and clearances made without PSI documentation, (d) inspect movements of good into and out of warehouses, and (e) analyze duties collected per customs point. However, with the elimination of preshipment declarations and the drastic reduction in the number of imports subject to PSI, the need for reconciliation diminished, especially because deficiencies in the statistical data made the reconciliation results unreliable.

The program of PSI was under review at the time this report was written. Two issues appeared to dominate the agenda. The first issue was the role of PSI once Mozambique adopts the WTO Agreement on Customs Valuation. Clearly, PSI activities are compatible with the agreement. However, application of the agreement requires more evidence to create reasonable doubt than had been required under the Brussels definition of value, which Mozambique had previously used to justify rejecting the invoice price as the customs valuation and moving to the alternative method allowed under the Agreement on Customs Valuation. This difference will require additional information and training for all agents involved, a process that has started with the support of Crown Agents and ITS in the areas of auditing and valuation training under Agreement on Customs Valuation principles. A specialist valuation unit has been created within the customs service, supported by a valuation module of the TIMS software that can carry out postimport audits of traders' records and a visiting control team that can determine value under the new procedures.

The second issue was that since January 2003, the scope of PSI inspections has been reduced to commodities that have been identified as sensitive—for instance, medicines and certain chemical products—to verify tariff classification, quantity, and quality. If the PSI company has doubts about the values declared, it advises the customs service so that customs officials can undertake appropriate postimport audits.

Physical Inspections

Mozambique's reform plans called for a drastic reduction of the rate of goods that are physically inspected so as to speed up the clearance process. Before the reform, all goods were physically inspected. This rate has been reduced to 40 percent since 1999, when the customs service and ITS agreed on a risk-based approach to select goods for inspection. This approach relies heavily on an analysis of data on the importer, exporter, and country of origin and on the Customs Code and can be applied even before the goods arrive in the country. In addition, a small percentage of goods is randomly selected for inspection. The PSI company produces monthly management reports that the customs service uses to determine the effectiveness of the PSI program.

Particular problems arise with secondhand goods, motor vehicles, and personal imports. To assist in the inspection of such goods, ITS has updated prices from the countries of origin on most of the goods and in some cases uses police records. The latter are used to detect smuggled secondhand cars, especially from South Africa.

Trade Procedures to Safeguard Revenues and Facilitate Trade

Mozambique's poor revenue performance before the reforms resulted largely from inefficiencies in collection and control procedures. Although measures were introduced to enhance revenue performance—for example, training along with reform of the customs administration—it would take time to produce results. In the meantime, the Crown Agents consultants focused on reinforcing the collection and control procedures that already existed.

Importation Process Import licenses were abolished in 1998, but importers must obtain importer identification and taxpayer cards. Since January 2003, if the goods to be imported do not appear on the list of sensitive goods that are subject to compulsory PSI, importers may proceed to import the products and submit their final declaration directly to customs agents. All goods that appear on the list of sensitive goods must be submitted for PSI. In such cases, importers notify the PSI company directly by lodging their suppliers' pro forma invoices and informing suppliers of the need to submit the goods for inspection. The PSI company performs a physical inspection of the goods. If the results are satisfactory, then the PSI company issues certified single documents that the importers will use to clear the goods through customs. Currently the PSI company does not intervene in exports.

Special Import Regimes TIMS software is used to process declarations for special customs regimes, including temporary admission for imports and exports, free trade zones, and bonded warehouses. Since 1996, duty exemptions have been limited to imports that are covered by the Code of Fiscal Benefits; are going to free trade zones; or are imported by nongovernmental organizations dealing with humanitarian aid and medicines, diplomatic missions, and multilateral organizations. The government has heightened controls over duty exemptions, and abuses are now rare.

Mozambique has two free trade zones: Mozal, which is located five miles outside Maputo and specializes in aluminum smelting, and Belita, which is located in Beira and manufactures textile products and apparel. The Free Trade Zone Law requires that at least 85 percent of the production of companies operating in free trade zones be exported duty free. Permission to sell locally is given for up to 15 percent of the previous year's production in accordance with customs regulations. Both Mozal and Beira have honored this obligation. Trained customs officials are stationed inside the free trade zones to monitor the movement of goods using computerized records. Customs audit teams periodically examine the records. Free trade zones enjoy an exemption from customs duties on the importation of goods and merchandise under the terms of free trade zone regulations.

Approval for exemption from duties under the Code of Fiscal Benefits is carried out at the ministerial level, following an appraisal of investment projects by the Investment Promotion Center. The principal aim of the exemptions is to attract foreign investment that will both generate local employment and reduce the country's dependence on imports. The government pays duties on its own imports. Government departments include their requirements in the state budget, and until November 2003, the Ministry of Planning and Finance issued Treasury orders to settle the duties as imports were received. The arrangements aim to ensure that ministries budget properly and plan their expenditures in line with their budgets. The use of Treasury orders has since been abandoned and accounting notes are now used to pay duties.

Mozambique does not use a drawback system, and adoption of such a system in the future is not advisable. However, temporary admission is permitted for a wide variety of specified goods, especially those used during international exhibitions. Such goods are secured by cash or bank guarantees, which are refunded when the goods are reexported.

Transit Trade Mozambique has transit trade with Malawi, South Africa, Swaziland, Tanzania, Zambia, and Zimbabwe under SADC and COMESA. Trade is guided by protocols that depend on the regional membership of the particular country. The authorities recently approved new transit procedures, and the procedures are being implemented. Guarantee centers are being established in each region to be responsible for acquitting guarantees once the transit process has been completed. In addition, intelligence systems identify transit traffic that either fails to move on or takes an abnormally long time to do so, and they notify frontier locations to seize such shipments on sight, pending further investigation. COMESA and SADC are implementing a regional customs bond guarantee system that will be cost effective and will be able to control transit traffic in each member country.

Border controls at Ressano Garcia and Namaacha, the frontier points between Mozambique and South Africa and Swaziland, respectively, had been quite weak. Both facilities needed to have their infrastructure upgraded to enable installation of the latest technology so they could better control transit traffic. The authorities have undertaken a number of investments to strengthen those border control points, and in the case of Namaacha, the facilities at the border have been totally rehabilitated.

Most goods imported through the border posts of Ressano Garcia and Namaacha are transported by truck and must proceed for customs clearance to the privately owned road cargo terminal on the outskirts of Maputo. The terminal charges a daily storage and parking fee that traders consider to be exorbitant and that the government does not regulate. The prospect of building clearance facilities at the frontiers has been raised periodically, but no firm plans to do so have been prepared.

Outcomes to Date

The following paragraphs describe the outcomes to date.

Revenue Performance

Customs reforms have contributed to improved revenue performance. Between 1997 and 2001, customs revenues, including VAT collected on imports, increased from 3.6 percent of gross domestic product to 6.0 percent (table 5.4). The largest increase was due to the introduction of the VAT in 2000, which reduced the share of customs duties in total revenues managed by the customs service from 63 percent in 1995 to 33 percent in 2001. Despite tariff reform that entailed a substantial lowering of nominal rates, the ratio of customs duties to the value of total imports rose slightly from 8.9 percent in 1995 to about 10 percent in 1998, 1999, and 2000, with a drop to 8.6 percent in 2001. The increase was due partly to the reduction in the volume of goods previously imported under an exemption regime and partly to more effective customs administration. However, with the introduction of the VAT, the effective import tax (customs taxes plus VAT over imports) rose from 12.3 percent in 1995 to 22.6 percent in 2001. Limitations placed on exemptions and better control of the remaining exemptions led to a drop in the share of exempted imports from 26 percent of all imports in 1995 to 8 percent in 2001.

TABLE 5.4 Customs Revenues, 1995–2001

Category US$ Millions	1995	1996	1997	1998	1999	2000	2001
Circulation tax/VAT	10.2	10.7	19.6	21.5	74.1	112.3	104.9
Consumption tax on imports	14.4	14.2	15.5	18.2	16.9	14.3	12.2
Custom duties	64.8	62.5	70.3	80.2	81.5	82.3	71.2
Total customs revenue	102.5	106.3	125.4	146.1	198.1	236.0	213.5
Taxes on imports	89.3	87.5	105.3	119.9	172.5	208.9	188.3
Value of imports	727.0	783.0	760.0	781.0	790.0	821.0	832.0
Percent							
Customs duties as a share of the value of imports	8.9	8.0	9.0	10.2	10.3	10.2	8.6
Total taxes on imports as a share of the value of imports	12.3	11.2	13.9	15.4	21.9	25.4	22.6
Customs revenue as a share of total fiscal revenue	—	—	—	—	43.9	52.7	51.1
Customs revenue as a share of gross domestic product	—	—	3.6	3.8	4.9	6.1	6.0

— Not available.

Note: The VAT replaced the circulation tax.

Source: Mozambique Customs Bureau data.

Enforcement

The new enforcement systems have reduced illegal imports. The number of seizures of illegally imported goods by customs agents increased from 559 in 1997 to 1,709 in 1999. In 1999, 1,602 cases of diversion of duties, 61 of wrongdoing in relation to importing goods, and 46 of smuggling were brought before customs courts. Consumer goods and alcoholic beverages—items that attract the highest tariffs—represent the largest categories of goods caught in antismuggling activities.

Customs Clearance Times

Even though measurement of total clearance time does not seem to be fully satisfactory, the reforms appear to have shortened overall clearance times, because several steps in the import procedure now seem to be carried out more rapidly. Goods are now cleared 40 times faster than before the reforms.

The profession of clearing agent is strictly regulated, and entry into the profession of clearing agent is restricted. These restrictions undoubtedly undermine the quality of services provided to traders and negatively affect clearance time. In 2000, the International Finance Corporation's Foreign Investment Advisory Service estimated the average clearance time in Mozambique at 18 days, substantially more than in Botswana, Lesotho, South Africa, and Swaziland but fewer than in Kenya and Zimbabwe (figure 5.1). The situation has improved since then, and Crown Agents estimates that in mid-2002 clearance times had fallen to an average of 8 days. This estimate is based on the time elapsed between when customs declarations are lodged and when delivery orders are provided, which can be done only after duties are paid. Having a clear indicator of clearance time that is periodically communicated to private sector operators would enhance transparency and could serve as an indicator of success or the lack thereof.

Anticorruption Measures

All customs personnel sign a personal integrity commitment declaration, in accordance with the requirements of the Public Sector Employment Law. A staff handbook and a code of conduct have been prepared and are awaiting approval by TURC's director general. In addition, in 2002 the Customs Board approved an anticorruption strategic plan. Overall procedures to detect staff misconduct have been strengthened. Between 1997 and

Figure 5.1 Average Number of Days Required for Import Clearance, Selected African Countries, 2000

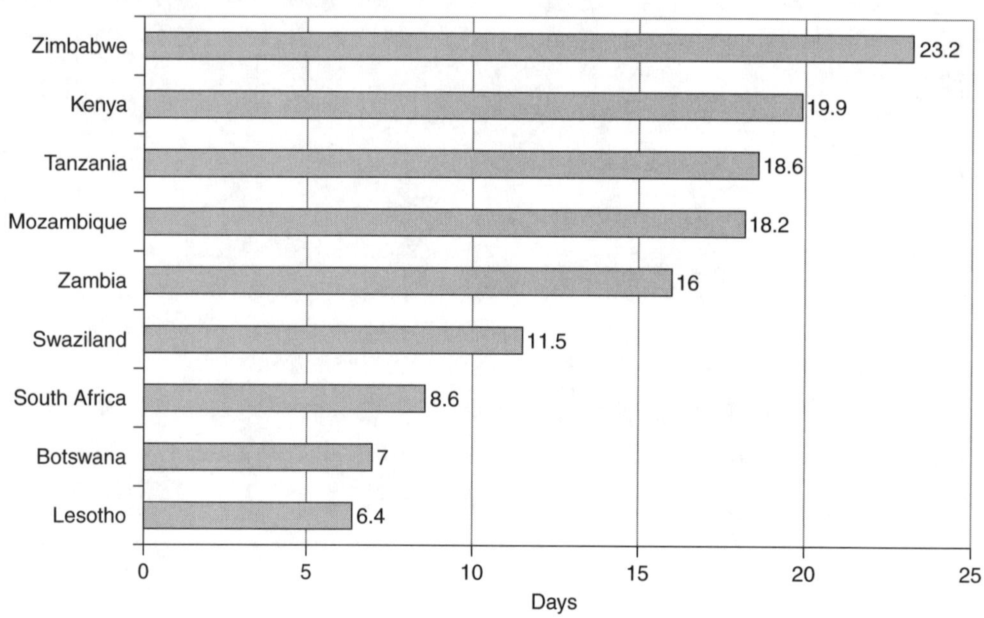

Source: Foreign Investment Advisory Service 2001.

TABLE 5.5 Penalties for Misconduct, 1997–June 2000

Penalties	Old Staff	New Staff	Total
Expelled	20	15	35
Dismissed	58	35	93
Demoted	24	15	39
Other	16	5	21
Acquitted	45	26	71
Under investigation	81	82	163
Total	244	178	422

Source: Mozambique Customs Bureau data.

June 2000, 188 cases of gross misconduct involving both old and new staff members at middle and lower levels were detected and dealt with, while a further 163 are under investigation (table 5.5). By the end of 2001, a further 102 disciplinary cases had been closed, with 55 expulsions and dismissals.

Even though the Customs Tribunal has been in existence for some time, it has gradually been reconstituted to bring it in line with the new Customs Law and the new career plan set out in the tribunal's regulations. The Customs Tribunal deals only with matters of a fiscal nature. Human resources personnel resolve disciplinary matters, and these matters are subsequently referred to the Adjunct General Directorate for Operations and Organization. TURC advises the Directorate when necessary. This system needs to be strengthened to be fully effective.

The application of sanctions to corrupt customs officials is further hampered by the fact that corruption must be dealt with under criminal law, over which the Customs Court has no jurisdiction. Delays at the level of the Administrative Court are lengthy, undermining the credibility of the campaign to enhance integrity. Further undermining the anticorruption program is the failure of disciplinary action to always swiftly follow conviction.

The seriousness with which Mozambique views corruption in the customs service is illustrated by the March 2002 invitation to the WCO to hold an international conference in Maputo on Integrity in Customs: The African Experience. This meeting resulted in participants issuing and signing the Maputo Declaration, a commitment to integrity in customs services.

Users' Reactions

The Customs Higher Technical Council was created as a forum for consulting with trade association representatives and clearing agents regarding their views on progress under the customs modernization process. The Customs Higher Technical Council meets quarterly, or more frequently when the situation demands it. Participants consider it to be a good forum for discussing and exchanging ideas on a whole range of topics, from proposed legislation to the effectiveness of the reforms. The Chamber of Commerce organizes an annual private sector conference, during which participants discuss constraints on private sector development, including those related to customs operations.

Although the community of private sector users appears to have no formal measures of improvement, general user opinion is that overall customs performance has made substantial progress. Users also believe that corruption in the customs administration has declined somewhat but has not been eliminated. They are optimistic that the reform process will help to close the gap between the performance of Mozambique's customs administration and that of more advanced neighboring administrations, such as those in South Africa, Swaziland, and Zambia.

Importers and their representatives look forward to the possibility of making electronic customs declarations and electronic payments for assessed duties and taxes. The customs administration intended to enable electronic declarations by the end of 2002, and TIMS was reengineered accordingly.

Selected Issues that Deserve Immediate Attention

The following are selected issues that deserve immediate attention.

Debt Management

A review of debt management systems reveals that large amounts of money are owed to the government. Those amounts include about US$500,000 in uncollected fines and penalties for 2002 imposed by the Customs Tribunal and about US$850,000 in guarantees where importers have not fulfilled their legal obligations. To address the outstanding debt issue, the government should introduce changes in the customs structure that would lead to the creation of a secretariat responsible for collecting such debts. Regarding the Customs Tribunal, the government has appointed 11 justices and assigned them to the tribunals of Beira, Maputo, and Nacala.

Change Management

With the extension of Crown Agents' contract, the authorities must monitor the progress that Crown Agents makes in implementing its key assignment of upgrading management skills—including at the highest levels—in order to establish a sustainable national customs service.

Mozambique's tax administrations, including the customs administration, are to be transformed into the Central Revenue Authority by 2005, much like the organizational structure of customs administration in Kenya and Uganda. Studying the experiences of those countries would be useful, so that Mozambique could benefit from the lessons learned.

By mid-2003 all technical customs positions that go through a selection process were fully staffed by local officials, except for the position of director general. In June 2003, a new customs director general was appointed and added to the management team.

Staff and Management Issues

The process of staff renewal has been completed, meaning that the process of retrenching the 263 staff members earlier identified for retrenchment has been expedited. Nevertheless, the human resources strategy to deal with retrenchment, recruitment, and staff discipline needs to be strengthened. Staff training also deserves more attention, and the establishment of a revenue academy deserves priority attention within the context of government plans for creating the Center for Public Finance as part of the Ministry of Planning and Finance.

The operations of key border posts and terminals are deficient, because managers are not supervising their staffs adequately and are not following guidelines. If unchecked, this situation will lead to corruption and other illegal activities. The backlog of disciplinary cases in which staff members have been convicted but no disciplinary action has been taken is reaching an unprecedented level. In mid-2002, it stood at 109 cases. This situation undermines the achievement of the integrity objectives. Also, the sanctions imposed may not be sufficient deterrents.

Infrastructure

The development and upgrading of communications facilities to manage transit traffic require urgent attention. TURC should act on available, specific proposals to redress the situation.

Customs personnel continue to live and work in extremely poor conditions, especially at some of the border posts that lack even water and electricity. Decisive action to remedy this situation is warranted.

In addition, to achieve the objectives of the bridging phase of the customs reform program, key infrastructure projects need to be completed, especially the communications infrastructure required to complete the installation of TIMS at all customs offices.

Smuggling

Policies to check smuggling by informal sector traders need strengthening, and arrangements need to be made early on to manage such risk in a sustainable manner. Elements of such a policy, some of which are under consideration, could include (a) encouraging greater cooperation between the customs administration, the police force, and frontier guards; (b) attempting to sustain pressure at key locations over a number of weeks; and (c) mobilizing the elite mobile rapid-response teams that have been specially trained by the police and provided with quality equipment. To strengthen antismuggling efforts, the government approved regulations for the Council for Customs Policy Coordination, which brings together the different ministries involved in antismuggling activities. The private sector, through the Mozambican Association of Sugar Producers, which represents all enterprises in the sugar sector, coordinates with the customs administration in such efforts.

Lessons Learned

The reform and modernization project on which Mozambique embarked in 1996 was unique in its comprehensiveness and its reliance on expatriate consultants to whom the government granted managerial powers. However, the initiative turned out to be more ambitious and complex than initial planning suggested, and as a result, the initial contract with the consultant firm was extended twice. The acid test for the success of the reform will be a successful transition to a sustainable customs service that is completely run by Mozambican staff and the smooth integration of the customs administration into the envisaged Central Revenue Authority.

Mozambique's experience underlines the importance of developing a detailed feasibility study of the management tasks to be entrusted to an outside agency before any contract is agreed. Such a study would reduce the need for repeated contract extensions, while greater flexibility in relation to contract length could be useful for tasks related to capacity building.

The following are key factors in the success of the customs modernization initiative to date:

- The willingness to rely extensively on external companies, trainers, and facilitators to support the process of reform to supplement the acute shortage of experienced local customs officers.
- The prudent and gradual approach that placed revenue collection above other reform processes to avoid jeopardizing the relatively fragile advances made in the overall context of economic reforms. The decision to adopt a gradual and phased approach to reforms was helpful in that it led to the introduction of new systems only when adequate support for their functionality was guaranteed. Examples are the reliance on PSI and its move to greater selectivity and the phased introduction of the ICT system by Crown Agents.
- The careful planning of the reform, with progress rigorously reported and monitored by domestic leaders and external donors. This factor gave added flexibility and authority to the process and contributed to donors' willingness to extend their support beyond the period originally envisaged.
- The benefits provided to the reform by adequate political support.

The sustainability of the reforms will depend greatly on actions taken during the bridging phase of the customs reform program before the withdrawal of the Crown Agents and on how the customs administration is readying itself to take on the task of valuation. Several issues deserve to be highlighted in this regard.

First, with all the key management roles now performed by nationals, the challenge is to enable managers to provide effective leadership in a modern and efficient public service organization and to develop customs strategies and policies to achieve the reform objectives, particularly the integration of the customs administration into the Central Revenue Authority.

Second, provisions should be put in place to ensure that the TIMS software is maintained and further developed so as to accept customs declaration information electronically. To that effect, an ICT strategy will need to be developed that will include recruiting skilled personnel and upgrading training. Eventually a system should be designed to permit trade information to flow between the customs administration and other trade participants, such as freight forwarders, importers, exporters, port operators, and carriers over a wide area network or the Internet. Electronic payment of taxes should also be made possible.

Third, the newly created valuation unit should be closely monitored to ensure that it will be able to operate autonomously from the PSI company over time. Staff policies should be implemented without delay so that the new customs administration does not inherit the thorny problem of staff turnover and can concentrate on enhancing staff efficiency and enforcing staff integrity. Attention to staff training should be given greater priority than at present.

Finally, civil service reform that improves the performance of the police, the immigration service, and the local administration at border points would greatly benefit the performance of the customs service.

Reference

Foreign Investment Advisory Service. 2001. *African Competitiveness Report 2000.* Washington, D.C.: International Finance Corporation.

APPENDIX 5.A. SADC and COMESA Country Tariff Structures, Selected Years

Country or Entity	Tariff Structure (percent)	Simple Average Rate (percent)	Trade-Weighted Rate, SADC and COMESA (percent)	Number of Tariff Lines
Malawi (2000)	0, 5, 10, 12.5, 15, 25, 30	5.16	14.05	5,443
Mauritius (2000)	5, 10, 15, 20, 30, 40, 55, 80	24.36	n.a.	5,481
Mozambique (1998)	0, 2.5, 5, 7.5, 35	15.74	10.69	5,172
Mozambique (2001)	0, 2.5, 5, 7.5, 30	13.80	8.70	5,243
Tanzania (2000)	0, 5, 10, 20, 30	24.00	19.84	6,215
Southern Africa Customs Union (2000)	279 different taxes, both specific and *ad valorem,* with rates from 0 to 72 percent	n.a.	n.a.	7,804
Zambia (2000)	0, 5, 15, 25	13.59	12.87	6,066
Zimbabwe (2000)	0, 5, 10, 15, 20, 25, 30, 40, 60, 65, 70, 75, 80, 85, 100	20.14	19.25	7,099

n.a. Not applicable.

Source: Various national and regional databases.

6

PERU

Adrien Goorman

In 1990, the Peruvian government launched a major customs administration reform. The reform transformed what was generally considered to be an inefficient and "bad" customs administration into an efficient and modern administration that observers see as a model for others to follow. Moreover, the improvements resulting from the reform have been sustained to date, consolidated, and deepened.

The most important steps that would eventually ensure the success of the reform were taken at the very beginning and during the initial years of the process, when the legislative basis for reform was laid. With the support of the highest authority, reformers were able to work toward achieving their vision of a professional, modern customs administration characterized by integrity. Rather than tinkering with adjustments or improving existing systems and procedures, the reformers started with a clean slate; went for the best in organizational, managerial, and operational systems; and largely achieved their objective through quality design and planning. The customs administration changed dramatically within a few years, and the consolidation and deepening of the reform process continues today.

The modernization of a complex administration is, by its nature, a gradual process. One cannot pinpoint a fixed date when the new customs administration was established. The most intense years of reform were 1991–94, when the basics were developed and put into place, and 1995–98, when the reforms were consolidated and deepened. Following a brief leveling-off period, in 2000 the reformers made a push for further modernization, increased administrative efficiency, and better service to the trading community with a program of second-generation reforms that were based largely on more intensive use of technology. Today the customs administration continues to renovate itself in light of changes in the trading environment and technological developments.

Although Peru's achievements are formidable both in substance and in sustainability, continued vigilance and effort will be needed to prevent the quality of the customs administration from deteriorating. Risks are mainly economic and political, but some of a systemic nature may also arise.

This chapter begins by reviewing the circumstances and factors that stimulated the reform and underlie its success. Skeptics might reason that being perceived as successful is easier when a country starts from an extremely low point of departure and establishes what should have existed in the first place, but Peru's success in customs reform is much more than that. By starting from scratch, in many ways Peru surpassed the degree of modernization and the quality of management systems that can be found in many industrial countries. That is not to say that the system is perfect, and improvements and adjustments are possible or needed in a number of areas, but that situation is characteristic of customs administration. Given its position in the middle of foreign trade operations, customs administration needs to be flexible and able to adapt to changes in the sector.

Background and Origin of the Customs Reform

This section summarizes the characteristics of the trade and tariff regime and the customs administration in 1990 and how the economic crisis that erupted that year led to important policy and institutional reforms, including the customs administration reform.

Trade and Tariff Regime in 1990

In 1990, Peru's trade regime was characterized by intervention, regulation, and protection. The import tariff regime was complex, consisting of 39 different rates, ranging from 10 percent to 84 percent, along with 14 different surtaxes. In combination, the tariffs and surtaxes amounted to 56 rates ranging from 10 to 110 percent. The overall rate level was high. The unweighted, average, nominal tariff rate, excluding surtaxes, was 46.5 percent. Multiple exemptions and numerous nontariff barriers added further complexity. Peru also had 130 special exemption regimes. Nontariff barriers included quantitative restrictions, prohibitions on 539 tariff items, licenses, importer and exporter registration, authorizations, and administrative requirements. Exports were subsidized.

Customs Administration in 1990

In 1990, Peru's customs administration was disorganized, inefficient, and corrupt, and it had a negative public image. Out of 4,700 personnel, only 2 percent were professionals. Salaries were low and training was inadequate. In addition, discipline was poor and the incidence of corruption was high. Laws and regulations were uncoordinated and contradictory, and neither customs personnel nor the private sector were familiar with them; as a result they were not properly applied. Working without guidelines or instructions, personnel acted on suspicions rather than on good faith. Discretionary action was the rule. Procedures were bureaucratic and cumbersome, with excessive clearance controls. Customs valuation was subjective; thus the duties and taxes charged on import shipments were unpredictable. On average, goods were not released from customs until more than 20 days after the presentation of declarations. Such delays substantially increased costs for import and export businesses.

Computing equipment was inadequate, and the customs administration lacked professional staff members with adequate computer skills. The customs process was almost entirely based on paperwork. Statistics were processed through a mainframe computer at the Ministry of Economy and Finance (MEF) that served the entire ministry. Statistics, prepared only after huge delays, were obsolete by the time they were ready. Infrastructure was precarious and, at some customs offices, nonexistent. Vehicles were not available for operational activities, and communication links between headquarters and field offices were lacking.

The customs administration's collection function was not effectively controlled. Revenue collection procedures lacked rigor and resulted in a large number of disputes and litigation cases. In addition, many payment checks lacked deposit coverage, but the customs administration failed to take action to recover revenue. Customs policy was not clearly defined, and institutional development plans did not exist. Also the customs administration failed to provide the public with information about rules, procedures, and activities. Personnel changes in senior management positions were frequent. Finally, the customs administration depended on the MEF for its budget. There was no investment budget, and budgetary programs were not properly implemented.

The 1990 Economic Crisis

The Peruvian customs reform came about as a result of the 1990 economic crisis. In 1990, Peru faced an unprecedented collapse of its public finances. Tax revenue, which had averaged between

15.0 and 17.0 percent of gross domestic product (GDP) in the mid-1980s, had fallen to 8.7 percent of GDP, and GDP itself was also falling. Those developments coincided with hyperinflation and increasing terrorism by the Shining Path. To bring Peru out of the crisis, newly elected President Alberto Fujimori launched major policy and institutional reforms. The old trade policy of interventionism and protection was replaced by a policy of deregulation, openness, and liberalization. Within a year, quantitative restrictions and other nontariff barriers had been virtually eliminated, the tariff structure had been simplified to only a few low rates, and most exemptions had been abolished.

On the institutional side, a January 1991 decree mandated the reform of all public entities of the central and regional governments and decentralized public institutions. Customs reform was considered urgent because of the fiscal emergency and the need to reduce obstacles to trade. A March 1991 decree empowered the customs administration to reorganize itself. The subsequent Legislative Decree Number 680 stipulated that the reorganization must encompass the redefinition of a national customs policy, a new organizational structure, the professionalization of staff, the implementation of an integrated computerized system for administrative and technical operations, an overall moralization of customs staff, the reactivation of foreign trade, and an increase in budgetary revenue.

Laying the Foundation for Reform

This section reviews important initial measures taken to establish a solid basis for sustainable reform.

Fully Dedicated Reform Manager and Team

In December 1990, President Fujimori appointed Carmen Higaonna as superintendent of the customs administration with a mandate to reform the agency. Higaonna was eminently qualified for the job. After obtaining her degree in economics, she worked for 10 years in the MEF's Tax Office, where she gained experience in tax policy and administration. For the next 10 years, she worked in the General Auditor's Office, where she was responsible for auditing the customs administration and gained in-depth knowledge of its workings and failings. During that period, she also obtained a certificate as a customs technician after attending a three-month course sponsored by the German Technical Assistance Agency. In 1990, Higaonna and her team prepared a report for the president on the state of the customs administration.

Thus, when Higaonna was given responsibility for reforming the customs administration, she was in the excellent position of already having considerable insider information about every component of the administration. In addition, she had no political affiliations and was given a high degree of freedom in carrying out the reform. She put together a reform team consisting of 20 officials, whom she had brought in from the General Auditor's Office. They had worked together auditing the customs administration for many years, and 17 of them also had obtained the German Technical Assistance Agency's customs technician certificate. That core team was later strengthened with officers retained from the existing customs administration, following a stringent selection process. The team worked full-time on the reform for about five years.

Support from the Highest Authority

Opposition from vested interests was strong during the initial stages of the reform. The policy of opening up the economy and reforming the customs administration to facilitate trade did not sit well with business lobbies that were used to import protection and other special treatment. Customs officials also opposed the reforms, albeit for other reasons: they wanted to protect their jobs and privileges. Congress strongly opposed the reforms, which would have affected some well-entrenched vested interests.

Despite such opposition, the reformers went ahead, thanks to personal and unrelenting support from the president, who met with Higaonna frequently during the initial years of the reform and protected her from political interference. As the reforms progressed, opposition decreased. Opposition from Congress disappeared because the president disbanded Congress in 1992. Opposition from customs personnel disappeared with the new staffing and working conditions that were introduced in the first year of reform. Business and industry began seeing the gains from reform and eventually gave it their support.

External Support and Financing

In 1991, the reform received a substantial budget of US$3.4 million from the technical cooperation component of a trade adjustment loan financed by the Inter-American Development Bank (IDB). The IDB provided this support for Peru to prepare new customs laws and regulations, establish a new organizational structure, streamline and computerize operational procedures, upgrade the physical infrastructure, adopt a new salary scale, and implement training programs in the National Customs School. The support covered the hiring of international and national experts; the acquisition of computers, communications equipment, and laboratory equipment; and the hiring of highly specialized instructors for the National Customs School.

The IDB continued its support with three more loans: a US$1.5 million loan in 1994 to consolidate the reform, a US$750,000 loan in 1997 to establish a certified quality system, and a US$1 million loan in 1999 to consolidate and extend the quality system and introduce the World Trade Organization (WTO) Agreement on Customs Valuation. The reform was also financed internally through the customs administration budget. Approved legislation granted budgetary autonomy to the administration. Two percent of customs revenue was allocated to finance operational expenses, and 1 percent was allocated to the annual investment plan designed to modernize the customs system.

Design, Planning, and Monitoring

Members of the reform team took study trips to countries that had modern customs administrations or had successfully reformed their customs services to learn about best practices in customs administration and reform. The reform team designed the reform plan, working closely with the MEF and with IDB experts in the context of the technical cooperation program. Throughout the reform, MEF and IDB experts monitored implementation.

Reform Objectives and Strategies

Given the chaotic state of the customs administration, a piecemeal approach to reform would evidently have been insufficient and an integral restructuring and transformation was needed. The reform team set out to develop a strategy and program to convert the administration into a professional, dynamic, modern, and efficient one that would be an effective instrument of fiscal policy and foreign trade and would have a positive public image. The program was constructed around three basic themes: moralization, professionalization, and modernization. The envisaged outcome was a customs system that would (a) facilitate trade; (b) operate on the basis of good faith; (c) limit the discretion of customs officers; (d) be fully computerized; (e) implement a self-assessment system of duty liability; (f) selectively check transactions, with a maximum of 15 percent of transactions undergoing physical inspection; (g) rely on postrelease checking; (h) delegate functions to the private sector, such as banks (to collect duty payments), privately operated warehouses, customs brokerage services, and preshipment inspection (PSI) companies (to help establish the customs value of imports); (i) be professional; and (j) be quality certified (International Standards Organization 9000).

The team planned to achieve this system by such means as revising and systematizing customs legislation, restructuring the organization of the customs administration, adopting modern management systems, revising personnel and training policies and systems, streamlining and computerizing operational procedures, and modernizing infrastructure. The reform team concretized the specific objectives and strategies in its reform plans for the consecutive phases of the reform.

Reform Measures

The key measures that resulted in successful reform involved legislation, organization and management, personnel recruitment and development, and computerization and other information and communication technology (ICT) applications that supported clearance procedures and the new customs control strategy.

Legislation

At the beginning of the reform process, fundamental legislation was passed to change the trade regime, thereby enabling and supporting the customs administration reform.

TABLE 6.1 Tariff Regime, Selected Years

Aspects of the Regime	1990	1997	2002
Number of rates	56	4[a]	7[b]
Highest rate	110	25	25
Lowest rate	10	12	4
Nonweighted average nominal rate	47	14	11
Prohibitions	539	25	—
Nontariff barriers	Numerous	—	—

— Not available.
a. Basic rates of 12 and 20 percent and surtax of 5 percent combine to 12, 17, 20, and 25 percent.
b. Basic rates of 4, 7, 12, and 20 percent and surtax of 5 percent combine to 4, 7, 9, 12, 17, 20, and 25 percent.
Source: National Customs Service data.

Trade liberalization policies not only made reform of the customs administration necessary to remove administrative obstacles to trade but also enormously simplified customs administration, thereby creating conditions needed for the reform to succeed. Significant steps toward liberalizing and simplifying the tariff and trade regime were made during August and September 1990 and were continued in subsequent years. Table 6.1 highlights the key elements of the tariff regime in 1990, 1997, and 2002.

In relation to customs administration, crucial legislation was passed at the beginning of the reform process, including the following:

- In 1991, a supreme decree and Legislative Decree Number 680 set out the objectives and direction of the reform. Those decrees are of utmost importance because they provided the customs administration with the autonomy to reorganize itself. Such autonomy was crucial because it greatly facilitated the development and implementation of measures needed to achieve reform objectives in such sensitive areas as personnel policy and management. It also allowed the customs administration to use its budget effectively and flexibly to operate and, thus, to achieve its goals much like a private business.
- Decree Number 659 of August 1991 introduced the Import Verification Program, the first measure geared toward outsourcing customs functions to the private sector.[1] The measure met with intense opposition from importers, not only because they had to pay for inspections but also because it made corruption more difficult. The customs administration itself perceived the measure as demonstrating a lack of confidence in the administration. However, the program proved useful because it provided price and product information that would otherwise not have been available. The Import Verification Program has been renewed annually, although its continuation has remained controversial.
- The new General Customs Law and Regulations and the new Organizational Law on Customs became effective in March 1992 and December 1992, respectively. Customs legislation was updated as the reforms progressed. The General Customs Law of 1996 (Legislative Decree Number 809) has been the basis of customs administration to date.

The new laws provided the necessary legal basis for the professionalization, moralization, and modernization of the customs administration. They harmonized and systematized customs laws and adapted them to international norms and standards and to the requirements of an open trade regime.[2] The laws enabled the effective

1. This measure was not part of Higaonna's program but was imposed by the MEF.

2. Peru has been a contracting party to the World Customs Organization since 1969, the multilateral agreements included in the Uruguay Round decision since 1994, and the Harmonized Commodity Description and Coding System since 1998.

FIGURE 6.1 Organizational Structure of the National Customs Service

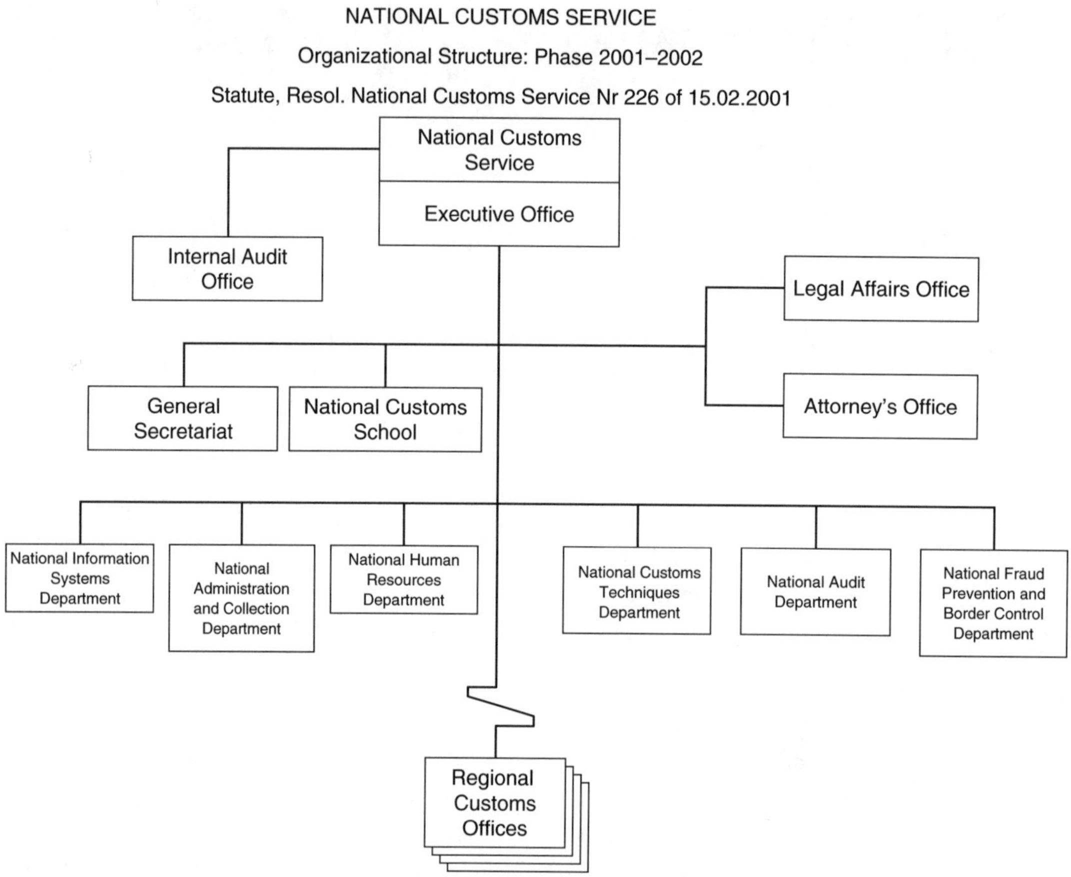

Source: National Customs Service.

organization of the National Customs Service (NCS, see figure 6.1); the effective management of human, budgetary, and physical resources; and the introduction and implementation of modern administrative and control procedures and systems. They also established the principles of good faith and presumption of innocence and were geared toward minimizing discretion in customs administration, providing for reliance on postrelease audits, and facilitating trade. Finally, they regulated the functions that the private sector was to perform, such as acting as customs agents, warehouse operators, and shipping agents.

Organization and Management

The objective of the reform was to establish an organizational structure that would be functional and modern, have the necessary infrastructure and equipment, and allow management to achieve administrative goals through autonomy and accountability.[3]

The March 1991 supreme decree provided the customs administration with administrative autonomy on a temporary basis and in broad terms. The organizational law of March 1992 rendered that autonomy permanent and defined it more specifically. The law established the customs administration as a decentralized public institution under the MEF with administrative, economic, budgetary, financial, and technical autonomy. The president selects the superintendent of the NCS on the recommendation of the minister of economy and finance,

3. A July 2002 decree stipulated the integration of the NCS and the Internal Revenue Service, to be effective within 90 days. The objective was to expand the tax base through improved revenue control, including more intense cross-checking of information, and to realize economies of scale in such areas as computerization.

and the superintendent is appointed by a cabinet resolution. The superintendent has the power to hire and fire customs personnel at any level.

Economic, budgetary, and financial autonomy allows the NCS to finance its operations and investments. The law allows the NCS to retain 3 percent of customs revenue collections and to charge fees for its services. There is no nominal upper limit. Two-thirds of that income is to be used for operations and one-third for investment in customs modernization. In general, the NCS decides autonomously how to use its budget; however, in addition to the requirement that it use part of its budget for investment, the MEF's Office of State Institutions and Organisms must approve the salaries of customs staff. Furthermore, budgetary autonomy depends on governmental approval: at the request of the executive branch, the allocation of 3 percent of customs revenue can be changed by a simple act of Congress.

That extensive autonomy has been a decisive factor in bringing about reform. It has allowed the NCS to accomplish the following:

- Set and implement its personnel policy independently, including firing and laying off staff; implement a new, rigorous recruitment system; and adopt a private sector employment regime that allows the NCS to pay much higher salaries than those prevailing in the public sector and reduces incentives for staff members to engage in corrupt behavior.
- Develop administrative and operational norms, systems, and procedures that largely eliminate discretionary decisionmaking; reduce interactions between customs officers and foreign trade operators to a minimum; and make customs administration transparent and predictable.
- Develop norms and procedures that are independent of the standard rules set for public administration in general and freely adapt them to the needs of a modern customs administration.
- Operate like a private business, unencumbered by rules set by other agencies concerning travel, procurement, and so on.

Every year, the NCS and the MEF sign a management agreement that commits the NCS to the pursuit of institutional objectives and management targets. The agreement provides for periodic evaluations to assess whether the NCS is achieving its objectives in a timely manner. It also enables the NCS to pay productivity bonuses to its personnel subject to certain conditions. More on this agreement is included in appendix 6.A.

In 2003, the NCS and the Internal Revenue Service were consolidated into a single organization. The objective of this recent organizational change was to expand the tax base through improved revenue control, including more intense cross-checking of information, and to realize economies of scale in such areas as computerization.

One of the objectives of the reform was to establish an administration characterized by openness and transparency. To this end, the NCS closely involves foreign trade operators, customs agents, and the public in its reform plans and consults with them on its proposals for changing customs law, regulations, and procedures. For instance, meetings that included representatives of the NCS's Legal Department and foreign trade operators led to the realization that the Customs Law needed to be revised. Following the drafting of an initial set of revisions, the NCS will solicit the opinions of foreign trade operators, other users, and the public and will prepare a new draft that will reflect their comments.

The NCS makes information about rules, regulations, activities, and programs available through its Web site. Detailed data on foreign trade operations, including the details of every customs declaration that the NCS processes, are also available. In addition, the customs valuation data bank is also accessible to anyone interested in the value of specific imports.

The transparency of customs operations not only supports the customs administration's operations and reform plans through consultation and information but also helps preserve integrity and gives the customs administration a favorable image. That is an important factor in securing the sustainability of the reforms.

Personnel Recruitment and Development

The first important reform measure was the removal of all nonperforming, underperforming, and corrupt personnel. A voluntary withdrawal program was introduced whereby such personnel were offered significant monetary amounts as an incentive to leave. Personnel who opted not to leave under this arrangement were required to pass an external examination that was organized in cooperation with the National Engineering University.

Those who did not pass had to leave the customs administration. Those who passed had to take a one-year course at the National Customs School and pass another test at the end of the course. Those measures allowed the NCS to get rid of 60 percent of its staff in 1991 (and more during the next few years) and to retain only the best.

At the same time, the responsibilities of the National Customs School were expanded to include recruitment. Before the reform, admission to the customs administration was regulated under civil service rules, and no more than a high school degree was required. Since 1992, recruitment has been controlled by internal NCS regulations. Under the new system, only university graduates who graduated in the top third of their class could enter the customs service. In addition, candidates had to pass a one-year National Customs School course. Candidates were required to pay for the course, but they were guaranteed immediate employment if they passed the examination.

Those measures resulted in a substantial increase in the number of NCS staff members with university degrees and a specialization in customs administration, while the total size of the staff was greatly reduced. By 1993, the number of customs personnel had decreased by some 30 percent (table 6.2). By 1997, about 50 percent of the personnel were professionals, and this ratio has been maintained.

With the March 1992 Organizational Law of Customs, the NCS was changed from a public sector employment regime to a private sector one. This change placed customs employees on the same salary scale as those at financial institutions, and their salaries increased by 600 percent. In addition to regular salaries, personnel are also eligible for productivity bonuses. Bonuses are based on performance under the Customs Quarterly Operational Plan, and the amount available to be paid out as bonuses depends on the operational cash flow balance at the end of every six-month period. Individual bonuses are based on performance evaluations, which are carried out every six months. The management agreement that the NCS signs with the MEF every year establishes the criteria and parameters for distributing bonuses.

Individual performance evaluations of customs personnel use such criteria as quality of work, cooperation, discretion, knowledge, adherence to rules, meeting of targets, initiative, and interpersonal relations. In addition, group evaluations are carried out on the performance and achievement of objectives determined every six months for every administrative area under the Customs Quarterly Operational Plan.

Almost every measure taken in the context of the customs reform can be considered a measure to ensure or promote integrity, because together the measures create an environment that is conducive to integrity. In addition, the reformers took a number of specific measures to ensure or promote integrity in the service, including the following:

- Issuing a code of conduct.
- Carrying out background checks to ensure staff members' quality and honesty. Those checks cover their academic levels (authenticity of diplomas), criminal records, family situations, and kinship (this measure, aimed at identifying cases of nepotism, was introduced more recently).
- Requiring a sworn declaration of income and assets. In 2002, the superintendent of the NCS requested 81 management staff members to make such declarations.

TABLE 6.2 Customs Staffing, Selected Years (number of employees)

Type of Staff	1991	1992	1993	1994	1997	2000
Professionals	67	552	686	1,065	1,280	1,440
Unspecialized technical staff	1,303	534	472	469	454	420
Technical specialists	0	118	134	198	231	250
Administrative staff	1,289	813	611	505	596	519
Total	2,659	2,017	1,903	2,237	2,561	2,629

Source: National Customs Service data.

The National Customs School has played an important role in professionalizing the customs service by means of its role in evaluating and training recruits, in developing and implementing in-service training programs and specialized activities for customs personnel and customs agents, and in publishing pertinent information. In combination with the increase in the number of personnel with university degrees, the continuous training of staff, and the performance evaluation system, the overall quality of NCS staff has been significantly enhanced.

Since 1991, 2,244 staff members have graduated from the National Customs School. Although the majority of courses are given in Lima, since 1997 the school has increasingly organized courses in the provinces.

In recent years, the school has also increased its focus on training personnel in institutional management. About 250 NCS staff members have participated in a senior management training program at the University of Piura. The program is funded by the PSI companies that have been approved under the Import Verification Program. The PSI companies are required to train those customs personnel who work on valuation. The program includes inspection techniques and administrative and organizational procedures. In 1992–95, approved import verification companies delivered some thirty 15-day courses. Customs officers believe that those courses have been useful in such areas as inspection techniques, goods classification, and valuation. About 15 percent of the courses were held abroad, bringing personnel into contact with customs systems in other countries and with officials with whom they could maintain relationships afterward. Since 1999, training has centered on the introduction of the WTO Agreement on Customs Valuation.

The various measures taken in the areas of recruitment, training, salaries, bonuses, evaluation, and integrity have been crucial in attracting and maintaining a professional staff, encouraging honesty, strengthening management, increasing administrative efficiency, and improving performance.

Information Technology and Customs Control and Clearance Procedures

An integrated computer system was developed at the NCS that encompasses all customs regimes, operations, control functions, audits, administration, exchange of information with foreign trade operators, statistics, and management. Its main components are the Customs Management System, the Payment Control System, the valuation data bank, and the Audit Management System.

All customs operations are computerized. Customs offices are interconnected through a system of 1,600 computers, 50 servers, and an e-mail network. This computerization has permitted the following:

- The NCS has a Web site that provides access to institutional and operational information and a place for electronic commerce.
- Trade and revenue statistics are now produced quickly and efficiently through electronic means.
- Cargo manifests are transmitted electronically.
- Declaration processing and clearance procedures are fully automated. A program of risk assessment and management selects shipments for red, orange, or green channels with payments made through electronic or other means. By law, no more than 15 percent of shipments can be physically inspected. Clearance times have been reduced from an average of 20 days to 24 hours for the red channel (physical inspection), 12 hours for the orange channel (document verification), and 1 to 2 hours for the green channel (immediate release). An advance clearance system is in place for operators in good standing.
- Postrelease checking of shipments or operators, as selected through the Audit Management System, complements the clearance process. Penalties for fraud are stiff.

For more details about the declaration processing and customs clearance system and the NCS Web site, see appendix 6.B.

The extensive application of ICT has been a crucial element of the reform by helping to achieve and support several objectives:

- automating, simplifying, and establishing uniformity of operational procedures
- implementing modern customs control strategies based on selective checking at the time of importation supported by postrelease audits
- minimizing contact between customs personnel and foreign trade operators
- eliminating or reducing discretionary action by customs personnel

- selecting shipments for inspection
- reducing clearance times
- tightening revenue controls
- improving and accelerating the availability of management information
- permitting rapid and efficient production of trade and revenue statistics
- increasing overall efficiency.

Audits

One of the objectives of the reform was to shift the emphasis of customs control from controls at the time of importation, exportation, or other transaction to postrelease audits. That objective lies at the heart of the new customs control strategy and is based on the view that the customs service should be a second-story administration, in which many functions are outsourced to the private sector while customs personnel concentrate on postrelease controls. The reform included the creation of the National Audit Department. The department's activities are divided into two main branches: the Intelligence Management Branch, which is responsible for risk analysis and audit programming, and the Audit Management Branch, which is responsible for carrying out inspections and audits. During 1999–2002, the number of customs auditors was increased from 25 to 60.

The risk management system is used in the customs clearance process through electronic alerts or orders to retain shipments in terminals or through the assignment of shipments to the red or orange channels. It is also the basis for postrelease controls.

Audits are carried out in line with an audit plan and audit program. The audit function is well developed, organized, and managed, but it needs to be strengthened further. All the elements for the Audit Department to work efficiently and effectively are in place; however, periodic amnesties granted by the government are negatively affecting the results of audits and may eventually undermine the entire new customs control strategy, which hinges on the effectiveness of postrelease audits.

Valuation and the Import Verification Program

Legislative Decree Number 659 of August 1991 established the Import Verification Program, which requires importers to obtain certificates of inspection issued by authorized PSI companies before goods are shipped from the country of exportation. In the certificates, the PSI company certifies the nature, quantity, value, and tariff classification of the goods. Under the original procedure, those data were to be used by importers in their import declarations and formed the basis for the payment of duties. Customs officers verified the consistency of import shipments with the data on the inspection certificates. In cases of discrepancy, the goods were released with security required for any additional duties, and the case was submitted to the NCS Valuation Division for a decision.

The Import Verification Program was originally created to address the failure of the old customs administration to effectively carry out its core responsibility of verifying import shipments for duty assessment and collection. Furthermore, the program was consistent with another reform objective that called for outsourcing certain administrative functions to the private sector and leaving the responsibility for supervising and monitoring the outsourced activities to the customs administration.

Even though the Import Verification Program was originally presented as a temporary measure that would help prevent undervaluation and fraud until the NCS could build up sufficient capacity to carry out the valuation function without PSI assistance, it is still in place. However, in view of the adoption of the WTO Agreement on Customs Valuation and the WTO Agreement on Preshipment Inspection, the use of PSI services in the area of valuation has changed.[4] The role of PSI is limited to that of risk indicator, and importers are no longer required to declare the value verified or observed by the PSI company. Customs officers question the declared value whenever they have reasonable doubts about the accuracy of the declared value or of the documents presented in its support. Reasonable doubt may arise on the basis of the PSI companies' verification reports, the indicators from the Risk Assessment System, or the valuation data bank. When customs officers have reasonable doubts, they use the procedures laid down in the Agreement on Customs Valuation to arrive at an acceptable value.

The NCS's Valuation Division oversees the activities and performance of the approved PSI

4. As a signatory, Peru implements the WTO Agreement on Preshipment Inspection and the WTO Agreement on Customs Valuation and has incorporated the agreements into national law.

companies. The division is also responsible for developing, interpreting, explaining, and supervising the application of the valuation norm and developing, maintaining, and updating the valuation data bank. The division deals with all valuation matters and has a staff of 24. The price information that is provided by the approved PSI companies has greatly facilitated the valuation work of the NCS. About 80 to 85 percent of import shipments are subject to PSI intervention. Imports with a value below US$5,000 (US$2,000 for goods particularly vulnerable to fraud) and those that fall in certain other categories are exempt. From the implementation of the Import Verification Program in 1992 until March 2002, the approved PSI companies issued 1,351,544 inspection certificates or verification reports, all of which have been used as a basis for duty assessment. According to data from the PSI companies, the NCS found irregularities in the quantity, quality, or value of shipments in only 2,291 cases, or 0.17 percent of the total.

The customs valuation data bank was created in 1992 and was gradually developed on the basis of inspection certificates and, since 1999, of verification reports. It now contains some 40,000 entries. Declared values, whether declared by importers or observed by a PSI company, are automatically checked against the values in the data bank, which is continually being updated.

The Import Verification Program was helpful in (a) providing the NCS with the elements needed for duty assessment (for example, value, tariff classification) for every shipment at a time when it lacked the capacity to perform these functions properly on its own; (b) supplying those data during the subsequent years of the reform, while the NCS was building up that capacity; (c) providing most of the price information that allowed the NCS to create and build up its valuation data bank; (d) dissuading importers from misrepresenting the actual customs value of their imports; and (e) training valuation officers.

Ten years after the introduction of the Import Verification Program, the NCS has greatly increased its capacity by training personnel, computerizing its activities and making extensive use of ICT applications, maintaining an updated valuation data bank, and ensuring stable organization and management. It also has gained experience since 1999 in implementing the Agreement on Customs Valuation. Thus, the questions that now arise are whether the NCS is ready and able to perform the valuation function without the assistance of the approved PSI companies and whether doing so would be more cost effective than the present system. Opinions vary widely among both public and private sector representatives. The cost of the Import Verification Program amounts to some US$45 million per year. On the basis of its findings and analysis, the mission that carried out this reform evaluation believes that the NCS should now carry out its valuation function largely without assistance from PSI companies. PSI assistance could still be useful on a limited basis, especially in relation to shipments vulnerable to fraud and in the context of risk-based management of the pre- and postclearance verification process.

Outcome of the Reform

This section evaluates the overall effect of the reform and examines its influence on revenue collection.

Overall Effect

Today the customs administration is a modern, effective, and efficient system that compares favorably with other customs administrations in South America, which operate in a broadly similar economic and trade environment, and with customs administrations worldwide. According to both public and private sector representatives interviewed during the evaluation mission, the customs reform has been a great success. The gains in trade facilitation, revenue collection, service to foreign trade operators and the public, and administrative efficiency are indisputable. Table 6.3 outlines the achievements of the reform by comparing the situation in 1990 with that in 2002.

There remains room for improvements and further gains in efficiency, but if those gains have not been made yet, the lack of improvement has more to do with Peru's economic realities than with any inability to implement further reforms, particularly with respect to trade facilitation. The economic reality is that substantial incentives to evade customs duties and taxes still exist, and the degree to which further reforms can be achieved must be weighed against the risk of evasion. For instance, the desirability of reducing the number of physical inspections of imports to less than 15 percent of shipments is not obvious at this stage, even though it would be desirable from a trade facilitation point

TABLE 6.3 A Comparison of the Customs Administration, before and after the Reform, 1990 and 2002

1990	2002
Objective of customs	
Revenue collection; no explicit or implicit objective to facilitate trade	Revenue collection and trade facilitation
Legislation	
Tariff and trade regime	
• 39 tariff rates, 14 surtaxes, combining to 56 different rates	4 rates (7 rates including surtax)
• Range of rates: 10–110	Range of rates: 4–25
• Prohibitions: 539 items	Prohibitions: 1997: 25 items
Administration (laws and regulations)	
• Contradictory and dispersed	Clear and coherent
Organization and management	
No autonomy; public sector regime	Administrative and technical autonomy
No institutional development plan	Institutional development plan in place
Inadequate and bureaucratic structure	Structure adapted to the needs of a modern customs administration and the dynamics of foreign trade, with clearly established functions for each organizational subdivision and unit
Centralized decisionmaking	Delegation of functions and responsibilities
Budget depends on the MEF and determined through a national budgetary process; no investment budget	Budgetary, financial, and economic autonomy; 3 percent of customs revenue to finance customs operations and investment
Precarious or nonexistent infrastructure	Modern physical infrastructure
No annual investment plan	Annual investment plan
No acquisition program	Existence of an acquisition program
Personnel and training	
Total staff: 4,700	Total staff: 2,540
Professionals: 2.5 percent of staff	Professionals: 60 percent of staff
Recruitment: no strict requirement	Recruitment: rigorous evaluation process
Low salaries	Salaries equivalent to those in the private sector
No career plan	Career plan
No training program	One-year full-time course at the National Customs School as a condition of entry; special and refresher courses during career; 1,573 staff trained at the National Customs School by 1999 and 2,240 by 2002; training under the PSI program
No training provided to customs agents	One-year full-time course at the National Customs School for customs agents required for certification
Computerization	
No computerization	All customs functions and operations computerized; 1,600 computers and 50 servers; interconnection of all customs offices through an e-mail system; interconnection with foreign trade operators online through electronic data interchange and e-mail
Huge delays in trade statistics and obsolete when ready	Statistics in excellent shape and produced rapidly
Electronic commerce	
Not available	Electronic customs auctions, acquisitions, and sale of statistics via the NCS Web site

TABLE 6.3 (Continued)

1990	2002
Customs control and clearance process	
Incoherent procedures	Uniform, computerized procedures
Paper declaration, clearance process, and transactions	Electronic declaration lodging and processing
Control system based on suspicion	Good faith principle
100 percent of shipments checked	Selective checking based on risk analysis; by law maximum of 15 percent of shipments physically checked; in 2001 18.9 percent were physically checked, documents were checked for 44.4 percent, and 36.7 percent were not checked[a]
Multiple procedural steps	Automated procedure
Payment at customs	Payment at bank, electronic or otherwise
Process discretionary and unpredictable	Predictable, set rules and procedures virtually without discretion
Multiple contact with foreign trade operators	Little or no contact of customs officer with importers or exporters
No facilities for reliable foreign trade operators	Facilities for reliable importers and exporters: advance declaration system, temporary admission regime for export processing
Clearance times: over 20 days	Clearance times: red channel 24 hours, orange channel 12 hours, green channel 1–2 hours
Revenue collection not effectively controlled	Revenue collection tightly controlled
Poor quality of service	Quality certified (ISO 9000)
Postrelease audits	
No postrelease audit; customs control system relies on 100 percent checking at time of clearance	Customs control system relies heavily on postrelease audit; audit function established and fully operating with a staff of 50 based on the audit selection system and audit program
Valuation	
Brussels definition of value system	WTO Agreement on Customs Valuation introduced in 2000
Valuation discretionary and subjective	Strict valuation methods and rules
No valuation data bank	Valuation data bank operated by customs on the basis of PSI and other data
Revenue collection	
US$626 million	US$2,403 million
23 percent of budgetary revenue	36 percent of budgetary revenue

a. Although the law stipulates that no more than 15 percent of shipments should be checked physically, achieving exactly 15 percent in practice is difficult. The 18.9 percent rate resulted from adjustments of the declaration or the duty liability in 6 percent of cases.
Source: International Standards Organization (ISO).

of view. Customs administrations in industrial countries routinely inspect only 2 to 5 percent of shipments, but they operate in an environment where incentives to evade are weaker and where audit-based controls are solidly entrenched.

Furthermore, as Peru's customs administration was built up anew under the reform beginning in 1991, the fact that customs managers are still working on improvement of, and refinements to, the administrative and operational systems that were established over the past 10 years or so is not surprising. Although the trading sector lauds the achievements without exception, it is not satisfied 100 percent of the time.

TABLE 6.4 Value of Imports, Customs Revenue, Rate of Increase, and Average Collection Rate, 1990–2001

Year	Value of Imports (US$ millions)	Rate of Increase (percent)	Customs Revenue (US$ millions)	Rate of Increase (percent)	Average Collection Rate (percent)
1990	2,726	n.a.	626	n.a.	23.0
1991	3,476	27.5	1,001	59.9	28.8
1992	3,791	9.1	1,283	28.2	33.8
1993	4,024	6.1	1,505	17.3	37.4
1994	5,435	35.1	2,032	35.0	37.4
1995	7,584	39.5	2,676	31.7	35.3
1996	7,774	2.5	2,726	1.9	35.1
1997	8,341	7.3	2,846	4.4	34.1
1998	8,042	−3.6	2,838	−0.3	35.3
1999	6,718	−16.5	2,402	−15.4	35.8
2000	7,344	9.3	2,502	4.2	34.1
2001	7,252	−1.3	2,403	−4.0	33.1

n.a. Not applicable.
Source: NCS data and author's calculations.

Influence on Revenue

Customs reform has had a substantial positive effect on revenue. Table 6.4 shows the value of imports, the revenue collected, the rate of increase, and the average collection rate for 1990–2001. During 1991–93, the first three years of the reform, customs revenue increased from US$626 million to US$1,505 million. The rates of increase in revenue were substantially higher than the rates of increase in the value of imports. In interpreting those data, note that several factors were at play, the effects of which are difficult to isolate because adequate data are not available for 1990 and 1991. Apart from the value of imports, those factors include tariff rate reductions, which had a negative revenue effect with a given value of imports; eliminations of exemptions, which had a positive revenue effect with a given value of imports; and changes in rates of and exemptions from the sales and consumption taxes. However, those factors cannot account for the substantial increases in revenue from 1991 to 1993, a large part of which must therefore be due to the improved customs administration. After 1993, the rate of increase in revenue was slightly lower than the rate of increase in import value, but this change is mainly an outcome of further tariff rate reductions.

Conclusions

In addition to summarizing the main factors underlying the success and sustainability of reform, this section also highlights some risks to its longer-term sustainability and suggests a number of areas where reforms should now focus.

Success Factors

A number of factors account for the success of the reform, including the following:

- The political will and the continued and unrelenting support of the highest authority was the overriding and single most important factor, a view unanimously shared by all those interviewed.
- The trade regime was drastically simplified and most exemptions, restrictions, licenses, authorizations, and other nontariff barriers were eliminated. Those steps simplified administration, reduced bureaucracy, and eliminated opportunities for bribery.
- The creation of a dedicated reform team allowed it to take ownership of the reform and work on it full-time for several years.
- The definition of clear objectives and strategies geared toward the establishment of best practices led the reform in the right direction.

- An adequate budget to implement reform was made available to the reformers through a self-financing arrangement and external support.
- The administrative, economic, budgetary, financial, and technical autonomy gave the reformers virtually a free hand in designing, establishing, and developing modern systems.
- The establishment of a simple, clear legal framework for customs administration supported all the changes needed for the modernization and put the customs administration on a firm footing for the future.
- The removal of corrupt and unqualified personnel from the customs administration by means of a strict evaluation and testing process allowed the reformers to begin with a clean slate. Only the best personnel stayed, becoming the foundation on which the reform was built.
- The professionalization and moralization of customs staff members were achieved through a comprehensive set of human resource development and management measures, including an effective personnel recruitment, development, and management policy; a private sector employment system, which permitted a much higher salary structure than that of the public service; a performance evaluation every six months, with these evaluations serving as the basis for merit or productivity bonuses; and an effective integrity policy.
- An environment for integrity was created through the establishment of a simple and transparent trade regime; clear, straightforward customs norms and regulations; computerization and ICT applications that left little or no room for negotiation, influence, or discretion in customs processes; strict staff evaluation and selection procedures; professional training; good salaries; performance bonuses; internal control; a code of conduct; background checks; and appropriate and attractive infrastructure. All those factors combined to (a) create incentives for personnel to work well, (b) give them an institutional identity and sense of belonging, and (c) strengthen them against temptations to engage in corrupt behavior.
- A modern customs control system was adopted. The system was based on self-assessment, selective checking, risk assessment and management, and postrelease audits.
- The privatization of activities that could be executed more efficiently or effectively by the private sector allowed the NCS to concentrate on its core tasks of assessing and collecting duties and managing and supervising the customs control system. The Customs Law mandates the delegation of activities to the private sector.
- The computerization and the extensive use of ICT applications allowed for less contact between personnel and foreign trade operators, less discretionary decisionmaking, and uniform and speedy processing.
- The professionalization of customs agents helped smooth the clearance process and contributed to the achievement of operational efficiency.
- The legal obligation of the NCS to obtain certification under the International Standards Organization 9000 norm (Article 3 of the Customs Law and Article 8 of Customs Rules) helped achieve a high level of quality in systems, procedures, and overall service.

Sustainability Factors

Factors underlying the stability of the reform included the following:

- The continuity in top management at the NCS ensured perseverance in the implementation of the reform. The NCS had only two superintendents during the reform, one from 1992 to 1999 and one from 1999 to the present. The change of superintendent did not change the direction of the reform but rather continued the process and gave it new strength.
- The NCS has built-in mechanisms for good performance, timely adaptation, and renewal, including administrative, financial, and budgetary autonomy, whereby customs personnel all have an institutional and direct personal interest in performing well, increasing revenue collections, and keeping standards high. Indeed, revenue collections determine the size of the customs budget, which in turn supports salaries, bonuses, equipment, and infrastructure.
- The reform has been hard-wired into the customs administration's organizational systems, culture, and performance expectations. It has

been comprehensive and thorough, changing the normative, structural, administrative, managerial, and technical components that all interact to make up the customs administration and allow it to perform well.

- The improvement in customs revenue collections, much of which can be ascribed to the reform, should be a guarantee against government actions that might endanger customs revenue.
- The enhanced service—in particular, the reduced clearance times, the overall gains in efficiency and cost reduction achieved by means of ICT applications, and the transparency of the whole system—is likely to encourage the continuation of support for modernization by most of the business community.

Risks to Sustainability

Potential risks to the sustainability of the reform include the following:

- Lowered commitment to trade liberalization and facilitation would undermine the drive toward customs efficiency. Several representatives from both the public and the private sectors who were interviewed for this study expressed concern in this regard.
- Future governments may be less supportive of an efficient customs service and may appoint superintendents who are less dedicated to continued modernization and high performance standards. Decreased support might also interfere with personnel management and recruitment, thereby undermining the professionalism of the staff.
- During periods of economic downturn, the customs service budget may be cut to the extent that it cannot ensure the proper operation of the NCS, thereby causing a spiral of deterioration in performance and prestige.
- Periodic amnesties whereby duties and penalties resulting from audits and other enforcement activities are forgiven could undermine the effectiveness of the control strategy, thereby affecting the morale of the auditors and the prestige of the customs administration.
- The NCS may become overly strict in applying its rules and procedures and become rigid in its operations. That rigidity could build up resentment against the customs service and entice trade operators to influence customs staff to solve problems informally. Such an approach would breed corruption.

Areas to Monitor

Discussions with senior customs staff members and private sector representatives, as well as the author's own findings, suggest that the following areas may warrant careful monitoring:

- Improve human resource development and management further to motivate and improve the staff.
- Improve the distribution and allocation of staff members (for example, by moving personnel from handling files to more operational work, including audits).
- Strengthen the training programs at the National Customs School, particularly in the areas of valuation and audits.
- Be aware of the limits of extremely strict application of rules, which was a reaction to the chaotic situation that existed before 1990 in relation to customs operations. Customs staff members make great efforts to go by the rules and are closely controlled by the General Controller's Office. That approach works well for routine matters; however, the mechanical application of rules and regulations is at times counterproductive. Foreign trade operators complain that customs personnel delay clearance procedures in cases, for instance, in which the documentation contains small errors that have no effect on either duty collection or other essential matters, and that they have to solicit authorizations from superiors for routine matters. Also, customs personnel frequently demand additional copies of documents they already possess or that are available on the Internet. To counter this mind-set, customs personnel should be made more service oriented through training that emphasizes solving operational problems expeditiously within the limits of rules and instructions.
- Monitor the need to continue outsourcing the valuation function to PSI companies. The cost of such outsourcing should be weighed against

the feasibility of the NCS undertaking this task itself using risk analysis and postrelease audit methodologies, while further building up and updating its valuation data bank and occasionally consulting PSI companies. In any event, a case can be made for exempting from PSI inspections those importers that have an excellent reputation with the tax and customs authorities.

- Coordinate the inspection activities of standard-setting agencies (such as those concerned with agriculture and health) with customs clearance activities to prevent delays in the release of shipments that could result from the need to comply with all those agencies' regulations. This coordination could be accomplished by means of a temporary inspection facilitation committee consisting of representatives of the relevant agencies, who could be given a mandate to work out a solution within, say, two months.
- Improve revenue collections by further strengthening the audit function.
- Improve management information to help managers make timely and adequate decisions in a constantly changing trade environment.
- Enhance cooperation and coordination with the Internal Revenue Service.[5]

5. The integration of the NCS and the Internal Revenue Service, stipulated in a July 2002 decree, should facilitate the exchange and cross-checking of information on taxpayers' activities and obligations.

Appendix 6.A. Management Agreement between the National Customs Service and the Ministry of Economy and Finance

Every year, a management agreement is signed between the superintendent of the National Customs Service and the Ministry of Economy and Finance. The purpose of the agreement is to commit the NCS to the pursuit of institutional objectives and management targets for the year, with a view to improving the quality and coverage of the customs service and increasing the efficiency, effectiveness, and quality of the management of its resources. At the same time, the agreement is an instrument for quarterly evaluations, through control and follow-up of partial targets established for the achievement of the objectives, and for encouraging personnel to reach the targets on time.

In the 2002 agreement, the NCS declares the objectives of the customs budget for the year and determines management indicators. The NCS is committed to the following:

- achieving performance targets and using agreed units of measurement
- presenting a report to the MEF's national budget director on progress toward achieving the targets and performance indicators
- presenting information on the execution and evaluation of the budget
- informing the MEF about the personnel evaluation system and the criteria for assigning productivity bonuses
- agreeing not to increase salaries and bonuses during the year, except increases that result from collective negotiation or from the productivity bonuses provided for in the agreement
- making progress in overall management by designing and implementing measures to increase the quality and coverage of the customs service in the following areas: human resources, services to users, strategic planning, and transparency and availability of accounts.

The signing of the management agreement enables the NCS to pay productivity bonuses to its personnel subject to the following conditions:

- A maximum amount is determined, as a fraction of personnel expenditures.
- The bonus has to be financed through savings in the NCS's current expenditures for the year; that is, a positive operating balance is needed from which the bonus can be paid.
- The NCS must be in good financial health, and it must have sufficient liquidity so that its operations and the quality of its service are not affected.
- The performance targets must be met at an average level of at least 95 percent.

Failure to present the information about performance indicators and about the execution and evaluation of the budget on time is penalized by a 10 percent reduction of the bonus.

Appendix 6.B. The Application of Customs Information and Communication Technology and Control and Clearance Procedures

Integrated System

An integrated computer system was developed that encompasses all customs regimes and operations, control functions, audits, administration, exchange of information with foreign trade operators, statistics, and management. Its main components are the Customs Management System, the Payment Control System, the valuation data bank, and the Audit Management System.

Declaration Processing and Customs Clearance Procedures

Cargo manifests are transmitted electronically to the customs agent and to the NCS. The lodging of the customs declaration is also electronic. Customs declarations and supporting documents, including value declaration, input-output data, appendixes, and cargo manifests and their amendments must be sent electronically from the foreign operator's office to the customs office. This process takes no more than five minutes. The system operates through public e-mail services and through the e-mail systems of the Customs Brokers Association (a private company) and the NCS. Validation service for the declarations operates 24 hours a day and is available throughout the country.

The customs agent (broker) verifies the value declaration electronically by accessing the customs valuation data bank. The Customs Management System verifies and validates the data, issues a single declaration number, and prints the declaration. Using a program of risk assessment and management, the system selects shipments for the red, orange, or green channels. Payment is made to the bank by electronic or other means. Inspection can be documentary and physical (red channel), documentary only (orange channel), or not required (green channel). Goods are released from warehouses after verification of payment.

Clearance times for imports are as follows: 24 hours for the red channel, 12 hours for the orange channel, and 1 to 2 hours for the green channel.

This process is complemented by postrelease checking of shipments or operators selected by the Audit Management System. Penalties for fraud are stiff.

Advance Clearance System

Importers that have not incurred a penalty higher than US$897 in the preceding 12 months are allowed to process import declarations in advance of arrival of shipments and to have the shipments delivered directly to their warehouses without a customs inspection. The importers are required to have their accounts audited every three months by a private audit company, at their own expense.

Electronic Payment Through Banks and Control over Collection

Payment of duties and taxes must be made to the bank electronically, through the e-mail system, or in another form. Electronic payment requires registration of the operator and identification of the bank and account the operator wants to use for automatic debiting.

The Payment Control System brings together information from the NCS, banks, and warehouses, thereby permitting tight control over the accuracy and timeliness of duty and tax payments. Revenue collections are checked daily, monthly, and annually for all customs offices. The system allows for effective control over payments and for rapid action in case of error or fraud.

Customs Web Site

The NCS has a Web site through which it makes available to users and to the general public information on customs rules, regulations, activities, and programs; its valuation data bank; and detailed data on foreign trade operations, including the details of every customs declaration. Recently the NCS has begun using its Web site for both customs auctions and procurement. The NCS also sells statistical information over the Internet. In that way, more information is made available to more buyers at a lower cost.

7

PHILIPPINES

Guillermo L. Parayno Jr.

The period 1992–98 was one of golden opportunity for reform and modernization in the Philippine customs service. The country had just conducted a national election that had brought into power a government whose priorities included matters directly relating to the efficiency of the customs service. In his first state of the nation address, President Fidel V. Ramos noted his intent to strengthen tax and customs collections.

Background

Responding to Ramos's policy direction and to the president's earlier instructions to the Bureau of Customs (BOC) commissioner to "clean up customs," the BOC prepared the *Blueprint for Customs Development Towards the Year 2000.* The previous administration under President Corazon Aquino (1986–92) must also be given credit for sowing many of the seeds of change. Loan negotiations with the World Bank; preparatory work with the International Monetary Fund (IMF) on the Philippine Tax Computerization Project (PTCP); and two important and reform-minded laws, the Republic Act Number 7650 and the Republic Act Number 7651, were initiated under Aquino's administration. Even the main underlying philosophy that guided the massive reengineering of the customs environment and the methods of work were based on the philosophy of the Public Ethics and Accountability Program, which was crafted and implemented early in 1987.

However, other factors also created an opportunity for reform. An experienced staff, whose uninterrupted tenure enabled it to introduce projects with long gestation periods, led the reform. The staff had the full trust and confidence of the president and his cabinet and was also supported by the business community. With the economy performing well from 1992 until mid-1997, many of the development funds required to provide impetus to the reform became readily available. In addition, the private sector contributed as part of a genuine collaborative effort with the government. This collaboration was a major factor behind the 1992–98 Customs Reform and Modernization Program.

The program was basically successful, and it was recognized in the national business community, the country, and internationally for its significant outcomes. However, the reform was not fully sustained, as progress was reversed under the administration of President Joseph Ejercito Estrada (1998–2001).

An investment climate study (Pernia and Gupta forthcoming) points out that customs and trade regulations ranked seventh out of 18 specific constraints evaluated by firms. Exporters and foreign firms ranked customs as the major constraint on business operations. The survey also noted that bribery is typically used to speed up the process of getting government authorization or permits, thus encouraging public officials to slow down the process.

Efforts are under way to revitalize the reforms and recover lost ground. As before, the key is to harness private sector support for the program, obtain full political commitment to the reform, fully implement the measures identified earlier, and work on removing all the constraints that hinder the achievement of those objectives. Issues that should be addressed include adequate personnel compensation, staff retention, and continuity of direction and management even when the political leadership changes.

Focus of the Study

The BOC observed its 100th anniversary in February 2002. During its existence, its top management has changed about 40 times, and each administration has claimed to have undertaken reform and modernization initiatives. During 1972–86, many corrupt customs officials were sacked. In 1974, the valuation methodology was drastically revised, shifting from export value to home consumption value. In 1976, a mainframe computer system was installed to generate databases of important customs transactions such as customs bonds, orders of payment, and customs declarations. In 1986, a new purge of corrupt BOC officials was undertaken. That same year the BOC engaged a preshipment inspection (PSI) service for the first time. During the 1986–92 administration, the Public Ethics and Accountability Program was launched to increase the risks and reduce the rewards of engaging in corrupt practices. Attempts to exempt certain key customs positions from the civil service law that regulated those positions failed.

This chapter focuses mainly on the changes implemented from July 1, 1992, to June 30, 1998, because that reform was the only one that was preceded by the publication of a well-thought-out reform program. This publication was the *Blueprint for Customs Development Towards the Year 2000,* which proposed a clearly identifiable program, was approved by the president and the cabinet, was disseminated to the public, and was updated over the years. The World Bank supported the program, which also benefited from regular assessments by IMF customs experts.

Origins of Customs Reform and Modernization Program

The 1992–98 Customs Reform and Modernization Program started when the new government took office and appointed a commissioner of customs, who received full support from the president and enjoyed direct access to him. Because one of the new government's immediate concerns was the budget deficit—the BOC was behind its revenue target for the first six months of the year by more than P 3 billion—the initial work program concentrated on removing revenue leakages. This work entailed intensifying antismuggling operations; disposing of seized goods more frequently and efficiently; and collecting tax arrears, including those from government corporations and agencies.

The Blueprint for Customs Development

Work on the blueprint began toward the end of 1992. From a thorough analysis of the environment projected for customs service operations until the end of the century, the BOC carefully defined the objectives of the service and mapped out the strategies for achieving them. In addition to the primary target of revenue generation, other equally important reform objectives were set, including attaining a better business and investment environment, protecting people's health and the environment, and streamlining the bureaucracy.

Some of the factors that were perceived as helping the program achieve its objectives were as follows:

- The introduction of PSI and the Comprehensive Import Supervision Scheme (the mechanism for reviewing imports within the customs administration), which was seen as an opportunity for the BOC to gradually assume full responsibility for all customs administration.
- The World Bank loan and the PTCP, which were already in the final stages of deliberations and were expected to provide technology that would allow the BOC to overhaul its systems and procedures to better support organizational objectives.
- The widespread use of information and communication technology (ICT) by customs

partner entities, such as the shipping and airline industries, port operators, and banks, which would permit sharing databases and automating cargo clearance processes.
- The readiness of many business groups, such as the Federation of Philippine Industries, the various domestic industry associations, and the chambers of commerce, to collaborate with the BOC for more effective enforcement of customs laws.

The following were the major strategies and development principles lined up to achieve the objectives:

- The BOC would increasingly rely on clients' self-assessments and voluntary compliance with customs laws, rules, and regulations.
- The clearance of low-risk shipments and passengers was to be expedited, while enforcement resources would be concentrated on high-risk shipments through increased reliance on postrelease clearance procedures and other postaudit processes.
- Information, communication, and other technologies would be used extensively to advance customs processes well ahead of the arrival of cargo, to automate processes, and to reduce human intervention to a minimum.
- Information and other resources would be shared extensively with clients, partners, and stakeholders both in the Philippines and abroad.
- A high degree of harmony and complementarity would be attained by means of extensive consultation with all affected groups.
- A climate that promoted involvement, commitment, integrity, and professionalism in the customs service would be cultivated.

The blueprint was presented to the president and his cabinet for approval and then disseminated widely to the public as well as to the BOC's rank and file. The public welcomed the blueprint's objectives but was somewhat skeptical that it would ever benefit from them. Few commented on the blueprint.

The Shape of Things to Come in the Bureau of Customs

Subsequent documents were prepared and issued to the public as well as to the BOC. Those documents provided more details and amplified the development plans outlined in the blueprint. One such document suggested a number of development activities, including the following:

- Introduce by 1997 remote lodgment of declarations, mainly by means of electronic data interchange.
- Carry out advance screening of cargo manifests for suspicious and high-risk shipments.
- Ensure computer connectivity between the BOC and major port operators by the end of 1993.
- Establish the BOC as a major hub for all trade-related information in the country, such as trade statistics, shipping schedules, and cargo locations.
- Reduce progressively the percentage of shipments undergoing physical clearance to, at most, 20 percent by 1998 and to less than 5 percent by 2000–05.
- Develop an intelligence module as part of the Automated Customs Operating System, which is based on the latest version of the United Nations Conference on Trade and Development (UNCTAD) Automated System for Customs Data (ASYCUDA), and also develop an automated examiner assignment routine.
- Strengthen the customs service to assume increasing responsibility for examining shipments, and focus the service on gathering information about the value of imports.
- Procure fixed and mobile X-ray machines capable of detecting prohibited drugs, firearms, and other controlled articles, as well as highly dutiable goods.
- Reduce the number of customs staff members through attrition and through the reclassification of positions to fewer but better-paid jobs. ICT specialists, accountants, chemists, and management professionals would increase in number relative to other position classifications.

Cargo Clearance

The principles that were to be adopted to speed up customs clearance for cargo were announced under the acronym SPACE, which stands for selectivity, postaudit, advance clearance, client self-assessment, and electronic data processing, and information about the program was widely disseminated. A publication titled "2000 Today" provided a detailed description of the various projects included in the SPACE Program. The various customs techniques advocated were already in widespread use in advanced customs administrations and were some of the main principles that underlay the reform and modernization program of the Philippine customs service. The projects making up the SPACE Program included the following: (a) green lane processing, (b) electronic manifest system, (c) secure and electronic transmittal of bank payments, (d) automated matching of payments and payables, (e) postrelease review, and (f) automated computation of payables.

Tracing the Seeds of the Reform

A summary section tracing the seeds of the reform follows. The subsequent subsections summarize the key elements of those seeds.

Revenue Base

The government's Medium-Term Revenue Program (1993–98) required the BOC to increase its revenue collections by 16 percent per year, whereas the economy was expected to grow at no more than 14 percent per year in nominal terms. The government had no plans to introduce new measures that would expand its overall revenue base. On the contrary, in an effort to boost business, the new administration planned to phase out two emergency revenue measures that the preceding administration had imposed, the special import levy and the special levy on oil, which had provided 24 percent of total customs collections in 1991.

The government's tariff reform program, which it started in 1981 and which had drastically reduced tariff rates on imports and lowered the customs revenue base, was accelerated in the 1990s in compliance with the country's commitments to the World Trade Organization, Asia-Pacific Economic Cooperation, and the Association of Southeast Asian Nations Free Trade Area. Before the initiation of the program, 27 percent of the tariff lines had rates ranging from 55 to 100 percent, and 16 percent had rates between 35 and 50 percent. By 1985, the 55 to 100 percent rate bands had been abolished, although the majority of tariff lines remained in the high-rate range of 30 to 50 percent. By 1995, 51 percent of tariff lines were in the 0 to 15 percent band, and virtually all the rest were in the 20 to 30 percent range.

Average nominal tariffs were reduced from a high of 41.0 percent in 1980 to 26.0 percent in 1992, 10.7 percent in 1998, and 8.0 percent in 2000. The number of tariff lines that were on the restricted list was reduced from 32 percent before the liberalization to 8 percent in 1980 and 3 percent in 1992.

A related positive factor in relation to the customs revenue program was the lifting of foreign exchange controls and the legalization of other sources for funding imports. Combined with tariff restructuring and import liberalization, those policy measures resulted in a drastic shift of trade from illegal and undocumented channels into legitimate and official channels. Thereby they helped offset other factors that were eroding customs revenue.

The government's trade liberalization programs strained the BOC's ability to achieve its programmed level of collections. Although customs collections continued to rise except for the years following the 1997 Asian financial crisis, they generally declined as a percentage of both overall tax revenues and revenues from other sources. Collections fell from 25 percent of total tax revenue in 1990 to 17 percent in 2001. The relative decline of customs duties coincided with the increase in importance of the value added tax. The value added tax equaled about one-third of customs duties in 1991 but almost as much as all customs duties by 1997. As a percentage of gross domestic product, customs collections fell from 4 percent in 1996 to 2.7 percent in 1998.

Changes in the macroeconomic environment since the beginning of the Customs Reform and Modernization Program in 1992 have magnified the customs dilemma. On the one hand, the ambitious revenue program set against a backdrop of a shrinking revenue base compels the BOC to take measures to control revenue leakages and to improve its collection efficiency. On the other hand, the liberalization programs compel the BOC to embrace trade facilitation as an objective and to adopt more appropriate control measures.

Revenue Leakages and Collection Inefficiencies

The challenge that the macroeconomic environment posed to the customs revenue program was the reason that the Department of Finance sought a World Bank loan in 1990 to fund a computerization program at the BOC and the Bureau of Internal Revenue.

Plugging customs revenue leakages and improving collection efficiency has been a primary concern of the Department of Finance. In 1989 the department estimated that revenues that were actually collected were as high as revenues that went uncollected.

Other estimates broadly agree with the extent of the tax leakage (Parayno 1995). For example, estimates indicate that the extent of underinvoicing ranges from 12.2 to 53.0 percent of recorded imports. The World Bank supported the PTCP, which was aimed primarily at revenue mobilization, a key component of the 1992–98 Customs Reform and Modernization Program.

Preshipment Inspection Program

The seeds of reform may also be traced to certain programs that were undertaken before the new wave of reforms. The engagement in 1987 of a PSI company to conduct import inspections at the country of export helped increase revenue. The company also provided training, observation tours abroad, consultancy, and equipment to improve the efficiency of the Philippine customs service. Moreover, the PSI program opened up trade facilitation possibilities for the BOC by waiving inspection for 10 percent of all packages, as mandated by the Tariff and Customs Code, because the Department of Justice considered inspections performed by the PSI company abroad to be in compliance with the examination required under the code. A 1988 law recognized the prerogative of the BOC to undertake only a selective examinations of goods.

Public Ethics and Accountability Program

The Public Ethics and Accountability Program, which the Aquino administration introduced to combat corruption, had a major influence on the shape of the 1992–98 Customs Reform and Modernization Program. Customs transactions provided opportunities for as many as 40 million face-to-face interactions each year, each one of which was fertile ground for corruption. In keeping with the philosophy of the Public Ethics and Accountability Program, systems and procedures covering customs transactions were reengineered to use the following techniques:

- automating processes to avoid intervention by customs officers in 80 percent of all transactions, with the percentage to be increased gradually to 95 percent
- repositioning controls to the points where they can be most effective, without obstructing business and trade
- providing remote facilities for lodging declarations
- introducing paperless and cashless processes throughout the customs service
- privatizing certain operations
- linking all the agencies participating in the system electronically
- using clear and simple rules.

A number of private sector groups called for the strict enforcement of customs controls because of the unfair competition that smuggled goods presented for domestically produced goods. Companies engaged in both manufacturing and exports complained of the excessive bureaucracy and the high cost of doing business, which made exports uncompetitive and discouraged investment. Legitimate traders complained of being pushed toward underground and illegal trade channels. The media were also clamoring for reforms. Occasionally the media prepared special reports about sensational corruption cases and demanded meaningful and long-lasting changes at the BOC.

Harmonization of Customs Procedures and Adoption of International Best Practices

The call by international and regional organizations for customs administrations to adopt international best practices and to harmonize their procedures and practices was a strong motivation for developing the Customs Reform and Modernization Program. Documents by such bodies as the World Customs Organization, Asia-Pacific Economic Cooperation, and Association of Southeast Asian Nations Working Group on Customs Matters highlighted best practices, including just-in-time inventorying, electronic commerce and paperless transactions, remote entry lodgment of declarations, risk management and selectivity, electronic funds transfer, advance clearance, and postaudits. Catching up with the leaders in advanced customs administration and making headway in relation to efficiency benchmarks have become matters of national pride and matters of survival in global trade competition.

Sponsors of Reform and Modernization

The following paragraphs discuss the key sponsors of reform and modernization.

The Private Sector

Other than the networked computers strategically located in the central areas of customs buildings, the most visible proof of customs modernization is the newly built or renovated customs buildings across the country. Before modernization, customs offices were in such poor shape that it was unrealistic to expect personnel to pursue such ideals as customer service and dedication to good service delivery. The reform process targeted the improvement of offices not only to provide better working conditions but also to harmonize the physical infrastructure with automated and computerized work processes. The renovated customs offices became better than most government offices and were as good as or better than offices in the private sector.

Because the amount allocated for facilities improvement by the PTCP was insufficient, private sector sources supplemented the resources available to renovate buildings. Among others, port operators, the banking community, chambers of commerce, and port users such as brokers, forwarders, and transportation companies contributed to the effort and embraced the reform's objectives.

The Government

The secretary of finance and senior officers of the Department of Finance provided support by regularly citing the reforms being undertaken in the BOC in their speeches and press conferences and by ensuring that budgetary resources were made available in a timely fashion. The Civil Service Commission also played an active role in expressing support for the program. Its chair cited the effectiveness of the reform in her weekly radio program and showcased the BOC in the commission's national symposiums of successful reform programs. However, it was the president who really brought customs reforms to the public's attention, by organizing the presentation of the reform process blueprint to the cabinet and announcing that, henceforth, the cabinet was to consider the plan as the government's program for the customs service. He also called on other government agencies to consider the plan as a model for developing their respective blueprints for reform.

In addition, the president demonstrated his political commitment by publicly calling for everyone's support, particularly that of customs officials, and warning in the strongest terms that those who would not cooperate would be subject to severe sanctions. Expressing his support for the leadership and its program in clear terms, he publicly commended all who supported the program and issued public citations to private sector individuals and groups who provided support. The president dipped into his social funds to augment the resources available for the program and exempted the BOC's modernization program from the general moratorium on government capital expenditures in 1998. The president provided strong moral support to the BOC's commissioner, especially when threats to his leadership and to the reforms he was pursuing were reported. In the final analysis, the strong expression of political support enabled the program to overcome the obstacles it faced.

The Legislature

The House of Representatives and the Senate approved the BOC's annual budget and left it essentially intact, particularly those elements related to the implementation of the reform and of modernization. Budget committees assisted by holding investigations "in aid of legislation." The BOC commissioner took those investigations as opportunities for taking drastic measures. However, many individuals in the legislature harmed the program by making unfavorable declarations to the media and by using their power to summon customs officials for investigation. The legislators appeared to be seeking to gain influence and control and to solicit favors and gifts indirectly.

The World Bank and the International Monetary Fund

The centerpiece of the Customs Reform and Modernization Program was the PTCP. The World Bank provided a credit for about one-third of the cost of the PTCP and provided technical advice. Equally important were the calls made by the World Bank and the IMF for vigilance, sustainability, and continuity in relation to the reform program.

Those organizations objectively reported on slippages and deviations from the program.

The IMF sent a team to the Philippines in 1991, accompanied by a World Bank consultant, to assess the BOC's existing organization and procedures and to review the plans for computerization. To follow up on the implementation of the PTCP, the IMF assigned a customs adviser, a former comptroller of the New Zealand customs service who had served two stints in the Philippines as an adviser. Groups were organized in the BOC to assist the adviser and to pursue individual components of the PTCP. Most of the IMF's recommendations were incorporated into the BOC's customs reform program, and the IMF tracked the implementation of its recommendations during successive visits to the Philippines.

The Media

In general, newspapers and television networks provided support by disseminating information pertaining to the reform. The media gave the public good accounts of the developments, at times issuing not just news reports but in-depth coverage. However, the media's propensity for sensationalizing the news sometimes took the upper hand, and gradual improvements in service delivery were not deemed newsworthy. As the customs leadership did not have a policy of paying for news coverage, some elements of the news media ignored significant developments or even reversed their presentations in favor of opponents of the reforms who paid for media coverage. Luckily, those stories were printed mainly in newspapers with a limited circulation.

The Reform Process

The following provides a summary of the main elements of the reform process.

Leadership

Because customs managers risk being overwhelmed by day-to-day emergencies and policy issues and often do not have the time to plan for the future, the BOC commissioner took it upon himself to manage the reform and provide guidance on the direction to be taken. The reform used a strong top-down approach, with relatively few consultations with stakeholders or BOC management. To free himself of such routine matters as dealing with personnel promotions and mobility, the commissioner rationalized procedures so that they would require less direct input from him. He also instituted a clear delegation of authority to his deputy commissioners in relation to personnel and procurement matters. The commissioner tracked the progress of the reform in detail and personally intervened to address problems as necessary.

Public–Private Sector Cooperation

In mid-1992, while the decisionmaking process on the PTCP was still under way, early measures were required to step up revenue collection, intensify enforcement, combat corruption, and improve trade facilitation and the investment climate. The BOC felt compelled to call on the private sector for assistance. The BOC reached agreement with private sector groups on solutions that were implemented at no cost to the government. In cooperation with freight forwarders, the BOC put in place the online release system to counter the illegal release of shipments through the use of spurious documents and to ease the lengthy and time-consuming release process. In cooperation with the Philippines Banking Association, the BOC launched Project Abstract Secure. It uses encryption technology to electronically transmit payment data from the banks to the BOC, with the objective of reducing the massive revenue leakage resulting from the introduction into the payments system of spurious documents or documents that have been tampered with. The advance submission of manifest information through the facilities of the Société Internationale de la Communication Aéronautique, the port operators' computer systems, and the consolidator's data exchange center were all solutions that did not cost the government anything. A number of other customs operations were outsourced in a similar fashion.

The private sector, which had urged the BOC to reform, at times thought that the reform was going too fast and that the BOC was changing habits too briskly. The private sector's suspicions about the BOC's intentions were aroused when the BOC introduced mandatory payment to banks as the first step in the cargo clearance process, when it simplified the formula for computing port charges and the landed cost of goods, and when it initiated the electronic lodgment of declarations through the electronic data interchange and direct trader input systems. However, the BOC explained the rationale for those changes and gradually received full cooperation from most elements of the private sector.

Selective Inspection, Risk Assessment, and Other Regulations

In preparation for the automation of the cargo clearance process under the PTCP, the BOC sought legislation to abolish mandatory physical examination of all shipments. It would be incongruent to fully automate and speed up the computational segments of assessment but then allow the process to be caught in the gridlock of physical examinations of all shipments at the docks. The Republic Act Number 7650 of April 1993 abolished the mandatory inspection of all shipments. In lieu of 100 percent inspection, the BOC was allowed to inspect cargo selectively on the basis of risk analysis and threat assessment. Automation of the entire cargo clearance system and full electronic services at remote sites are facilitated by a risk assessment and selectivity approach that decides which consignments will be extended green lane processing—that is, do not require intervention by customs officers.

Even before the Republic Act Number 7650 was passed, Customs Memorandum Order Number 96-92 stipulated that full container load shipments that the government surveyor at the port of exportation had inspected and sealed should be deemed to have been examined for customs purposes. Such shipments therefore would not have to be reexamined upon arrival in the Philippines. Separate acts of legislation strengthened customs enforcement and the BOC's ability to collect the targeted revenues by removing a number of legal loopholes that traders had used to reduce their tax liability. The reform process thus used all available avenues to ensure that revenue generation would be protected.

From March 1993 to June 1998, the BOC commissioner issued 277 regulations. Many of the regulations concerned the Automated Customs Operating System and the manual processes surrounding each of its subsystems. Many others pertained to control systems designed to reduce the opportunities for engaging in irregularities, to heighten the capability to detect wrongdoing, and to increase the chances of successfully prosecuting offenders.

One set of regulations allowed the customs service to implement paperless and complete automation of the cargo clearance process even before the e-commerce legislation was enacted. At that time, the Tariff and Customs Code had 52 sections explicitly requiring the submission of paper documents for customs clearance. Legislation on e-commerce passed the lower house in 1997 but failed to pass the Senate before the change in government in 1998. Nonetheless, the BOC issued a regulation allowing the fully automated processing of an electronic declaration without requiring importers or their representatives to come to a customs office.

Legislation pertaining to the implementation of the World Trade Organization Agreement on Customs Valuation came into effect in 1998, with export value used as an interim basis for customs value. In addition, the BOC formed the Management Information System and Technology Group and charged it with developing ICT for use by customs operations.

Funds and Resources

The government appropriated 18 percent of the BOC's total budget for the customs component of the PTCP for 1994–99. Because of judicious handling of the procurement process and tight controls on expenditures, the amount actually spent was significantly less than the amount budgeted. For example, the amount budgeted for hardware was about US$21 million, but the winning bid came in at less than US$9 million. Also US$2.3 million was budgeted for software acquisition and development, but a balance of US$300,000 remained at the conclusion of the contract with the supplier. The government borrowed 35 percent of the funding for the PTCP from the World Bank and obtained the remainder from local counterpart funds. Ten information systems specialists from the BOC's Information Technology Group were assigned full-time with UNCTAD. More than 100 mid-level and senior customs managers were assigned to various task groups to support system development and implementation.

Work on the PTCP commenced in the third quarter of 1994, although several projects were started early in 1992, including ICT initiatives that did not use PTCP funding. Support for those projects came mainly from private sector groups that benefited from them, such as the airlines and shipping lines, the foreign trade operators, the banking community, and the chambers of commerce. Those private sector groups contributed technical personnel, hardware, and even office furniture and equipment.

External Consultants

The BOC engaged the services of two external contractors: UNCTAD and Unisys. The BOC selected UNCTAD to develop and implement the application systems following its decision to use ASYCUDA as the main software for the PTCP. ASYCUDA was chosen over the French information solution software (known as SOFI), primarily because of its compatibility with the BOC's hardware and because UNCTAD agreed to upgrade its version 2.0, then the most widely used customs software in the world, to meet the BOC's requirements. Some staff members inside the BOC contested the decision to use ready-made customs software, claiming that the Philippines had a large pool of experts that the BOC could have tapped to develop a system. The BOC defended its outsourcing decision on the basis of the speed with which ASYCUDA could be introduced and argued that the modules lacking in the UNCTAD system could be developed locally.

Tenders for computer hardware, facilities management, and systems integration were selected on a competitive basis, using tender documents that had been prepared with the assistance of Crown Agents. The contract was awarded to Unisys after two other contenders submitted proposals that were twice as expensive. Prior to approval by the secretary of finance, the bid was evaluated by the Customs Technical Committee, the Bids and Awards Committee, and the Department of Finance's Advisory Committee, which was represented by recognized ICT professionals from the private sector.

Change Management

The BOC undertook a change readiness survey to measure the readiness of the staff for reforms and to develop communication strategies to overcome opposition. The main objection to the reform program was the loss of control by customs employees that resulted from the reengineering of the clearance process and the shift from a manual and paper-based system to an electronic, paperless, and automated system. Examples of activities in which the staff lost control included the following:

- For green lane shipments, customs officers were required to work on unaccompanied electronic documents instead of paper documents, which importers' representatives used to carry from desk to desk and from office to office.
- Electronic documents submitted in the green lane channel were processed without interruption until completion, whether or not the customs officer actually viewed the electronic documents.
- Officers who scrutinized the electronic documents and were convinced that a violation had occurred had to obtain clearance from their superiors before they could hold the shipment, through an alert system that makes the process transparent.

Before the reform, the handling of clearance papers and the discretion to hold shipments were the source of customs officers' power and control over the transacting public. The face-to-face interactions that characterized the manual and paper-based systems created opportunities for customs officers to obtain gifts and favors. The reengineering eliminated much of the paper handling, enabled clearance without face-to-face interaction, and allowed most transactions to bypass customs procedures completely. Many of the traditional customs activities could now be undertaken by the customs computer system, including the computation and collection of duties and taxes, the determination of payments made, the issuance of release instructions for shipments to the cargo handler, and the keeping of document receipts and releases by various offices. The computer system even determined which shipments were to be examined and assigned the customs officer who would conduct the examination. Some staff members resisted the reforms and brought their grievances to the media. In response, BOC management met with those opponents and repeatedly presented the gains that the Philippine economy would realize from a streamlined and modern customs service.

Personnel

A year before the reform, the Attrition Law was passed. It prohibited for seven years new hiring by the government and the replacement of staff members who left for any reason. The customs leadership used the law to downsize the workforce and to force it to adapt to automation and modern work methods.

After a review of the workload, estimates indicated that—assuming the introduction of modern customs techniques as planned by the reform—a staff of 4,300 would be adequate, or 200 fewer staff members than the number on the payroll at the time. Such a finding led to much debate, because most could not imagine a customs service that did not rely on labor-intensive techniques. Contributing to the perception that the customs service was undermanned was the highly uneven distribution of personnel. In general, the line offices where contacts with importers and their representative were frequent—and where the opportunities for making extra income were plentiful—were heavily overstaffed, but many other offices were practically deserted. For instance, the management information system office was in theory manned by more than 50 people, but fewer than 20 were actually in place. Interest was high in staffing those positions that could benefit from "facilitation money," as was political meddling on behalf of individual staff members.

Modernization efforts, in combination with the law against new recruiting in the civil service, led to a reduction in staff size by 1,000 between 1992 and 1998, as the number of positions rendered unnecessary by the new work procedures exceeded the number of new positions required by the postaudit and ICT functions.

Restrictions on hiring new civil servants ended in 1998. When the new government came into office, about 300 new recruits entered the service of the BOC almost overnight. Political meddling in the hiring, assignments, and promotions led to widespread demoralization, and frequent reassignments in staff destabilized the customs service. A fiscal crisis led to the adoption of a new hiring freeze in the BOC.

The Civil Service Law states that a staff member rated unsatisfactory for two consecutive rating periods may be let go. Although that would give the BOC's management greater flexibility in managing its human resources, implementation of the law has been delayed because, under the present rating system, no one has been rated unsatisfactory.

Remuneration

The blueprint identified the low pay of customs personnel relative to the temptations they encountered as one of the threats to the achievement of development objectives and called on Congress to address the threat immediately. Stakeholders had attacked the salary of customs personnel as corruption in itself, because the salaries of nearly half the staff members were below the official poverty line for an income earner with a family of six. Allowances added little to customs officers' low salaries. The blueprint's proposal would have exempted customs employees from the Salary Standardization Law and would have provided remuneration equivalent to that in the private sector to those holding sensitive customs positions, such as examiners and appraisers. However, both the commissioner of the civil service and the chair of the Senate Civil Service Committee rejected the proposal on the grounds that approving it would remove the security of tenure for the customs officials concerned and that making an exception to the law could lead other civil servants to ask for higher salaries. In addition, many lawmakers believed that customs personnel had access to other sources of income—mostly illegal—because of their positions and that they therefore did not need a salary increase.

Anticorruption Measures

The reform and modernization measures drastically reduced the opportunities for bureaucratic corruption, strengthened the system against the vulnerabilities that had facilitated fraud and reduced the BOC's revenues, and enhanced the visibility and transparency of the customs service. However, staff members initially resisted the changes and at times referred to the reform measures as World Bank and IMF impositions in conspiracy with the Société Générale de Surveillance, the government-appointed PSI company. Staff members often paid lip service to the reform program but did not give it any real commitment and support.

Value formation workshops and training were provided in parallel with the main reform measures to promote integrity and to add an internal dimension to the "external impositions." Various offices down to the division level were required to develop anticorruption programs and put them into effect. Neither the training nor the programs had any significant effect on corruption. Parliament's failure to improve staff compensation undermined internal motivation. Weak organizational support resulting from inadequate compensation is the main vulnerability of the reform program, especially given the level of material benefit available if the status quo is maintained.

Funding for Information and Communication Technology

The BOC was among the earliest government entities to use ICT. In the 1960s, through reparations for World War II, the BOC acquired the first Fujitsu automatic computer model in the country, ahead of even the National Computer Center. In 1976, the BOC built a computer center and a Burroughs 700 mainframe computer became operational essentially to capture transaction data and generate management information. However, the low value that management attached to the outputs led to the early demise of the system.

Before the start of the 1992–98 reforms, the only system still running was the manifest clearance system. This system entailed encoding paper cargo manifests to create an electronic file into which declarations and cargo claims were posted, in order to generate shipment reports. The new ICT systems introduced at the start of the reform focused on the BOC's core business of cargo clearance, which involves assessing and collecting duties, taxes, and fees and implementing cargo control objectives. Those ICT systems have proved extremely useful.

Management's decision to use generic software rather than to build a custom-tailored system initially faced strong criticism from certain quarters, such as academia, for not making use of the country's ICT professionals. However, the decision cut the waiting time for the implementation of the core functionalities and allowed the BOC to focus on implementation rather than on design and development. Customs officers participated in customizing the system to the BOC's business and process rules and in developing other systems that were then attached to the core software. The ICT achievements during the reform years were the outcome of a coordinated and harmonious implementation of the generic and homegrown systems. By 1997, practically all segments of the cargo clearance process had been fully automated.

The various components of the Automated Customs Operating System have been fitted together into one seamless whole. Only part of the system uses the UNCTAD customs software, ASYCUDA. The rest makes use of software developed and operated through the joint efforts of the BOC and its partners in the private sector. By the end of 1997, the BOC was recognized as a leader in electronic governance in the country. In 1993, the government made arrangements for a five-year budget for the PTCP; however, the budget did not include funds for system maintenance after that period because the later periods were considered a responsibility of the next administration. That failure to provide for system maintenance beyond 1998 was the biggest oversight of the government and of customs leadership at that time.

The BOC commissioner proposed several measures to ensure additional funding for ICT activities:

- The introduction of an entry encoding charge to raise substantial amounts that would be used to finance some costs of daily operations, facilities maintenance, and support for the BOC's other ICT requirements. However, funds levied in this way were badly managed and were not used for the intended purpose.
- An increase of the import processing fee from P 250 to P 1,000, with P 500 of the increment earmarked for ICT maintenance and upgrading. The business community objected to this increase, and it was introduced only much later, with revenues not earmarked for ICT operations.
- The private sector group that benefited the most from particular new projects would contribute the most to the projects. Recently, the Automated Customs Cargo Transfer System, adopted by the Philippine Economic Zone Authority, was implemented at the customs house at Manila's Ninoy Aquino International Airport for transferring shipments from the airport to the various special economic zones in the Calabarzon area.[1] The private sector, notably the semiconductor and electronics industry, defrayed the total amounts involved. The BOC's only contribution is the use of ASYCUDA. Even the configuration of ASYCUDA for use in this customs regime was

1. Calabarzon stands for the four provinces near Metro Manila: Cavite, Laguna, Batangas, and Rizal.

spearheaded by private sector ICT professionals. The private sector also paid all the costs for implementing the automated export documentation system, from the server, router, and firewall to the operating, communications, and frame relay systems. Private ICT practitioners designed the application system and worked with customs staff to configure ASYCUDA.
- The BOC organized golf tournaments, known as the customs commissioner's golf cups, to raise funds for particular projects.

Preshipment Inspection

The government introduced the PSI service in 1986 and contracted it to the Société Générale de Surveillance. From its initial coverage of three supplying countries, the program was progressively expanded to more countries until it became global in 1992, before the new administration assumed office. The government undertook the progressive expansion in both geographic coverage and types of goods subject to inspection in an attempt to reduce the level of smuggling.

The PSI addressed two major problems in customs operations: valuation and classification. The downsizing of the country's diplomatic offices abroad and the recall of many diplomatic officials because of budgetary constraints, along with the removal in 1985 of the requirement to present commercial invoices for goods imported to a consulate or embassy abroad, left the BOC with few means of gathering home consumption values in the countries of exportation. With no reliable basis for contesting submissions, customs officials generally had to accept whatever value importers declared. As a result, customs officials increased declared values by an insignificant 0.81 percent of invoice values.

In 1997, the BOC established a study group to evaluate the PSI contract. The group noted that if the service were to be terminated at that time, the following negative impacts were probable:

- an estimated P 2 billion per year—net of inspection fees—uncollected (that is, the difference between the Société Générale de Surveillance's estimated valuation of shipments and the declared invoice values)
- a deflation of the repetitive effect of Clean Report of Findings values on declarations and the loss of deterrence to incorrect payment provided by the report, which contains the estimated duty and tax payable
- the loss of deterrence to smuggling provided by cargo inspections abroad.

The following are among the lessons the BOC learned in relation to PSI:

- The utility of PSI can be maximized by identifying areas where it is ineffective or not deployed and then deploying customs resources to fill the gaps. For example, PSI cannot improve controls on bonded warehouse operations or other suspense regimes. In addition, in the Philippines, oil and oil products are exempt from PSI, and therefore qualified customs personnel need to be deployed to control imports of those commodities.
- The use of PSI should be for a fixed term only and should be accompanied by a clear exit strategy. The Philippines only developed an exit strategy during the reform years, and ultimately that strategy was not implemented properly. As a result, the customs service was still unprepared to assume sole responsibility for all customs work by the time the PSI contract ended.
- The customs service must make it clear right from the start of any PSI program that it owns the database developed from the inspections, and an adequate ICT infrastructure must be made available to the customs service so that it can make proper use of the data gathered.
- A clear system for verifying whether PSI services have actually been rendered must be established and agreed upon before the start of the service to avoid disputes about the payment of fees.
- A dispute settlement system for good value and classification is essential for the proper functioning of PSI. Adequate system support is essential, including ICT for the dispute settlement process.
- The benefits of trade facilitation may outweigh the additional revenue that a PSI system can provide.

Assessment of the Reform

The overall results of the 1992–98 Customs Reform and Modernization Program were encouraging. Its achievements were recognized not only by the country's trade community in particular and the public in general, but also by such prestigious organizations as the World Customs Organization and UNCTAD and by numerous regional customs groupings.

Evaluation

The evaluation of the reform can be divided into local opinions and international experts' evaluations.

Local Opinions The media's reviews of progress in customs administration were generally positive. At the time of the presentation of the legislation, an article in the *Philippine Star* provided a good example of how the progress and promises of the reform measures were reported:

> One of the most sensible bills now pending in the House of Representatives is that authored by Quezón City Rep. Feliciano "Sonny" Belmonte: The Customs Modernization Bill or HB 8687. The modernization of customs processes, as envisioned by Sonny Belmonte's bill, will mean faster release of goods and more efficient collection of revenues for duties and taxes. It will also make it easier to identify suspicious customs transactions including under collection. In other words, the use of computers and information technology will make customs processes safe from external manipulation. And the network of computers covering customs offices across the nation will deal a major blow to smugglers and grafters. Fully computerized operations would also allow for cashless transactions. The BOC can levy the tax via computer, and the importer can then instruct his bank to remit the amount directly to the designated customs bank electronically, via telephone (modem) instructions. Which will mean elimination of third parties into whose hands the customs collections go into. The business community is pushing hard for the enactment of the Belmonte Bill. The businessmen say that its passage will not only benefit the traders, manufacturers, and importers but also the national economy. And there is sense in their observation that in all modern and economically emerging societies, the buzz words are paperless, queueless and cashless transactions available 24-hours a day and 365 days a year.

An article in the *Business Star* (1994, p. 4) noted:

> The strategy being followed by Customs to move out of the way of the business process is indeed the most sensible way of addressing bureaucratic red tape and for the first time [the business community] expressed confidence that this social ill [smuggling] will be finally addressed in the BOC.

Some small publications (no more than 1,000 copies per issue) that were published irregularly and distributed to customs personnel went against the assessment of the national dailies and other media to express strong opposition to the reforms in the BOC, especially those components that significantly reduced opportunities for corruption. Those tabloids were apparently financed by customs staff members and their sympathizers.

The reform has substantially improved how the public views the BOC's services. In 1990, a survey by the Social Weather Station, a polling organization, showed that those interviewed considered the BOC to be the most corrupt agency of all those surveyed, with 74 percent of respondents considering corruption to be a big problem (24 percent perceived the level of corruption to be small and 1 percent had no opinion). In that survey, the BOC tied with the police force in registering the lowest margin of satisfaction on the issue of what was being done to reduce corruption (56 percent dissatisfied, 7 percent satisfied, and 36 percent undecided). Those findings were reconfirmed in the Social Weather Station survey of December 2001. However, by 1996, according to testimony by Civil Service Commissioner Ramon Ereneta Jr. before the Committee on Civil Service and Professional Regulation, the BOC no longer appeared in the list of the top 10 most corrupt and bureaucratic government agencies.[2]

Evaluation by Foreign Experts UNCTAD praised the program, as did an unpublished IMF review, which noted that the strategy followed by the BOC over the past five years has resulted in significant improvements in terms of both the implementation of more effective controls and the reduction in the time it takes to process transactions (70 percent of imports are processed through the green channel in two to three hours). It is not just the extensive use of automation that has produced this change

2. Although the 1996 source was not comparable with the 1990 survey, it was at that time a generally accepted fact that the population's perception was that corruption at the BOC had been reduced.

but, more important, the implementation of simplified procedures supported by automation. The review goes on to state that the BOC has put in place a good foundation from which it can now move to develop and implement a modern customs administration.

Performance

The BOC's overall revenue performance was influenced by the drastic drop in imports caused by the Asian crisis and by the substantial trade liberalization measures introduced during the reform period. The Department of Finance measures the BOC's efficiency in terms of its collection rate, which stood at about 100 percent in 1992–94 and averaged 87.5 percent during 1995–96. These figures compare favorably with an average collection rate of 65 percent in 1986–91.

As far as entry processing is concerned, the president's mandate to clear shipments within 48 hours has been achieved. In the case of entries lodged electronically, the results have been even more dramatic. Green channel processing was extended to 95.4 percent of shipments, with assessment completed instantaneously and payment matched in less than 19 hours.

Primary Success Factors

The following were among the factors that contributed to the success of the reforms:

- *Strong government support.* Never in the BOC's history has the government allotted so many resources for ICT development. The government made funds available not just for procuring hardware and software, but also for improving customs facilities, training, and managing change.
- *Private sector involvement and support.* Knowing that strong government backing was not enough, the BOC also relied on substantial support from the private sector. In addition, procurement for the PTCP had to follow a set legal process and schedule and, therefore, could not respond quickly to pressing ICT needs; in this connection, the private sector helped accelerate the implementation of reform components.
- *Strong leadership.* Customs leadership provided the vision for the customs community and enlisted the support of key stakeholders. National leadership, for its part, lent its full support to the program and provided backing for the leadership, even as it warned all those who would not cooperate of the dire consequences of noncooperation.
- *Generic customs software.* Adopting a generic customs software solution rather than building a system from scratch cut the waiting time for implementing the system's core functionalities and allowed the BOC to focus on implementation issues rather than on design and development. Customs officers participated in customizing the system and in developing other systems that were then attached to the core software. By June 1998, the system was already running at all the major ports, with some ports already offering electronic lodgment technologies. By comparison, the Bureau of Internal Revenue's component of the PTCP, which started at the same time as the BOC program, was not yet operational by mid-1998.
- *Analysis and selectivity.* The benefits of ICT in terms of facilitating trade and reducing bureaucratic corruption would not have been realized without the legislation that permitted selective inspections based on risk analysis.

Threats to the Program

An opinion survey conducted in December 2001 by the Social Weather Station accorded the BOC the most unfavorable rating of its sincerity in fighting graft and corruption among the government agencies surveyed. Seventy-one percent of respondents rated the BOC as the most insincere agency in fighting graft and corruption. Also the investment climate survey (Pernia and Gupta forthcoming) suggests that clearance times have lengthened again; at the end of 2003 clearance times were 9.1 days for imports and 6.6. days for exports.

Many reasons could account for the return of the BOC's unfavorable image, including the following:

- *Failure of the PTCP's sustainability measures.* Appropriate and specific measures introduced from 1996 to 1998 assured the funding institutions (the World Bank and the IMF), business groups, and the government that the ICT program would function adequately no matter who ran the BOC. One measure was the establishment of the Management Information Systems and Technology Group, which was to be responsible for continuing the reform process. Another was the creation of the Change Management Group, which was to identify and train ICT champions among BOC officials. The continued active participation of the Philippine Chamber of Commerce and the Bankers Association of the Philippines was formalized with the privatization and transfer of the lodgment declaration and payment systems to those private groups. However, the momentum of modernization has not been sustained in more recent years. Although the hardware contractor has been able to extend the geographic reach of the network to more ports and customs stations, the coverage of the application system has stagnated. Attempts to add new capabilities have had questionable success, while ICT application systems have suffered setbacks on practically all fronts. Most heavily damaged have been the selectivity and remote lodgment systems, and interfaces with other government agencies. The private sector has tried to reach out to the new management to offer the same partnership it had had with the previous leadership, but the incoming management has ignored those offers or even viewed them with suspicion.

- *Change in leadership.* A major sustainability measure, which was introduced in April 1998, was the BOC's appointment of an ICT and management professional from the private sector to head the Management Information Systems and Technology Group. Unfortunately, the manager was among the first to leave following the change in administration in July 1998. For the next two and a half years, the BOC suffered from an ICT leadership vacuum, and several key ICT staff members became demoralized and eventually also tendered their resignations.
- *Depletion of financial resources.* A steady source of funds for the maintenance and further development of ICT was missing. With the high rate of technical obsolescence of ICT products, measures should have been taken from the start to provide a steady source of funds. Currently, the customs budget for replacing hardware that has reached the end of its useful life is insufficient.
- *Failure to obtain staff support.* Many customs personnel viewed the reform program as being imposed on them by international organizations and as counter to their own interests. Thus, most customs staff members did not support the program and were not committed to its success.
- *Failure to provide for adequate compensation for customs staff.* Passage of the Customs Modernization Bill and the Reward Laws would have provided customs staff members with adequate compensation and would have rewarded good performance. However, Congress failed to pass both laws and thereby failed to address employees' basic rights to fair and adequate compensation for the work performed.
- *Failure of trade sectors to keep pace with the move toward modernization.* Customs readiness alone is insufficient for the entire trading community to realize the benefits of ICT and e-commerce. The lack of readiness among partner agencies is a major stumbling block for the BOC. Unless those agencies enable e-commerce by improving the way they handle the processing of applications for all sorts of authorizations—such as licenses, permits, clearances, quotas, and certificates—this unreadiness will negate whatever improvements e-commerce can generate in the customs area.
- *Inadequacy of the BOC's performance management system.* Performance management could include indicators for evaluating and monitoring the progress of reform. The BOC could also pursue the concept of a report card, so that external and internal stakeholders could monitor the effect of improvements in the BOC's management systems and programs.
- *Inadequacy of audits and related judicial processes.* Audit reforms need to be given more emphasis, together with the swift and effective prosecution that should follow them. The reforms are crucial in sending a strong signal to corrupt people within and outside the BOC that the government means business.
- *Inadequacy of reform partnerships with nontraditional constituencies.* The BOC needs to build partnerships for reform with academia, civil

society groups, and other interest groups in order to develop a cadre of stakeholders that will promote the sustainability of the reform.

Conclusions

The achievements that the BOC realized and the extent of difficulties encountered in the implementation of reform and modernization were strongly influenced by a number of factors. The revival of the BOC's modernization efforts is more likely to succeed if particular attention is paid to the following factors:

- *Leader's role.* The most important determinant of a program's success or failure is the extent to which the leader owns the program and is engaged in hands-on management. Also important are the rewards and recognition that the leader dispenses to those who contribute to the program's success and the sanctions meted out to those who refuse to cooperate.
- *Private sector's role.* The business sector can be the BOC's strongest ally in the development and execution of reform. The BOC must try to directly involve the chief executive officers of businesses affected by the program. They are the ones who are in contact with top government officials and are in a position to impress on such officials the need for and the value of the reform, including the need for continuity and sustainability. The private sector must demand better service from and higher ethical standards among civil servants. At the same time, customs managers must inform their staffs that the BOC's policy is to encourage feedback from the private sector.
- *Multisectoral watchdog.* Foreign trade operators may have vested interests that would be harmed by the reform, and therefore the BOC should not rely on them to sustain the reform and modernization process. Thus, many private sector groups, including those not directly involved in trade operations, must join hands to pressure the government in general and the BOC in particular to sustain the reform process. The groups should designate a leader who could work directly with the BOC commissioner.
- *Negative reinforcement.* Until the BOC can obtain genuine support for the program and commitment to it from its rank-and-file employees—for example, by compensating them adequately for their work—it must make them aware of the negative consequences of corruption and other illegal activity and follow through with actual sanctions.
- *Regular audits.* A strong mechanism must be in place to monitor progress or the lack of it. The leadership should use external help for this activity, considering the propensity of BOC personnel not to present an objective picture of the level of corruption and to cover up for each other. An independent auditing unit that reports directly to the top leadership is desirable. The business sector should also carry out its own independent assessments of reform progress and the BOC's performance.
- *Resource availability.* If sufficient groups are concerned about the need for reform, resources will be made available. It is high time that the BOC experimented with creative funding schemes, such as pay-for-use or build-own-operate schemes.

The Philippine Customs Reform and Modernization Program, like many other undertakings in the country's history, might become another missed opportunity. However, opportunities exist for getting the reform back on track. The hope is that all concerned sectors of society can be mobilized to take a stand, resume the work from where it left off in a more coordinated fashion, and finish the job.

References

Business Star. 1994. "Parayno, A Rare Bird." January 14, p. 4.

Parayno, G. 1995. "Extent of Smuggling in the Philippines." *Futuristics* 7:70–92.

Pernia, Ernesto, and Arvind Gupta. Forthcoming. "Philippines: Improving the Investment Climate." Asian Development Bank and World Bank, Manila.

8

TURKEY

M. Bahri Oktem

This chapter reviews recent reforms undertaken by the Turkish Customs Administration (TCA) since 1993. The findings are based on a series of interviews with individuals who participated in the reform process from its outset, customs officials and other government officials who implemented it and were affected by it, and representatives of the trading community.

The reform was initiated as a result of both external and internal forces. They included the association agreement between Turkey and the European Union (EU), which required that Turkey's trade legislation be aligned with European practices. In addition, in the early 1990s Turkey's customs services were generally perceived as inefficient and corrupt. Public officials and traders alike viewed the situation as a major handicap to business that had to be eliminated in order for the country to integrate better into the world economy and benefit from international trade.

Government officials saw customs reform as part of a broader process of modernizing public sector management, and they included it in a request for support from the World Bank. The World Bank began preparation to provide such support in 1993, an effort that eventually resulted in the Public Financial Management Project. The International Monetary Fund was closely associated with the reform process and periodically sent missions to monitor its progress.

The broad objectives of the customs reform were to ensure that Turkey had modern customs laws that conformed with the EU's requirements, to simplify customs procedures, to adopt modern information and communication technology (ICT) that would help make customs clearance more efficient and predictable, and to ensure faster and more efficient production of trade statistics.

Background

Turkey's customs modernization initiative complemented its overall policy ambition of greater integration into the world economy, particularly into the EU.

Tariff Structure

Before 1992, Turkey levied multiple import taxes and surcharges. In addition to customs duties and value added taxes (VATs), those taxes included municipal charges; stamp duties; Promotion Fund, Mass Housing Fund, and Price Stability Fund taxes; and duties for transportation infrastructure.

Levying the additional taxes was complicated, and the government abolished them in 1992.

Turkey's policy of moving toward trade integration with the EU required that it adopt the EU's common external tariff. In 1995, the European Community–Turkey Association Council committed Turkey to adopting an entire body of legislation in the field of trade and adhering to conventions in the fields of intellectual, industrial, and commercial property rights. In 1996, Turkey entered into a customs union with the EU and incorporated the basic rules of the European Community's Customs Code into its customs legislation. At that time, the government removed all customs duties and quantitative restrictions on industrial products imported from EU countries. The EU–Turkey Customs Union currently covers industrial and processed agricultural products. After a five-year transition period, the government introduced the EU common external customs tariff in early 2001. Turkey's coding, description, and classification of goods became harmonized with the EU's system of combined nomenclatures. Turkey also implements the EU's preferential trade regimes, adheres to the Common Transit System and Single Administrative Document conventions, and signed the relevant protocols with EUROCUSTOMS. The application of the single administrative document was initiated unilaterally on January 1, 1996.

In addition to the EU–Turkey Customs Union, Turkey entered into free trade agreements with the European Free Trade Area, Bulgaria, the Czech Republic, Estonia, Hungary, Israel, Latvia, Lithuania, the former Yugoslav Republic of Macedonia, Poland, Romania, the Slovak Republic, and Slovenia.

The import duty regime is still rather complicated, because the TCA also administers the VAT and a series of other taxes that are intended for earmarked funds. The regular VAT rate is 18 percent, but basic goods are taxed at 1 percent or 8 percent and luxury goods at 26 percent. In addition, some excise taxes and earmarked taxes benefit the Agricultural Fund, the Tobacco Fund, the National Education Fund, the Fund for Promoting the Defense Industry, and the Price Stability Fund. The TCA also levies two lump-sum taxes per declaration: a charge contributing to education, which raises approximately US$2.7 million per year, and a special transaction tax, which raises approximately US$7 million per year.

Relations with the World Customs Organization and Other International Organizations

Turkey belongs to a number of organizations that seek to facilitate trade and strengthen customs operations. In 1953, Turkey became a member of the World Customs Organization, and it is a signatory of its major conventions and declarations. Turkey has also entered into mutual administrative agreements with many countries. Those agreements are based on the model bilateral agreement of the World Customs Organization.

With the EU, Turkey signed the United Nations–European Economic Council Convention on the International Carriage of Goods by Road, the 1954 Tourist Facilitation Convention, the Convention for Temporary Importation of Private Motor Vehicles, the Transport International Routier Convention, the Container Convention, and the Pallet Convention.

Turkey also participates in activities under the aegis of the South East Cooperation Initiative, the Economic Cooperation Organization, and the Regional Intelligence Liaison Office.

Membership in the World Trade Organization and Customs Valuation

Turkey became a member of the World Trade Organization (WTO) in 1994 and thereby accepted the WTO valuation principle, according to which imports are to be valued on the basis of their transaction value unless reasonable doubt permits the use of secondary valuation rules. Before 1994, the TCA used the Brussels definition of value and relied heavily on reference prices. Customs officials state that they are using the WTO definition of value for 99 percent of import transactions, an estimate confirmed by traders, who mentioned that this new valuation practice initially caused some delays and difficulties, but that those difficulties appear to have subsided substantially. Manufacturers, by contrast, are not pleased with this valuation system, because it deprives them of the protection granted under the prior system.

TABLE 8.1 Revenue Importance of Customs Duties and Taxes, Selected Years (percent)

Category	1994	1997	1999	2000	2001
Duties and taxes, collected by the TCA as a share of total tax revenue	15.25	17.41	13.36	16.18	13.96
Custom duties as a share of total tax revenue	3.73	2.61	1.62	1.46	0.96
VAT on imports as a share of total tax revenue	11.20	14.76	11.69	14.68	12.95
Customs duties as a share of the value of total imports	3.50	2.00	1.70	1.37	0.94

Source: TCA data.

Revenue Importance of Import Taxes

The importance of customs duties as a source of budgetary revenue has fallen considerably in recent years. By 2001, duties raised less than 1.0 percent of total tax revenue, down from 3.7 percent in 1994 (see table 8.1). That decrease is the result of the trade liberalization policies of the 1990s. By contrast, the revenue contribution of VATs on imports rose slightly, from 11.2 percent in 1994 to 13.0 percent in 2001. Because the TCA also levies VAT at the importation stage, the TCA remains responsible for about 14 percent of total tax revenue. Nevertheless, the share of total budget revenue managed by the TCA is much lower than that in most developing countries. Without neglecting its revenue mobilization role, the TCA could increasingly look for ways to enhance the efficiency of its operations and to manage its processes so as to reduce the burden that paying import taxes imposes on traders.

The Modernization Program

At the outset of the reform, the TCA prepared a four-year action plan that presented in chronological order the various interconnected activities that it intended to undertake to achieve the reform objectives. Those objectives focused on bringing customs practices in line with those prevailing in the EU and on easing the burden of customs operations on trading activities. The achievement of the objectives was to benefit substantially from the introduction of an up-to-date computerized import and export processing facility. Table 8.2 sets out the components of the four-year action plan.

The Reform Steering Committee, chaired by the deputy undersecretary of the TCA, was established to implement the program, but until 1997 it made virtually no progress. In 1997, the reform program was relaunched and a project unit staffed with customs employees was established to manage the reform and accelerate the decisionmaking process. The deputy undersecretary of the TCA was designated as the project coordinator.

The remainder of this section discusses the reforms as they affected customs law and import processes; reorganization of the TCA; improvement of physical infrastructure with support from the private sector; human resource management; automation; and customs controls, selectivity, and postrelease inspection.

New Customs Code and Simplified Trade Procedures

The modernization process included issuance of a new Customs Code and simplified trade procedures.

New Customs Legislation The reform of customs legislation began with the adaptation of the Customs Law to EU standards. Initial efforts in 1995 to ensure that Turkish customs laws conformed to the main principles of the EU Customs Code were not totally satisfactory, and in 1996 the government submitted a new Customs Code to the Grand National Assembly. Approval of this code was delayed; it was not obtained until 2000. The discussions during the last Assembly meeting lasted less than four hours, a tribute to the efforts of the state minister responsible for the TCA in convincing Assembly members of the advantages of the reforms ahead of the final Assembly discussions.

The TCA made a special effort to explain the practical implications of the new Customs Code to

TABLE 8.2 The TCA's Four-Year Action Plan

Year 1	Year 2	Year 3	Year 4
• Prepare the plan for modernizing the Customs Code. The plan needs to deal with the simplification of procedures; the production of the new forms required by these simplified procedures; the development and acquisition of a computer system; the training of customs staff; and the development of a public information program to acquaint traders and their brokers with the new procedures, in particular, the use of the computerized system. • Decide on the hardware, software, and telecommunication requirements of the IT system. • Prepare and issue tender documents for the hardware and software. • Acquire the electronic customs management system and begin development of the electronic import declaration processing system (e-base system).	• Complete development of the e-base system and launch it in a pilot office. • Assess the ability of customs facilities to operate the proposed IT system efficiently. • Develop and implement the public information campaign. • Develop and implement training for the e-base system. • Acquire hardware and software. • Roll out the e-base system in the largest locations. • Develop and implement simplified manual procedures for the sites that have not been automated. • Develop the remainder of the customs IT system, particularly the components related to export declarations, revenue accounting, manifest declaration, transit, and warehousing.	• Complete implementation of the hardware and software in the remaining smaller locations. • Complete the roll out of the e-base system. • Gradually phase in the modules of the overall customs IT system as they become available.	• Pilot test the computer system with the brokerage community. • Offer the computer system to all brokers. • Complete implementation of the computer system, including participation by other government departments, banks, and transport companies.

Source: TCA.

the trading community and to customs staff members. It started out by producing a publication that clarified the Customs Code. It also prepared a large number of documents for detailed guidance on specialized issues. Those documents led to the rapid production of decrees explaining the Customs Code, regulations, and general notifications, as well as to circulars and explanatory notes in relation to those circulars. Some of the documents were revised several times in 2000 to accommodate various issues that arose during the implementation of the new legislative framework. For instance, a decree was issued at the end of 2000 that explained the determination of the rules of origin; however, by March 2001, seven new amendments to the decree were issued. The regulatory framework that constitutes the legal basis for computerized customs procedures was promulgated in 1998. To consolidate the various updates of the regulations, the TCA published new customs regulations, consisting of 756 articles, in the *Official Journal* at the end of May 2002 and readied them for general distribution in July 2002. This publication reflects the TCA's desire to be responsive to comments from the public and to strive for transparency in the regulatory framework of its operations.

New Import Procedures Import transactions begin with the carrier's submission of the cargo manifest of goods to be shipped in from abroad to a customs office.[1] The cargo manifest and declaration data has to be entered into the Computerized Customs Management System (CCMS) through a kiosk or electronic data interchange (EDI) and registered by the CCMS. At that stage, customs personnel match the number of packages of cargo with the number that is declared in the cargo manifest. Goods that are not to be cleared immediately are promptly moved to temporary storage places and warehouses. The storage procedure causes serious disruptions and delays at several ports, particularly in Haydarpasa (Istanbul), Izmir, and Mersin, where port authorities have not computerized their warehousing procedures. Traders can clear their goods themselves, but they use brokers for 89 percent of their trade transactions because they still view foreign trade procedures as technically complicated, requiring the involvement of many organizations and entailing substantial paperwork.

In the past, customs declaration formalities had to be completed within 45 days in the case of sea freight and 20 days in the case of goods transported by other means. Today traders or their brokers submit their declarations electronically by using their dedicated user codes and passwords and by identifying the final importer of the goods, the documents attached, and the harmonized system code for the goods declared. This declaration needs to be made within 24 hours of the arrival of the goods, a period that some traders claim is too short to permit preparation of the necessary documentation. Traders also complain that they are often fined for small, inadvertent mistakes.

At that stage, the computer system verifies the declaration and assesses the risk that the declaration may be faulty or erroneous. This verification may prompt customs staff to ask for additional documentation. Traders interviewed for this study noted that this process often takes excessive time and is sometimes erratic. The computer system calculates the duties due, informs declarants of the outcome of the risk analysis for their cargo, and gives them a registration number. Goods are assigned different clearance channels: red for physical examination, yellow for documentary checks, blue for goods under postrelease controls, or green for immediate release. The risk rating is performed in light of details previously entered by customs headquarters staff members into the customs computer system through a risk analysis module. Goods are routed through the red channel only if they are included in the analysis list. Until 2001, declarants paid the assessed duties at the cashier's desk at the Ministry of Finance, but now they can make payments at banks. Traders have welcomed payment at banks, because they no longer need to transport large amounts of cash or obtain checks from the banks to present at the Ministry of Finance and wait for their clearance. An alternative process for clearing goods is to secure a bank guarantee. After the bank informs customs agents that the duties have been paid, the goods are released.

Besides having to comply with customs procedures, imports must conform to specific product standards that aim to protect public security, human health, and the environment. Organizations entrusted with establishing product standards and controlling conformity with the standards include the Turkish Standards Institution, the Ministry of Agriculture, the Ministry of Health, and the Undersecretariat of Foreign Trade. Each organization has its own laboratory and procedures for conformity checks. The Turkish Standards Institution inspects about one in five import declarations. Because the various laboratories are located at a considerable distance from customs offices, the verifications sometimes take months to finalize and thus result in considerable costs and delays. Traders

1. The Council of Ministers set up an importers' association in May 2002. All importers were instructed to obtain an import permit from that association, as is already the case for exports. The legislation was to become effective in July 2002, but it was postponed for one year. Traders oppose the new regulation because it is certain to delay import transactions.

interviewed for this study believe that the verifications act as nontariff barriers to imports. They noted that the inspections undertaken by the Ministry of Agriculture and the Ministry of Health are particularly burdensome. Because of recommendations by the World Bank's Foreign Investment Advisory Service, the TCA set up the Committee of Foreign Trade Standards and Customs to propose ways to simplify the procedures. The committee is to work in close association with the private sector and the standard-setting organizations.

Simplified Import Procedures for Certified Importers In accordance with the Kyoto Convention of the World Customs Organization, the Customs Code has provisions for accredited companies to benefit from simplified procedures. To qualify for the simplified procedures, enterprises must have clean records with the customs and tax authorities and must keep adequate records so that postclearance verifications can be performed. The simplified procedures specify that goods will be cleared without the usual documents required for customs clearance (invoices, certificates of origin, movement certificates, and administrative or other commercial documents). Importers have to keep those documents and make them available to the customs inspector if their transactions are audited. The procedures are expected to speed up the customs clearance process greatly. As of mid-2002, 289 companies had been certified for simplified procedures, but the simplified procedures had not yet taken effect. Importers anxiously await their introduction.

The trading community has welcomed the new import procedures but notes that progress is still somewhat uneven because manual procedures are still in place at a number of regional customs posts. They complain about the time it takes to satisfy organizations other than the TCA that are involved in goods clearance, because the control procedures of those organizations are lengthy and excessive and tend to undermine the progress made by the TCA. Traders claim that providing illegal "facilitation payments" at this stage to speed up the process is the current practice.

Export Procedures Export declarations must first be registered for approval by the Exporters' Association, a nongovernmental organization that is not associated with the TCA. Registration requires membership in the association (and a hefty membership fee), as well as a fee equivalent to 1 percent of the export value per registration, although some goods are exempt from the fee.[2] Once the declarations are registered, they are submitted to the TCA and are issued a computer-generated registration number. A customs official electronically verifies the declaration, and the computer system directs the shipment through a red, yellow, or green control channel, a process similar to the one used for imports except for the absence of a blue channel. Once checked through the assigned channel, goods are cleared for export.

As is the case for simplified import procedures, companies can be given the status of certified exporter and can thereby qualify for a simplified export processing formula. However, these certificates are issued by trade associations, not by the TCA. Some 70 companies have earned the status of certified exporters.

Reorganization of the TCA

In 1996–97, the organization of the TCA was reviewed in the context of the modernization program for which World Bank support was being mobilized. The review concluded that

- Customs offices with low efficiency, determined in accordance with economic and not political criteria, should be closed.
- Customs clearance and enforcement services are closely interconnected, and to enhance the coordination of their functions, the respective directorates should be integrated under a single regional directorate.
- Operational responsibility and authority should be delegated to regional and local offices.

Some 73 customs offices with low efficiency were closed in 1999. The consolidation or closure of other customs directorates is under consideration.

Measures to adjust the TCA's administrative structure have, however, encountered severe problems, because the Constitutional Court nullified

2. A plan to communicate export permissions electronically between the Exporter's Association and the TCA is being prepared but is not yet in place.

the decisions that the Council of Ministers made in 2000 to put a new administrative structure in place. A legislative proposal to adjust the administrative structure was again put before the government in mid-2002 and was presented for consideration by the Grand National Assembly. The most important change proposed by the Draft Law for the Reorganization of Customs Administration is that customs clearance and enforcement offices would be consolidated, thereby further streamlining the processing of import declarations.

As an integral part of the administrative reform of all public organizations, the number of directorates was reduced from 36 (18 customs directorates and 18 regional directorates) to 14 in 2002. The reform was also intended to delegate greater authority to regional and local offices. The goal of that change was to increase the efficiency of customs operations by reducing both operating costs and staff numbers, and it achieved its intended objectives.

Improvement of Physical Infrastructure with Private Sector Support

One goal of the modernization program was to refurbish and upgrade the physical condition of customs offices. Existing buildings needed to be adapted to meet workflow requirements and the use of ICT. Even though the Customs Fund and regional chambers of commerce and industry have contributed funds to improve the physical infrastructure, the programmed improvement of the infrastructure included in the World Bank loan was not realized because of budget constraints.

In a joint effort by the TCA and chambers of commerce and industry, the construction of modernized premises for the Kayseri, Gemlik, and Konya customs offices was completed in 2001–02. The regional chambers of commerce and industry and the Association of Transporters were also committed to building customs facilities on the basis of a build-operate-transfer model by the end of 2002 at the customs offices in Gürbulak (border post with Iran) and Ipsala (border post with Greece).

Human Resource Management

TCA personnel policies must follow the policies that apply to the overall civil service, which severely limits the TCA's flexibility in relation to human resources. Because of budget problems at the national level, the TCA could not hire any new staff members after 1996 despite major changes in operational procedures since that time. In light of that situation, the TCA undertook two major initiatives.

First, the TCA launched a major training and continuous education initiative to familiarize customs staff members with automated customs processing, with a special focus on training management staff members. Some 158 customs officials have been trained for total quality management under a protocol signed by the Undersecretariat of Customs and the Turkish Society for Quality in March 2002. Following training, continuous improvement teams were established to motivate personnel and provide more standardized services at central and regional units. However, traders indicate that, as of mid-2002, the results were mixed. Many customs personnel are unfamiliar with the new procedures and, therefore, do not apply the new regulations correctly, causing problems and delays in the processing of traders' goods. Traders also complain about the high staff turnover at regional customs offices.

Second, the TCA entered into contractual agreements with a number of experts—especially computer programmers, analysts, and controllers—whose expertise was required to implement the reforms. The contractual staff is located mainly at customs headquarters.

During 1996–2001, the number of staff members fell by 10 percent, with staff reductions concentrated at the regional offices, which were consolidated during that period. During the same period, the number of trade declarations rose by 40 percent (70 percent for exports and 24 percent for imports), reflecting a 54 percent increase in the number of trade declarations handled by each staff member.

The salaries of customs officers comply with civil service regulations, and thus the TCA has no flexibility in the matter; however, employees supplement their salaries with overtime work, which traders request and pay for. This practice is not without its inconsistencies and problems for traders, because some customs employees arrange to concentrate their work during periods that call for overtime pay. Overtime pay can amount to 50 percent of employees' base pay, so those who have the opportunity to work overtime can earn substantially more than other customs staff members or civil servants in general.[3] In addition to base salaries and overtime pay, customs staff members receive rewards for uncovering smuggling operations and also share in the fines levied on traders who provide erroneous customs declarations. Traders resent this practice.

The reform aimed to stem corrupt practices and appears to have made progress in that regard. One contributing factor has been the emphasis placed on the automatic processing of customs declarations, which has enhanced the overall transparency of transaction processing.

The TCA addresses corruption head on. In 2001, it disseminated a circular on ethics and conduct. The circular spells out the core principles of conduct and integrity for customs staff members and clearly defines what is meant by integrity. The circular instructs customs staff members not to accept any gratuities in the course of exercising their duties and not to engage in activities that could provide an appearance of conflict of interest. The circular permits customs authorities to use an unexplained accumulation of assets as an indication of "unjustifiable and illegal profit and possession." It explains in plain language what customs personnel are expected to do when offered a bribe.

Despite the wide publicity surrounding the circular's publication, many customs employees apparently still do not recognize that accepting gratuities on the job constitutes bribery. Indeed, in response to a TCA survey in 2001, 23 percent of customs employees noted that they did not regard gratuities as bribes. Although the TCA has successfully addressed significant payments of facilitation bribes, some petty corruption remains, and a significant number of staff members may not view these activities as corrupt practices. Traders stated that customs officials generally adhere to the strict application of customs legislation but at times request modest gratuities, which the traders routinely pay to prevent possible clearance delays. The gratuities are most frequently paid by brokers, who include their cost in the brokerage fee that they charge traders. Thus, traders may not even be aware that they are paying such gratuities.

Automation

A key component of the modernization project was the use of automated customs processes as much as possible to enhance efficiency and transparency. Until September 1997, the TCA's reliance on ICT was relatively insignificant and was limited to the production of trade statistics and a limited ICT clearance system that had been developed in-house. In 1997, the management of customs automation was entrusted to the Modernization Project Unit. The unit consisted of 3 senior managers, 14 customs experts, and 14 programmers and analysts. Its work program showed remarkable continuity, because its staff was unaffected by frequent management changes elsewhere in the TCA. This management continuity has contributed greatly to the success of the customs automation program.

The Computerized Customs Management System To save time and costs and to minimize implementation risks, the TCA decided to customize an existing software package rather than to develop a new system. Eighteen months of intensive work was needed to customize the selected software to the new streamlined operational procedures, translate the user interface into Turkish, and train customs personnel so that they could maintain and enhance the application source code.

The package chosen was the Solutions Françaises Informatiques (or SOFIX, UNIX), a derivative of the French computerized customs management system. In Turkey, the system is known as the CCMS. The software was provided by a consortium of French Customs and Bull S.A., with an initial contract that covered the provision of the software source code, of the customization of the software, of the hardware, and of the implementation support at a pilot site. It was successfully launched in mid-1998 in a pilot operation at Istanbul Airport, one of the busiest customs facilities in Turkey.

The CCMS is a client-server application based on an Oracle database that supports a full range of customs operations in real time, including an integrated tariff, accounting, import and export clearance, inspection selectivity, transit and other temporary admission regimes, and trade statistics.

3. At the local level, salaries range between US$400 and US$850 per month; the range for top management officers at customs headquarters is US$1,000 to US$1,300 per month.

The CCMS was installed in 65 customs offices throughout Turkey between 2000 and July 2003, following an international tender and contract award to a large Turkish firm. The firm installed a local area network and application and database servers at each site. A wide area network served as a backup system for all localities, centered at customs headquarters in Ankara, where a national data warehouse was established. The warehouse produces trade statistics and serves management information needs. The contractor successfully trained thousands of customs staff members and traders while the system was simultaneously rolled out across the country. Traders were consulted on the design and rollout of the CCMS through their representatives on the Consultancy Committee, which was established for that purpose at the outset of the computerization program. They note that the intensive training provided in the CCMS and EDI contributed to their acceptance of the system and its eventual success. As of mid-2002, about 99 percent of all customs declarations were processed through the CCMS.

Traders have a choice of three methods for entering their declarations. They can use a kiosk, EDI, or the Internet. Some 54 kiosks, equipped with a total of 800 computers and 400 printers, are made available to traders. Traders complain about the lack of personal computers and about continuous defects, mistakes, overcrowding, and congestion at these kiosks. The TCA encourages traders to use EDI and plans to close the kiosks eventually. Acceptance of EDI was more rapid than expected. First introduced at Istanbul Airport in August 1999, EDI was used in 42 percent of all declarations by the early part of 2002, with the share rising to 50 percent by mid-2003.[4] Traders rarely use the Internet to enter their declarations, largely because of inadequacies in the communications infrastructure. Initially, traders were opposed to the computerized declaration system, but they were quickly convinced that the system worked to their advantage. The media supported the new system.

The CCMS has received national and international recognition. It was named the best ICT project in a 2000 competition organized by INTERPRO in Turkey for leading ICT applications in the public and private sectors. At the 2003 European E-Government Conference, the modernization project was selected as one of the 65 best practices of public administration in Europe.

The CCMS is designed to share data with other government agencies. It already shares export data with the Ministry of Finance's Revenue Department and plans are to provide detailed import data as well. The CCMS uses a common tax identification number assigned to each taxpayer, thereby facilitating the cross-checking of taxpayers' records by the Revenue Department. The TCA also routinely shares data with the State Institute of Statistics. Plans are under way to extend data sharing to the undersecretariat of foreign trade, the banking sector, and the Exporters' Association, among others. The other entities appreciate this data exchange. For instance, the State Institute of Statistics notes that it can now produce accurate statistics more quickly and at the same time has been able to reduce the number of staff members working on trade statistics by 60 to 70 percent. To date, data exchanges have been undertaken by means of CDs. The State Institute of Statistics looks forward to having a direct link with the CCMS, which would make the exchange of data even more efficient.

The CCMS feeds its information into a data warehousing system that is available for analysis and other applications. One application that is scheduled for rollout is the management of the return of securities deposited for duty-free imports related to inward processing. To date the Ministry of Foreign Trade has provided permits for inward processing, and the Exporters' Association has carried out security procedures. That process, as it operated in mid-2002, was cumbersome and time-consuming, and thus it resulted in additional costs to processors. Drawing on the data warehouse to manage the release of the securities could drastically reduce those costs. Plans exist to exploit the valuation data stored in the data warehouse to construct a database that could help headquarters and regional staff members in their valuation work.

The total cost of introducing the CCMS was US$32 million, with the costs coming out of a

4. Traders note that their investment in EDI is rather high—\$300 to \$4,000—and that the transmission of messages is frequently not as fluid as it should be. The authorities are studying the possibility of introducing leased lines or other alternative technologies to improve the technology.

US$48 million World Bank loan (of which US$16 million remained undisbursed as of mid-2002). The government's budget covered VAT expenses and the costs of customs enforcement services.

Other Customs ICT Systems The customs administration uses specially designed ICT applications for tracking vehicles driven by travelers who enter Turkey and for transit procedures. In addition, a security system for customs borders was started in 2003 with the aim of improving transit traffic. It is based on a vehicle tracking system that uses license plate scanning.

Customs Controls, Selectivity, and Postrelease Inspection

Before the reform, all shipments were physically inspected. That process was intrusive and time consuming, and it often led traders to pay substantial facilitation money to speed up the process or to gain favor with customs officials in charge of their inspections. As part of its trade facilitation work, the TCA sought to develop its ability to undertake its control function without having to open every single cargo shipment while retaining effective control over the flow of goods and duties payable. The TCA sought to achieve those goals by carefully selecting the shipments that would undergo physical inspection upon arrival and those that would be inspected after the goods had been released to traders. A specialized selectivity module in the CCMS was prepared by the Risk Analysis Unit, which was established in 1998. The module checks each declaration against preselected risk assessment criteria and assigns the shipments to the green, yellow, red, or blue channels. Companies cleared for simplified procedures use the blue channel for all imports.

The selectivity system does not work exactly as intended, however. To begin with, the green channel is rarely used. In addition, customs staff members can modify the selectivity choices made by the CCMS, particularly by overruling yellow channel selections and orienting shipments toward the red channel so that they require full inspection before the release of the goods. In 2001, 25 percent of all goods were cleared through the red channel, 62 percent through the yellow channel, and 12 percent through the blue channel. For exports, the percentages were 10 percent for the red channel and 90 percent for the yellow channel. Those achievements are below the reform program's targets, which called for reducing red channel inspections to 12 percent for imports and 2 percent for exports. In relation to postrelease inspections, the CCMS allocates the personnel so that neither importers nor customs employees know in advance with whom they will be dealing, a procedure introduced to enhance the predictability and transparency of the inspection exercise. Some of the problems encountered with the implementation of the selectivity processes appear to be due to a lack of specialized training in these new procedures for frontline staff.

Performance of the TCA

The reforms can be evaluated on the basis of clearance times, transparency of operations, and efficiency.

Clearance Times

Customs clearance times have been reduced significantly, an achievement that represents the clearest sign that the reform has eased the burden on traders (table 8.3). The share of imports that

TABLE 8.3 Customs Clearance Times, 1996 and 2001 (percentage of total shipments cleared)

Clearance Time	*1996* Imports	*1996* Exports	*2001* Imports	*2001* Exports
Less than 24 hours	61	40	71	96
Less than 48 hours	68	60	83	97

Source: TCA data.

cleared customs in fewer than 48 hours rose from 68 percent of the total in 1996 to 83 percent in 2001, and for exports the share rose from 60 percent to 97 percent. Those increases were made possible by the reduction in physical inspections, which are gradually being replaced by postrelease verifications and audits. Laboratory inspections, which were a routine matter for a lengthy list of commodities before the reform, are now required only for imports that are assigned to the red channel. As a result, the share of total imports that undergoes laboratory inspection fell from 20 percent of total imports before the reform to 5 percent in the first five months of 2001.

However, traders note that delays caused by the Turkish Standards Institution, the Ministry of Agriculture, and the Ministry of Health slow the provision of documents to customs offices. In a sample of four tariff columns subject to certification by the Turkish Standards Institution, only 40 percent cleared customs in fewer than 48 hours. Hence, these inspections clearly slow down customs clearance substantially.

Transparency

The reforms have led to a substantial increase in the transparency of customs operations. The streamlined legislation is made available on the TCA's Web site (http://www.gumruk.gov.tr/), along with a large number of explanatory notes and circulars. As a result, traders and their representatives are fully informed about their obligations and are shielded from arbitrary decisions by customs staff members. The site provides complete details about the Turkish import tariff and explains how to register for access to the system for electronic submission of trade declarations. In addition, it provides contact information for all customs management staff members and a dedicated help line for general queries and for specialized questions about the ICT system. Some traders said that they rarely consult the official Web site but consult private Web sites that provide the same information.

The TCA aims to provide traders with binding tariff and origin information in a timely manner so as permit them to make long-term import commitments. Yet to date the decisionmaking process has been lengthy: it takes an average of 61 days for such information to be made available to importers.

Efficiency

As noted earlier, the number of customs staff members fell during 1996–2001, while the number of trade declarations rose substantially. As a result, the number of trade declarations handled per customs officer increased, a gain that was made possible by increased automation.

The 2001–05 Reform Program

The TCA's management is committed to continuing the pace of reforms. At the end of 2000, it announced a new five-year reform program (2001–05). Noting that substantial progress had been achieved in improving the application of the new Customs Code and in implementing the ICT support system, the TCA said that its goal was to ensure that the reform does not stall and to provide still better services to the trading community. The following are the main features of this program:

- Adapting customs services to developments in international trade so as to further reduce the cost of foreign trade through streamlining and accelerating customs formalities. This adaptation implies that ICT resources will be used more efficiently and that progress on risk management to reduce the number of physical inspections will continue. This effort will further improve the TCA's relationship with the trading community.
- Fighting against customs fraud and corruption through further staff training and strengthening of existing control mechanisms, including those applicable to transit trade, and making greater use of valuation databases and mutual support agreements with other customs administrations.
- Ensuring public security by emphasizing the protection of national security, health, and the environment.
- Assigning more resources to staff training, with the objective of retraining 25 percent of the staff annually, and improving the expertise of customs staff members in working with the virtual environment in which modern trade increasingly takes place.

- Striving for a proactive and democratic management system and for improved integration of customs personnel and customs partners into the decisionmaking process.

Conclusion

As a result of the modernization project, Turkey has had modern customs laws that are harmonized with those of the EU since 1995. Customs laws, including those pertaining to valuation, classification of goods, and rules of origin, have been made consistent with international standards. The processing of trade declarations has been simplified, and a computerized mechanism has been implemented, with an emphasis on selective inspections guided by an advanced risk analysis methodology. In this regard, the TCA has successfully reduced the level of corruption in customs operations.

Traders who were interviewed for this study were pleased with the progress so far. In particular, they cite their ability to access goods more rapidly than in the past because they can now submit their declarations electronically and are subject to lighter inspections. They hope that customs staff members will follow instructions more rigorously, particularly in the area of selectivity, where they do not strictly follow the CCMS-assigned channels. They would also like the other agencies involved in the customs clearance process to modernize their procedures. Doing so would further facilitate import and export processes and reduce traders' costs of doing business.

Additional benefits of customs reform include the provision of trade statistics with fewer delays and in full conformity with international standards, as well as the planned increase in the sharing of data on importers and exporters, which will allow other government bodies to perform their own responsibilities more efficiently. The reform is an ongoing process, and the decision to launch a new phase of the reform is a sign of the continued vitality of the TCA.

9

UGANDA

Luc De Wulf

During the 1990s, Uganda undertook a comprehensive economic reform program that included liberalizing external trade and modernizing its customs administration. As a result of those initiatives, Uganda's trade tariffs are now among the lowest and most streamlined in Sub-Saharan Africa. Moreover, the government created an independent revenue agency, the Uganda Revenue Authority (URA), to improve overall revenue collection. The initiatives have enabled the authorities to improve their revenue mobilization performance, ease trade operations, and initiate a fight against corrupt practices in the customs service.

This chapter begins by highlighting the key elements that led to the creation of the URA. It then turns to a review of customs reforms before looking at the future of reform. This chapter is based on a field study undertaken in June 2002 and was updated in November 2003 with information obtained from the URA.

The Uganda Revenue Authority

Toward the end of the 1980s, the minister of finance became frustrated with the ministry's revenue performance and looked for ways to strengthen revenue collection. In 1990–91 and 1991–92, Uganda's fiscal revenues were among the lowest in the developing world, averaging only 7.5 percent of gross domestic product (GDP). Following the turbulent years of President Idi Amin and President Milton Obote, corruption remained rampant, particularly in the area of revenue collection. In the context of periodic meetings of finance ministries organized by the Commonwealth countries, Uganda's minister of finance met with his counterpart from Ghana, who a few years earlier had established an autonomous revenue agency in his country. Such an approach to managing the customs service had been inspired by Margaret Thatcher's reform of the United Kingdom's public sector, which drew on a private sector business model.

The United Nations Development Programme supported the search for new approaches to make the customs service more efficient, provided the funds for a team from Uganda's Ministry of Finance (MOF) to visit Ghana, and commissioned a consultant study to define the steps needed to create an independent revenue authority. The United Kingdom's Department for International Development (DFID) supported the creation of the URA with a UK£4.6 million grant, UK£3.6 million of which was provided in the form of technical assistance, with the remainder as a capital grant. This United Nations Development Programme study compared salary levels in the private and public sectors with a view to suggesting a salary level for the customs service that would enable it to attract qualified personnel. Following internal discussions of the study, a new revenue regulation was drafted and presented to the parliament in early 1991. Following approval of this legislation, the ensuing legislation led to the creation of the URA in September 1991.

The main difference between the fiscal department that the URA was to replace and the URA itself was that the URA would pay better wages and would have greater flexibility in managing its human resources, including the ability to fire corrupt staff members. In establishing an independent revenue authority, Uganda led the way to similar initiatives in other Sub-Saharan African countries—Kenya, Malawi, Rwanda, Tanzania, and Zambia—that have also taken this important step to strengthen revenue mobilization. Efforts to enhance revenue and fight corruption were high on the URA's agenda, whereas trade facilitation received little attention. Moreover, the private sector was not consulted during the process of setting up the URA.

The URA was set up as an autonomous agency in the finance portfolio and was put in charge of collecting and accounting for all revenue provided for in the tax legislation. Initially, the URA was empowered to advise the government on tax policy issues, but later the *Cunningham Report* (DFID 1995) identified a number of institutional issues at the URA that prevented it from improving its operational performance to the desired level of effectiveness. In reaction to those suggestions, the government made some changes to strengthen the URA's management and autonomy. The government appointed a new board and a commissioner general, made other changes in the senior management team, passed legislation intended to clarify the role of the board and its relationship to the URA's management, and clarified the relationship between the MOF and the URA. The changes also granted the MOF greater authority in tax policy, while giving the URA greater flexibility in tax administration plus a somewhat larger budget. In addition, the government created the Tax Tribunal, which was intended to give taxpayers a means of recourse against disputable tax assessments and abuse by revenue officers. Clearly, those changes were largely intended to enhance the URA's revenue performance and the government's compliance with Enhanced Structural Adjustment Facility commitments related to the mobilization of larger budget revenues. The DFID supported the URA by providing an external adviser with line management responsibilities. Unfortunately, the changes did not yield the expected results.

Administration

The URA's Board of Directors consists of a chairperson, representatives of the MOF and the Ministry of Trade and Industry, a representative of the Uganda Manufacturers Association, and the URA's commissioner general (since 1998). The minister of finance is authorized to appoint two additional members on the basis of the professional expertise that they can bring to help the URA function efficiently. The minister of finance is also authorized to impart directives to the board regarding the performance of its functions, and the board must comply with those directives. The legislation was drafted in such a way as to give equal and conflicting power to both the board and the commissioner general to manage the URA. This allocation of power is likely to lead to conflicts and runs counter to effective management. Excluding the URA from the tax policy field would appear to be well intentioned, but its total exclusion from such discussion has at times been counterproductive.

The URA currently has a commissioner general, two deputy commissioners general, and four revenue departments: the Customs Department, the Domestic Indirect Taxes Department, the Domestic Direct Taxes Department, and the Expansion and Collection Department. The following departments support the revenue departments: Legal Affairs, Information Technology, Human Resources, Finance, Administration, and Internal Audit and Investigation. There is also a Staff Monitoring Unit.

Budget, Salary, and Staffing Issues

While the URA was being created, extensive discussions took place regarding the formula that would set its operational revenues so as to endow it with a solid revenue base that would ensure its efficient operation. Some argued that the URA should be allowed to retain a share of the revenues it collected. One formula would have established that the URA could retain 2 to 4 percent of collected revenues, depending on the amount specified in the budget each year, as a way to motivate the URA to enhance its revenue collections. Although the URA's budget is set during the regular budget process without any explicit reference to a share of collections, in recent years that share has amounted to 3.0 to 3.5 percent of revenue collected.

Staff salaries were adjusted upward and set at levels comparable to the highest salaries paid to the staff members of any large organization in the country, namely, those at the Bank of Uganda. However, since the URA's creation, salaries have been eroded by inflation and by a lack of the systematic adjustments called for by the URA's original provisions. By 1999, URA salaries ranked twelth in a sample of 50 private sector comparators, and by 2002 they had slipped even further, ranking seventeenth. Salaries at the Bank of Uganda are currently 40 percent higher than those at the URA. The wage compression that has been taking place over the years has affected lower-level staff more than management. Although the MOF was to approve a 10 percent basic salary bonus for all staff members in years when the URA surpassed its revenue target, this bonus was approved only in 1994 and 1998. In other years, the revenue target was set at an unrealistically high level. For 2002, the bonus formula was changed, and the staff was to share 15 percent of the revenue collected in excess of the budgeted amounts.

In 1991, all MOF Revenue Department staff members had to apply for their jobs at the newly created URA. A committee made up of MOF representatives and the URA's core team screened the applications, assisted by a human resource officer from the Bank of Uganda. About 70 percent of the applicants were accepted, and the remaining 30 percent were redeployed in other MOF departments, with some subsequently affected by the retrenchment polices of later years. Senior staff members—a total of 42 in 2002—were recruited on the basis of three-year contracts. The board is authorized to renew those contracts only once for people in the same position; thus managers who are not promoted must leave the URA. Nonmanagerial personnel are hired following a six-month probationary period, but few, if any, are not confirmed following the probationary period.

Customs Reform

The early customs reform involved import tariffs, legislation, procedures and clearance times, integrity and corruption, valuation and preshipment inspection (PSI), certificates of origin, personnel issues and training, information and communication technology (ICT), special import regimes, and goods in transit.

Tariff Policy Changes and Revenue Performance

Reform included the following changes in taxes and duties:

- The authorities streamlined customs duties in 1995. They now consist of three tariff schedules: 0 percent, 7 percent, and 15 percent. The zero rate is applied to agricultural inputs, pharmaceutical goods, school textbooks, and some basic consumer goods. Imports that are certified to originate from Common Market for Eastern and Southern Africa (COMESA) countries receive preference: rates for such imports are 0 percent, 4 percent, and 6 or 7 percent. Those tariffs resulted in a drop in the unweighted nominal protection rate for consumer goods from 30.8 percent to 16.5 percent. In some cases, the tariff depends on the use for which the imports are intended, as is the case with sugar imported by manufacturers, which is subject to determination by the Tax Department import quota. Such use-based tariffs easily lead to leakage and corruption, and customs experts discourage their use.
- A 10 percent excise tax is imposed on some goods—textiles, for instance—that are also produced domestically.
- A value added tax (VAT) is levied at a unified rate of 17 percent, but goods for which the customs duties are zero are exempted.
- A 4 percent tax is levied as a presumptive income tax on importers that are not listed as paying income tax.
- A presumptive 2.5 VAT is levied on importers that have no valid VAT registration. This tax generated US$800 million in revenue in May 2002.

TABLE 9.1 URA Revenue Performance, 1990–2002

Year	*Percentage of GDP*				
	URA Revenue	Taxes on Imports	Customs Duties	Sales Taxes and VAT on Imports	Duties on Imports as a Percentage of URA Revenue
1990–91	7.8	1.7	0.8	0.1	22.3
1991–92	7.0	1.6	0.8	0.1	23.2
1992–93	7.7	2.0	1.0	0.1	26.3
1993–94	9.5	2.8	1.5	1.3	29.7
1994–95	10.6	3.0	1.4	1.5	28.6
1995–96	11.5	3.6	1.5	1.7	29.2
1996–97	12.3	3.7	1.4	2.2	30.4
1997–98	12.0	3.6	1.2	2.2	30.3
1998–99	13.1	4.2	1.3	2.6	32.3
1999–00	12.7	4.1	1.4	2.4	32.1
2000–01	12.3	4.1	1.6	2.3	33.7
2001–02[a]	13.0	3.8	1.2	2.3	29.4

a. Provisional.
Source: URA data.

Kenya, Tanzania, and Uganda constitute the East African Community, which over time is expected to grant duty-free access within the community for originating commodities, with exceptions to accommodate the different levels of industrial development among the partner states. A three-band external tariff has been accepted (0 percent, 10 percent, and 25 percent) with the agreement that the 25 percent rate will be progressively reduced to 20 percent over a five-year period.

Uganda has accepted the transaction value definition of the World Trade Organization (WTO). In theory, Uganda does not use reference prices for administrative or protective purposes. It has also abolished export taxes, although the last budget reapplied them on exports of animal hides.

Since the URA was created, overall revenues have risen from 7.8 percent of GDP in 1990–91 to 13 percent in 2001–02 (table 9.1). That figure is still rather low when compared with figures in countries at similar stages of development. Total taxes on imports (customs duties, excise taxes, and sales taxes or VAT) increased from 1.7 percent of GDP in 1990–91 to 3.8 percent in 2001–02, an increase that was largely due to an increase in the relative importance of domestic sales taxes: domestic sales taxes on imports, which after 1994–95 include VAT, rose from 0.1 to 2.3 percent of GDP during the period under consideration.

In 2001–02, taxes on imports accounted for close to one-third of overall URA revenue. The reduction and streamlining in customs duty rates that took place in 1995 did not reduce customs duties revenues as a share of either GDP or total URA revenue. Even if the relative contribution of customs duties in the overall revenue structure were to fall in the future, the role of the URA in revenue generation would not decline, as the management of import taxation would still require that import values be assessed. In addition, the fight against corruption, false invoicing, undervaluation, and misclassification of goods would need to continue.

Effective tariff rates (that is, import duties as a percentage of total imports) were 6 percent in 2001, and total taxes on imports were 15 percent.[1] Average effective customs duty rates are lower than the unweighted average tariff because of exemptions that in 1997 still amounted to 17 percent of total imports. The exemptions include those granted to diplomats and those granted in the context of the Investment Code. Changes in tariff rates and the

1. In 1997, the import-weighted average collection rate was 8.0 percent, whereas the import-weighted average statutory rate was 11.4 percent. The total value of exempted imports amounted to 17.2 percent of total imports (Hinkle and Herrou-Aragon 2003).

Investment Code altered the relationship between statutory and effective rates, but no up-to-date estimates are available.

The MOF prepares annual revenue projections with tight targets. Yearly consultations with the International Monetary Fund are a major input into those projections, which are based on a set of assumptions that may or may not be realized. The URA carefully records the performance of all revenues under its purview on a monthly basis and explains the difference between the budgeted amount and actual revenue. With respect to the revenues from import taxes, the URA compares budget assumptions and actual results for the exchange rate, real GDP growth, inflation, and change in import structure.

In recent years, a shift toward zero-rated imports seems to have occurred—they accounted for 58 percent of total imports in 2001–02—alongside a growth of imports that benefit from regional agreements. The average unweighted tariff (that is, import duty revenues over import value) dropped from 8.9 percent in 1999–2000 to 6.5 percent in 2001–02. The URA is well aware that the importance of customs revenue will decrease over time and will have to be compensated for by greater reliance on domestic taxes. This shift will not reduce the burden on URA staff of ensuring that import values and volumes are correctly declared, but it will ease the problem of classification and origin somewhat. The URA is not penalized if its revenues fall short of targets, but the staff is rewarded if the URA surpasses its targets.

Legislation

During the URA's inception, the government did not introduce any new customs procedures, and the East African Customs Act of the 1960s remained in effect. New customs instructions were gradually introduced to streamline the existing procedures somewhat and to prepare for the introduction of the ICT system. Those instructions have yet to be consolidated in a new customs code. Doing so would improve the transparency of customs regulations, which are not readily available to importers, clearing agents, and customs officials. The lack of transparency leaves scope for individual interpretation of the procedures, negotiation, and arbitrary behavior on the part of URA staff.

Procedures and Clearance Times

The authorities do not keep detailed records on how long it takes to clear goods through customs even though the Automated System for Customs Data (ASYCUDA) of the United Nations Conference on Trade and Development (UNCTAD) could easily provide the data. Importers and brokers complain that the average of one week needed to clear goods is too long and adds substantially to their costs. Clearance times are long because of the multiple, tedious, and time-consuming import procedures. In addition, problems on the importers' side include poor preparation of import documents, low tax compliance, willingness to participate in corrupt activities, and poor understanding of customs. The inclination of customs officials to slow down the process in order to collect "facilitation money" also contributes to the slow pace of clearance. Finally, goods encounter major processing delays at the Kenyan and Tanzanian ports and borders, and transport from those borders to locations in Uganda is cumbersome and costly.

Simplification of Procedures Current customs procedures are excessively lengthy and require a number of verifications that do not contribute to good business practices. They do, however, increase the number of contact points between URA staff and importers or clearing agents, which provides opportunities for collusion. They certainly lead to a perception that importers need to provide facilitation money to ensure that their paperwork is handled promptly. Such facilitation money is included in brokerage fees, and importers report that this practice adds about U Sh 100,000 (roughly equivalent to US$50) per shipment if the shipment is to be processed in four days.

Beginning in early 2002, customs procedures were streamlined to accelerate the clearance of goods and fight corruption. Pilot tests are under way to see how well this simplification process is doing. The Association of Brokers has been closely associated with the review of those procedures. The simplification process involves the following:

- Trucks arriving at the border are cleared and allowed to proceed to Kampala individually. In the past, they could proceed only in convoys that traveled under supervision by the customs authorities, a procedure that could delay the journey for up to a day.

- Border documentation is forwarded to URA headquarters in Kampala in a more efficient manner.
- Document verification has been simplified to single verification at the internal container depot. For warehousing, the single verification is done at the bonded warehouse. This system cuts at least two days from the time it previously took to process goods.
- Verifications—because of the reduction in their number—now require fewer workflow managers, whose interventions caused delays and led to demands for facilitation money. This reduction, in turn, speeds up the paper flow.
- Secondhand cars are inspected at the border jointly by customs agents and internal revenue officers rather than being inspected by internal revenue agents separately in Kampala.

Clearing agents that use direct trader input (DTI) are allowed to use their own stationery, whereas others use bills of entry printed by the URA. DTI is not yet Web based. A pilot project was first done with two large clearing agents, but the URA anticipates that eventually all larger importers and clearing agents will use DTI from their premises. Smaller brokers are using privately established front-end bureaus for DTI. The pilot companies note that they would prefer to scan documents and forward them to the URA, but the URA does not have the equipment to receive scanned documents. Under the simplified procedures, single-item cargo is estimated to clear customs in one day, whereas mixed cargos take three days. However, the error rate of electronic data interchange declarations is significant (up to 50 percent), which slows down customs clearances. ASYCUDA++ was introduced and new customs clearance procedures were to come into effect by the end of November 2003. URA staff initially resisted these simpler procedures because of their implications for staff assignments and workflow. Despite management's awareness of the need for the rollout of the new import clearing procedures, to be accompanied by planned staff redeployment, no planning had taken place at the time of the initial rollout. Planning was expected to commence by January 2004.

Verification and Inspection of Cargo The inspection rate is currently close to 100 percent, causing considerable delays. As of early 2003, URA management was looking into risk-based, post-clearance inspection, and about 25 percent of employees have undergone pertinent training. Two PSI companies, Intertek Testing Services and the Société Générale de Surveillance, have given presentations to URA staff members on the support that they could provide in a risk-based approach to inspection. To date, the URA has not shown much interest in this approach; however, the customs administration has recently introduced a fast-track clearance procedure for some commodities and some importers. Now that ASYCUDA++ has been installed, it can be relied on to introduce a fully developed risk-based verification system, the advantages of which will be reaped only when staff are redeployed and training to effect postclearance audits has been completed.

At one point, the URA looked into using scanners in the verification process as one element of risk analysis. The URA solicited indications of interest from a number of scanner service providers and initiated a preliminary evaluation; however, this process has stalled.

Certification of Brokers Documentation submitted in relation to goods clearance is often completed incorrectly, and data are frequently missing, thereby slowing down the clearance process. To some extent, this problem is due to the presence of a large number of clearing agents, many of whom are small, part-time operators whose operational capacities and ethical standards are at times dubious. In many cases, the import documents are incomplete or incorrect, and the attachments—invoice, bill of lading, insurance certificate, importer's declaration, and certificate of origin—are incomplete.

The URA is currently rectifying this situation, and transparent accreditation criteria are being established to ensure that all clearing agents are capable operators. The URA manages the agent certification process, with full participation by a representative of the Uganda Freight Forwarding Association (created in 2001), which has about 27 members. The 12 criteria for certification include whether the qualifications of the applicant's board of directors and personnel are appropriate, whether the applicant has the financial capacity, whether the applicant is registered to pay VAT and income tax, whether an insurance bond is in place, and whether personnel are bonded. As a result of this process, the number of active clearance agents could drop from about 370 to 200. The certification process is taking longer than expected, in part because some clearance agents are not responding to the URA's requests for information. Some observers believe that the URA does not always adhere to the strict qualification standards it sets, possibly in reaction to political intervention.

Clearance and Transport of Goods from Kenyan and Tanzanian Ports Importers note that goods that are imported into Uganda mostly come through the ports of Mombassa in Kenya or Dar Es Salaam in Tanzania. Substantial delays occur at those ports. In Mombassa, the delays can easily amount to 10 days, even after the recent process of simplification that was put in place. For example, even though the number of required signatures was reduced from 13 to 4, importers still have to make 26 trips in and around the port to get their goods cleared. The customs clearance process has also improved in Dar Es Salaam, but Tanzania's railroad services are so poor that Mombassa is still the preferred route. There seems to be substantial scope for better regional cooperation, both to improve transit arrangements and to look into the possibility of arranging for customs clearance in the ports of Kenya and Tanzania. This effort appears to be on the agenda of the recently revived East African Community.

Integrity and Corruption

Uganda has signed the World Customs Organization (WCO) Arusha Declaration and has included an integrity section in the customs *Staff Handbook*. To date, this effort does not seem to have had any effect on corruption, which existed long before the creation of the URA and seems to be widespread, well beyond the customs staff. Both URA management and private sector operators share the perception of pervasive corruption, although the latter have suggested that corruption seems to have been reduced somewhat. According to URA sources, some 50 to 70 percent of URA employees working in the customs service are corrupt. Some interviewees suggested that the corruption issue has been brought much more into the open than before as some progress is made in fighting corruption. This visibility leads to a public perception that corruption is getting worse even though it may actually be decreasing.[2]

That perception can be reviewed in the context of Transparency International's 2000 corruption index, which reflects the perceptions of business sector managers.[3] On a scale of 10 (best) to 1 (worst), Uganda scores 2.3, above Nigeria (1.2) and Cameroon (2.0), but below Senegal (3.5) and South Africa (5.0). Transparency International does not keep track of perceived corruption in revenue departments, but survey data suggest that corruption in revenue departments is worse than in the government in general, and there is no reason to believe that the situation in Uganda is any different.

Efforts to stem corruption among revenue staff were high on the URA's reform agenda when it was created. To shelter staff members from the temptation of corruption, they were paid the highest salaries then prevailing in Uganda; however, as noted earlier, their salaries have stagnated. All URA personnel are required to fill in an asset declaration form during the selection process and must update this declaration every time a significant change in family status or asset ownership occurs. The Human Resources Department keeps the declarations, and the Staff Monitoring Unit, which has 6 to 10 members, is supposed to follow up. The URA is the only government unit or autonomous department that requires such asset declarations, even though civil service regulations require them for all civil servants. In theory, the nondeclaration of assets or a false declaration is reason for dismissal. In a few cases, the authorities have used asset declarations in the investigation of bribery. For instance, in 1997, 60 URA staff were accused of corruption, but 45 were brought back, in part because no illicit

2. One importer of steel products notes that he suffers considerably from fraudulent imports of steel products that compete with his. These fraudulent imports come in hidden among other cargo and benefit from fraudulent valuation and classification between the importer and URA staff. He notes that in recent years his business has improved because fraudulent imports, which the URA estimated to account for up 60 percent of total steel imports, have fallen back to 30 percent of total imports.

3. See http://www.transparency.org/.

gains could be detected on their asset declarations. One of the difficulties with the asset declaration is that female staff members often do not know the details of their husbands' assets and therefore cannot include them in their own asset declarations, making their declarations incomplete and difficult to exploit if disputes arise. Also, corrupt staff members can easily register their assets under the names of family members so as to escape future scrutiny.

The URA renewed its anticorruption efforts in 2002. In the process, it wanted to be explicit about the problem that corruption creates for society in general and the URA specifically, even if some found it embarrassing to acknowledge the prevalence of corruption in the URA so openly. The URA's management defends its position by drawing on the analogy of Uganda's approach to HIV/AIDS, whereby the government openly declared HIV/AIDS a major national emergency and organized a campaign against it even though doing so touched on delicate matters of sexual practices and morals. The anticorruption campaign was supported at the highest political level, and the government has created the new Ministry of Integrity to promote the cause of integrity across all spheres of public life.

The current URA campaign against corruption has several facets. The intended simplification of procedures is probably the most important, as it aims to provide greater transparency to transactions as well as reduce contacts between importers and URA agents. The transparency of customs operations will also benefit from the introduction of ASYCUDA++. The latter is supported by the following initiatives, which were to crystallize the campaign against corruption, although relatively little follow-up on the initiatives has taken place:

- The URA organized an integrity workshop in November 2001 to launch a new ethics and anticorruption campaign, during which the Ethics and Integrity Committee was created in the URA. The committee's objective was to help instigate behavioral change among URA staff members and thus enhance the overall image of the URA. One of several initiatives that were to follow from this workshop was the selection of ethics counselors from among URA staff members; however, their selection has not yet been completed.
- The Code of Ethics is being prepared. Drawn from the *Staff Handbook*, this code will set out the URA's operational values and principles in somewhat general terms. What the function or effect of the Ethics Code will be is still unclear. The code could focus more clearly on corruption and the penalties for violating the code, and it could include examples of what might constitute corrupt behavior, without blurring the message with other issues related to the need to deliver professional service. In addition, all URA staff members could be made to sign this simple code when they receive a salary increase.
- The campaign was publicized through announcements in the press and visible anticorruption signs posted at URA headquarters.
- The commissioner general sent a circular to all URA staff members in early 2002 inviting them to join in the fight against corruption and asking them for advice and details of corrupt practices. The message advised corrupt staff members that they could take the opportunity to resign with termination benefits paid—a type of amnesty for those willing to leave the URA. Responses were to be sent directly to the commissioner general within four days and were to be kept confidential. There is no indication that any staff members resigned.
- The Judicial Committee of Inquiry, headed by a high court judge, was created in February 2002 to look into corruption in the URA. Because of unresolved issues relating to its funding, the committee did not start work until June 2002. Its report was scheduled for the end of September 2002 but in mid-2004 was still being awaited. (Hearings were completed in February 2003.)
- A questionnaire was circulated to all staff members regarding their views about and attitudes toward corruption. So far, few responses have been collected, and the Human Resources Department has not carried out any analysis of those responses received.

Staff members can be sanctioned for corrupt behavior or other failures in performing their duties. The staff member's supervisor advises a disciplinary committee of the intended staff action. The staff member concerned can consult an appeals committee and can even appeal to the URA board. In 2001, 18 of the URA's 2,240 staff members were dismissed, of which 12 were from the Customs Department. Recovering ill-gotten wealth is extremely difficult, not only because the external judicial process is complex and corruption much more difficult to prove than in an internal URA process, but also because people in the private sector who offered bribes are involved. In such cases, the URA should start proceedings to claim payment of the correct amount of duties and taxes plus appropriate penalties, but such action appears to have taken place in few prior and current corruption cases. This lack of action explains why some corrupt URA staff members who were dismissed used their ill-gotten wealth with impunity to create visible businesses, a situation that undermines the credibility of the anticorruption campaign.

The URA also tends to move some corrupt staff members around rather than to dismiss them outright. Political interference is claimed to play a role in this practice, which private sector operators find extremely galling.

In mid-2002, some changes seemed to have taken place in the fight against corruption that involved actions outside the URA or the MOF. An external investigation looked into payments against faked drawback documentation. The case involved the head of the Large Taxpayers Department as well as several staff members of the Internal Audit Department. They were accused of falsifying drawback documents in which specially created companies obtained illegal duty drawbacks amounting to more than US$2.5 million. The accused were jailed pending further investigation (bail is not permitted for this kind of offense) and the next phases of the judicial process. Such well-publicized treatment is a stark departure from earlier practices and is likely to set an example for URA staff members at all levels. URA staff members and civil society at large are closely following the outcome of this case. Since then 12 more customs staff members, including an assistant commissioner, have been charged and were put on trial in late 2003.

Some Ugandans have argued that a more drastic solution should be adopted to counter corruption in the URA, one that would rely on drastically altering the composition of the staff, as has been done in Bolivia and as Uganda did when it first set up the URA. Employment in the URA is still extremely attractive, and the authority would have no difficulty recruiting highly qualified staff members that it could train in the new customs procedures and hold accountable to high ethical standards. These interlocutors do not believe that the current staff, which they perceive to be corrupt at all levels, is capable of reforming itself, especially because the supervisors tend to be accomplices in most corrupt practices. The observers note that, while better training and the recent progress in recruiting well-educated staff may reduce corruption somewhat, the scope of the problem appears to warrant a drastic solution.

Valuation Issues and Experience with Preshipment Inspection

As a member of the WTO, Uganda is a signatory of the Agreement on Customs Valuation (ACV) and, as required, notified the WTO in 2000 after the transition period had lapsed. Uganda notified the WTO of three sets of exceptions that it wants to apply: safety matches, dry batteries, and textiles. However, the URA does not apply the ACV widely. URA officials argued for a much longer transition period than the one provided by the WTO on the grounds that building capacity to implement the ACV effectively will take time.

Several reasons account for this situation. First, invoices presented by importers are largely false. A detailed audit—based on a raid of importers' records and their computer hard drives—of a sample of those invoices suggests that up to 70 percent are falsified in Uganda (that is, values or classifications are changed), are total fabrications, or are only partial declarations (that is, only free-on-board values are declared, not cost, insurance, and freight values). Even reputable firms provided partial and falsified invoices. Imports from Dubai and Kenya are particularly likely to be fraudulent. Second, URA personnel are complacent and participate in the fraud. Third, URA employees are poorly trained to challenge prices or classifications in invoices. A further problem that makes reliance on the ACV difficult is that more than half of the dutiable commodities imported into Uganda are secondhand goods, for which the ACV is particularly ill-suited. The secondhand goods include clothing; shoes; white goods (refrigerators, freezers, kitchen stoves, and so on); automobile tires; spare parts for motor vehicles; televisions; computers; and telephones.

In practice, the URA frequently relies on price lists that are based on the best information obtained from reliable importers. Private sector importers complain that the lists are arbitrary; however, they are concerned more about the secrecy surrounding the lists, which creates uncertainty for their businesses.

The URA is looking at alternative ways of finding a price basis that can be used to calculate the duties and taxes due at importation. The options exclude having recourse to PSI companies, which it sees as costly and as an option to which importers and URA staff would object. Although the imposition of this solution from outside the URA could restart a PSI program, its full benefits might not be realized if it ran into staff resistance. In this context, only demand-driven PSI support would stand a chance of working.

An alternative approach that the URA is investigating is the compilation of a price list using a transparent methodology. Importers and clearing agents appear to be inclined to go along with such an approach, as long as the price list is made public and compiled in a transparent manner. For them, what matters most is predictability and a system that avoids the present aggravations with URA staff. URA management indicated that it would welcome assistance in preparing a position paper that would spell out how developing countries apply the ACV. COMESA or the East African Community could submit such a paper to the WTO. A senior URA official has had private discussions with a South African consultant to investigate how the URA might draw on the price database from bar-code companies. In the process, a list of 12,000 bar codes was obtained from a Kenyan retailer. The list permitted the consultant to obtain wholesale prices for 80 percent of the items. When those prices were compared with invoice prices, the exercise suggested that invoice prices should be increased by 30 to 50 percent for customs valuation purposes.

One problem with the bar-code approach is that fake and imitation goods that bear the same bar code as the original product would be subject to the same import duties as real ones.[4] In the meantime, the Valuation Unit intends to have team leaders trained to become experts in particular commodities. Private sector importers and business people would support such a development. In some instances, customs agents are using chemical tests to identify the composition of commodities whose declared prices deviate significantly from similar commodities, as could be the case with cigarettes. Private sector importers, who claim that the effort to improve valuation has been piecemeal, acknowledge that the customs service is undertaking some initiatives, but they note the total lack of training of most of the people they are being asked to assist and the lack of continuity in their assignments.

Several interviewees noted that, given the absence of any reward for whistle-blowing, few customs staff members would volunteer to bring corrupt practices to the attention of the authorities, because they would be afraid of retaliation.

Uganda had an agreement with the Société Générale de Surveillance until 1996, when Intertek Testing Services won the PSI contract through competitive bidding. Intertek Testing Services operated PSI services until 2001, when the contract was terminated and the decision was made not to engage any PSI company. The private sector was extremely vocal about not wanting a new PSI contract. Both URA staff members and the private sector thought money spent on the PSI companies would be better spent on improving customs services. Critics also complained about inconsistencies in the PSI documentation regarding valuation and classification, although they offered no details.

The MOF had instructed the URA not to challenge the PSI findings, but later the URA started challenging PSI findings in isolated instances. No serious comparison of the PSI data and the data that were ultimately used to calculate customs duties and VAT was evident. Reconciliation occurred only sporadically and was complicated by long delays in the transmission of documents between the PSI company and the URA's Customs Department. Internal fraud also prevented the URA from making the most of the PSI documentation. In addition, the Treasury did not cooperate in making this reconciliation, in part because its cashbook was not computerized. URA personnel claim that they maintained a parallel value database that relied on invoices from earlier imports and on data provided by the PSI on earlier shipments.

The PSI company was supposed to have provided staff training and to have given the URA a database as well as computers. Aside from a little bit

4. One instance given was the case of a Barbie doll that has a wholesale price (verified with the bar-code process) of US$12. The importer claimed that it was an imitation product that cost him US$6.50.

of management and ACV training, URA officials claimed that the PSI companies did not honor their training commitments.

Certificates of Origin

Substantial abuse occurs in the use of certificates of origin, even though import tariffs are generally low. Only imports from COMESA qualify for tariff preferences. The preferences reduce the 7 percent tariff to 4 percent and the 15 percent tariff to 6 or 7 percent. The creation of the East African Community, with duty-free imports for commodities from member countries, has made the correct establishment of origin even more crucial, because the revenue loss from fraud could become significant. Uganda is a member of other regional agreements, but none has tariff preferences.

The ministries of trade or the chambers of commerce of exporting countries prepare the certificates of origin. Their main concern seems to be to please exporters and to facilitate the export process. Even if a certificate of origin has been issued according to regulations, the information is frequently either not reliable or false. Challenging the certificates is difficult and often beyond the capacities of URA staff. Also the cooperation the URA receives from customs departments in countries of origin is sometimes problematic. The cooperation agreement with Tanzania works well, that with Kenya works less smoothly, and countries like Egypt and the United Arab Emirates do not cooperate at all. Pursuing the veracity of certificates of origin is a lengthy process, and routine verifications exceed staff resources. This issue remains a major problem, and a ready solution does not appear to be available. One possibility is for customs offices in the countries of origin to become involved in issuing certificates of origin, a change that was proposed at the Doha WTO Conference and that the WCO is looking into.

Personnel Issues and Training

The URA has no difficulty recruiting university graduates, both because of its attractive pay levels and because of the high level of unemployment. Confirmation of URA employment and recruitment at the time of the URA's creation was a serious undertaking because it involved professional screening. After this initiative, new recruitment was based solely on interviews and was better isolated from the influence of politicians and from other nonprofessional criteria. In 1999, the last year of new recruitment, the applicants had to take a written examination before they could be selected for oral interviews. They then took an introductory course, and if their examination results were good enough, they were selected for URA employment.

Training for staff members who are already on board is weak. Most staff members have not received any formal training since joining the URA in 1991. Training facilities are underused, and the Customs Department uses the facilities less than the other branches of the URA. This lack of training is blamed in part on the reluctance of customs managers to release qualified staff members to prepare for and deliver training courses. Staff promotion is unrelated to job performance or to training. Because all involved see poor training as one of the shortcomings of URA staff, the issue needs to be addressed with some urgency. The training program was redesigned in 2003, but it has not yet been implemented. Some training could well benefit from a regional initiative. Recruitment procedures were revamped as of November 2003 and now rely on initial screening, written tests, further interviews, and psychometric testing (including integrity testing). Applicants are interviewed and, if qualified, undergo two weeks of introductory training, followed by two months of basic training in a revenue department. The latter training includes both practical and classroom training. After passing an examination, selected applicants are appointed for a probationary period.

Information Technology

At the time that the URA was created, the customs ICT that had been introduced in 1990 did not include a number of valuable functionalities. The URA launched a search for a better system in 1993 and settled on ASYCUDA version 2. However, the software was not installed at the Entebbe airport until 1997. Installations were later completed at seven more customs stations. Not all URA stations used all the functionalities of the system, a situation that could still be significantly improved. Not only was the new UNIX platform more stable than the platform it replaced, but it also helped the URA compile statistics and had the ability to randomly select customs officials to perform cargo verifications. However, the limitations of ASYCUDA version 2 became apparent over time: the data retrieval systems were complex, the software components for bond security management and risk management were missing, and UNCTAD was slow in responding to requests for support.

Staff resistance to the introduction of the ICT was initially high, but it dissipated substantially over time and with sensitization and training. However, difficulties in funding a training contract with UNCTAD complicated the installation process, which had to rely extensively on inadequate in-house support and on technical assistance from Zambia. Staff training was largely neglected, and most staff members had to learn the system on the job from more experienced agents. So even though computerization had been introduced, many employees continued to use a number of the old manual processes. The full benefits of the new ICT system, including those aspects of the system that would have helped fight corrupt practices, were not realized.

The URA has reviewed most of the customs ICT available on the market. For instance, it commissioned a detailed comparison of an alternative computerized customs management system and ASYCUDA++, then the most recent ASYCUDA version. On the basis of the results, the URA chose ASYCUDA++, which has most of the functionalities that were missing in its predecessor. Because other countries in COMESA had also adopted ASYCUDA++, the URA considered it wise to stick to that system, given its plans for the future integration and coordination of customs work in a regional context. UNCTAD's contract for training and some site visits ended in 2002, and the URA modernization program, financed by the DFID, has restarted the ASYCUDA++ program, which was expected to go live at the end of November 2003. The new modernization program is expected to closely follow the ASYCUDA rollout, so as to maximize the efficiency gains to be reaped from this ICT support to customs operations.

Full electronic data interchange is not yet feasible in Uganda because of poor infrastructure, but the new ICT system aims at close to 100 percent DTI. Two clearing agents already use DTI and, as noted earlier, DTI for smaller traders is in place at facilities made available through kiosks. Making full use of ASYCUDA++ will require staff redeployment and intensive training, issues that have not been adequately addressed in the past.

Importers pay duties through the banking system, which is connected to the URA by a wide area network. This system is operational in only two customs stations and does not yet work efficiently, because the network often breaks down. A new process is to be studied in a pilot project as part of the ASYCUDA++ rollout.

Special Import Regimes

The government must pay duties on its imports. Some URA staff members have suggested that the system could be improved to smooth the release of such imports.

The drawback system is intended to provide exporters with access to imports and VAT-free inputs. The system is part of the overall export procedure, which entails the following steps:

- The exporter prepares a packing list of exports and presents them to the clearance agent.
- The exporter presents the truck at the internal container depot, but trucks are rarely inspected because of the lack of proper weighing equipment.
- A copy of the export documents is sent to the appropriate border crossing point, but because truck convoys to the border do not leave every day, some delay occurs at this stage.
- The documents are stamped at the border, and the claim for the drawback of import duties and VAT is sent to the URA.
- The URA pays drawbacks after verification by the Commissioner General's Office, the Audit Bureau, and the Refund Section. Drawbacks are calculated on the basis of permitted wastage that occurs during the production process, which is often set at 3 percent, and an input-output coefficient that is proposed by the exporter.

The coefficient is recalculated every three months and takes the price of imports into account. Private sector operators have no problem with the calculation of duty drawback payments, but they do complain about the delays in obtaining refunds.

Refunds often take up to four months and would take longer if exporters did not systematically pursue them.

Goods in Transit

Uganda faces major difficulties in efficiently managing transit trade. Fraud tends to be high, and goods exported in transit to the Democratic Republic of the Congo are often fraudulently reimported into Uganda. This problem seems to be due to the lack of proper border controls on the Congolese side. Some of those interviewed suggested using electronic monitoring devices that could be installed in trucks and monitored in Kampala to detect any tampering. The URA has now called for tenders to supply electronic tracking seals for transit containers. Most URA staff members believe that an effective solution to the transit problem will require a regional approach.

The Way Forward

The URA is acutely aware that the performance of customs services can be improved within the context of the URA's revenue generation and trade facilitation responsibilities. To that end, it called on the DFID to continue the support it had provided since the URA's creation. A 1998 project memorandum spelled out the support that the DFID was prepared to provide to the URA; however, no real action was taken on this proposal until 2003.

The project document spells out a clear business plan for the URA, a plan that DFID support will help implement. The major objectives are to support the URA in its modernization program, which will ensure that, in relation to customs services, it (a) will provide accurate and timely trade statistics, (b) will clear goods efficiently in order to facilitate trade, (c) will be staffed by well-trained and honest officers, and (d) will protect society from undesirable products and substances.

The major components of the ongoing technical assistance project as it affects customs operations are (a) assessing training needs and delivering training modules to improve employees' technical knowledge of customs matters; (b) assisting in the installation of ASYCUDA++ and activating a good risk analysis module; and (c) supporting the URA's administration—in particular, the Investigation Department—to enhance integrity and antifraud activities. This work program was being implemented in November 2003.

Another task high on the agenda of the commissioner of customs is finding a solution to the vexing problem of customs valuation—that is, how WTO commitments can be reconciled with obtaining reliable valuation data for use in calculating customs duties and the VAT, so as to be fair to all importers while still protecting revenue collection. Private sector operators have a number of suggestions for improving the current situation:

- Have the private sector and the URA agree on the principles that should guide price lists and make the lists publicly available if they are to be used in the valuation process. Avoid giving price ranges on the lists because such ranges give individual customs officers too much discretion.
- Clear goods at the border, as was done for some goods four years ago. Doing so would require that the border posts be equipped with an internal container depot and other facilities, including banking facilities and housing for URA staff. It would help alleviate delays and would scale down the activities of the Revenue Protection Service, which stops trucks between the border and the internal container depot in Kampala. Private sector operators resent the activities of the Revenue Protection Service and special controls because they delay trucks and frequently (some say always) require payment of facilitation money.
- Look into regional cooperation for customs clearance. There is no reason why most cargo cannot be cleared in Mombassa or Dar Es Salaam. A well-functioning transit system is needed, something that should be easier to put into place once the East African Community is operational.
- Install one document verification room per internal container depot to speed up the clearing process.
- Provide a time frame and targets for managing the different import clearance documents and publish the results. Publish the time required for the release of goods on a monthly basis. The ASYCUDA system can provide these data, which could be used as a management improvement

and monitoring tool to reward those who improve release times.

- Move to accept electronic signatures.
- Disseminate customs procedures in detail.
- Invest in reliable weigh stations and bridges.
- Invest in scanners to use in a risk-based process that would reduce the number of physical inspections. Also, investigate the use of low-cost surveillance systems that could ease the transit of goods from Mombassa to Uganda and from the border to the internal container depot in Kampala.
- Make a clear distinction between reliable and unreliable importers so as to avoid performing 100 percent physical inspections. Make simplified import procedures available for authorized importers—that is, importers with a good record with the customs service and other fiscal authorities—as specified in the WCO Kyoto Convention.
- Standardize the penalties that are levied on discovered fraud by providing clear guidelines to URA staff, and publish information about infractions.
- Set up a system whereby payments for drawbacks are made out of URA revenue without having to wait for the MOF to make funds available. Such a procedure would still require that the MOF carefully audit transactions.

Key Conclusions

The customs administration is organized according to the rules of an independent revenue authority, and tariffs are low by regional standards, yet these features have not sheltered the URA from many of the problems that other customs organizations in developing countries face. Traders complain that clearing goods through customs is a slow and costly process. Many people inside and outside the URA believe that numerous URA staff members participate in or tolerate corruption, even though salaries in the URA are relatively better than those in the revenue agencies of other countries. In addition, the URA does not appear to have taken advantage of the management flexibility that it was afforded through its status as an autonomous agency. Finally, the valuation of imports presents a major problem. The URA has tested the PSI approach and has excluded it for the moment. It is currently searching for innovative approaches that would both satisfy the demands of the trading community and safeguard revenue collection.

Relations with the private sector are satisfactory, and the URA has invited the private sector to help find solutions to issues that plague the efficient functioning of customs services. Signs of this improving cooperation between the public and private sectors are the presence of representatives of the Uganda Manufacturer's Association on the board of the URA, the periodic meetings with freight forwarders invited to participate in simplifying the clearance processes, and the certification of clearance agents. These relations augur well for the agenda of trade facilitation, to which the URA is giving increasing attention.

The URA is fully aware that the reform agenda is far from finished and, with DFID support, is currently implementing a new modernization project. This project supports the definition of a business plan, provides training to URA staff, establishes a modern ICT support system, and provides management support. The issue of pervasive corruption is high on the agenda. A more focused approach may be needed.

References

DFID (Department for International Development). 1995. *Cunningham Report.* London.

Hinkle, Lawrence, and Alberto Herrou-Aragon. 2003. "How Far Did Africa's First Generation Trade Reforms Go?" African Working Paper 58a, 58b. World Bank, Washington, D.C.

INDEX

Boxes, figures, and tables are indicated by b, f, and t respectively.